Lost White Tribes

*The End of Privilege
and the Last Colonials in
Sri Lanka, Jamaica,
Brazil, Haiti, Namibia
and Guadeloupe*

Riccardo Orizio

Translated by
Avril Bardoni

The Free Press
New York · London · Toronto · Sydney · Singapore

*f*P
THE FREE PRESS
A Division of Simon & Schuster, Inc.
1230 Avenue of the Americas
New York, NY 10020

First Free Press Edition 2001
Published by arrangement with Secker & Warburg
Originally published in Great Britain in 2000 by Secker & Warburg

THE FREE PRESS and colophon are trademarks of Simon & Schuster, Inc.

Designed by Lauren Simonetti

Manufactured in the United States of America

10   9   8   7   6   5   4   3   2   1

Library of Congress Cataloging-in-Publication Data

Orizio, Riccardo.
Lost white tribes : the end of privilege and the last colonials in Sri Lanka,
Jamaica, Brazil, Haiti, Namibia, and Guadeloupe / Riccardo Orizio ; translated by Avril
Bardoni.—1st Free Press edition.
p. cm.
Originally published: London : Secker & Warburg, 2000.
1. Colonies—History. 2. Colonization—History. 3. Europe—Colonies—History. 4.
Whites—Developing countries—History. 5. Europeans—Developing countries—History. 6. Developing countries—Colonial influence. I. Title.

JV105 .O75 2001
909'.09'08691—dc21   2001023710

ISBN 0-7432-1197-9

Acknowledgments

Thank you to: my parents Roberto and Alda, the generous and patient Avril Bardoni and Geoff Mulligan, four people without whom this book would not have been possible.

Also, thank you to Marilyn Andree, Camilla Baresani Varini, Anna Cataldi, Martino and Francesca Cavalli, Renzo Cianfanelli, "Kaptein" Hans Diergaardt and all the Baster people in Rehoboth, my old friends Enrico, Carlo, Matteo and Checco, Frère Ernest of the Bibliothèque Haitienne des Frères de St. Louis de Gonzague, Alan Facey, Spencer Gardner, Father Bobby Gilmore, Chris Greet, Cleve Hacker, Jason Jacobs, Ali Isingor, Vince Kameka, Reverend Joseph Luc, Giorgio Meletti, Ettore Mo, Andrea Orizio, Camilla Orizio, Paolo Romani, Barbara and Dominic Sansoni, Tom Steagall, Danilo Taino, Hans and Barbara Thoenes, Francisco Vieira Daniel, Odeen White, Tony and Gisela Wool and family, Arturo Zampaglione, all my colleagues at *Corriere della Sera* and my Maasai friends Luca and Antonella Belpietro.

Special thanks to Ian Thomson, author of *Bonjour Blanc* (Hutchinson and Penguin), a book that I found invaluable when I was researching the last Poles of Haiti and a model for the other chapters too.

All my gratitude to those who, with their writing, inspired and encouraged me: Charles Allen, William Boyd, Bruce Chatwin, Mary Ann Fitzgerald, Kuki Gallmann, Eddy Harris, Ryszard Kapuściński, Aaron Latham, Claudio Magris, Francesca Marciano, Peter Matthiessen, Carl Muller, Shiva Naipaul, V. S. Naipaul, Michael Ondaatje, Mirella Ricciardi, Vikram Seth, Tiziano Terzani, Paul Theroux, Laurens van der Post, Simon Winchester.

Postscript: I have been a journalist for too many years to pretend to ignore the following: very seldom people do like the way they and their lives are portrayed. Even more often they don't like it when they are not portrayed. So, all my apologies to those who should have been mentioned and are not. Also to those who would have preferred not to be mentioned but are. This is not "the" truth, it's only as I saw it.

To Pia-Sophie,
the chief of my own tribe

Contents

Foreword

This book is very different from anything previously written about the relationship between the old colonial nations and the societies colonized by them. Riccardo Orizio's "journeys among the forgotten" puts into a different perspective that sense of guilt experienced by ex-colonial powers in the second half of the twentieth century, a guilt that has gone hand in hand with the whole decolonization process and maybe helped to distort it in our eyes. Here, instead of giving us yet another account of how the European nations exercised their power, Orizio sheds a completely new, fresh light on the interaction of colonizers and colonized. Among other things the author discovers that the colonials—or at least some of them—ended up defeated, too, despite or maybe because of the color of their skin, just like the colonized.

Lost White Tribes can be read on several different levels. It is packed with the history of colonialism, with detailed knowledge about how various empires developed in remote locations. But against this historical background the author highlights the fate of the white tribes he encountered, tribes lost in time who are now only the sad remnants of what used to be a vast and rich world.

A fascinating feature of this book is that Riccardo Orizio has chosen to concentrate not on the forces of colonialism but on the stories of the old adventurers, uncovering (in many cases for the first time) intimate details of their private history. This choice gives the book a strong human touch. It is, in fact, what I would call a *humanistic* book, revolving around tales of dying

places and dying communities, around people who live surrounded by old people, old furniture, old verandahs, old books.
The author shows them—his heroes—cocooned in the past, living lives based on nostalgia, on memories, on sadness, unable to
make true contact with the new reality.

The lost white tribes are in fact individuals still living a chapter of history that for the rest of mankind is forever closed.
Which is why, despite Riccardo's sympathy with these obscure
heroes, his is nevertheless an anticolonial book, a demonstration
of the fact that this particular human adventure can never be
relived. It belongs to the past and only to the past.

The lost white tribes of today live in a schizophrenic situation: having deliberately isolated themselves from the ambient
culture, they are yet part of it. They feel that they do not belong,
while the rest of the world sees them as typical of the very societies they reject. They are symbols, but not necessarily, or exclusively, of the past. In his journeys, the author visits communities
that appear to be centuries removed from the real world of
today. In fact they reflect, to a remarkable degree, the problems
inherent in modern societies where everything is mixed: color,
language, religion, culture. In a way, the fate of the lost white
tribes—far from being a historical oddity—anticipated the
twenty-first century with its growing multiculturalism. Through
the stories of the white tribes the author shows us how complicated, how difficult it is to achieve social equilibrium and how
much goodwill is needed to make coexistence function.

Above all, this book is a wonderful piece of reportage. It is
the work of a man who has traveled to remote places and come
back with a completely new map of the colonial world.

Ryszard Kapuściński
Milan, November 1999

Lost White Tribes

Introduction
Journeys Among the Forgotten

He was a year or two older than me. About twenty, naked to the waist, long hair tied back in a ponytail. He was serving drinks and dishes of rice and dried fish in the restaurant of a small hotel on a nondescript road in Sri Lanka. Like nearly everyone else in the place, he wore a red or purple sarong tight around his hips. The trees outside dripped with warm humidity. Sitting at a table, the De Silva family were noisily giving me the latest gossip about the acquaintances we were on our way to visit in a small town at the end of the road.

The boy brought some tea and walked quickly away without a word. But I had felt the rapid look of curiosity he had shot in my direction. As a white foreigner in a tropical country you soon learn to recognize this special look. To begin with, it disturbs you. Then, realizing that you do the same when you come across anyone markedly different from yourself, you cease to notice it. But there was something strange about that glance. A young European or American spinning out a holiday by working in a restaurant in Sri Lanka was much more likely to be struck, if at all, by my Sinhalese friend, dressed as he was in immaculate cricket whites and looking as if he had just stepped out of a picture postcard of the colonial era.

"Who is he?" I asked.

"Him? A waiter," Dilsham replied.

But my curiosity was aroused. "What nationality, would you say? German? English?"

"Him?" he repeated. "I told you, he's a waiter. Local chap."

1

I was still mystified. "But he's white, Dilsham."

Ignoring me, Dilsham continued his account of a group of friends from the Lions Club who had recently thrown a memorable party where the arrack had flowed like water and only Subash Fernando, who never touched alcohol and was known as the "milk boy," had abstained.

I persisted: "He can't be local."

"He can and he is," said Dilsham at last. "He's a Sri Lankan like me. Hear how he speaks the language? He's only a Dutch Burgher. Don't bother your head about them. Strange people. Dutch, or something of the sort. Maybe Portuguese. Some of them live in crumbling old grand houses. Nothing to cook with, roof falling in, but that's where they like to live. As if this was still the eighteenth century. Perhaps, although they're trash, they think they're better than we are."

That was how I found my first White Tribe: by the side of a tropical road, more exotic than all the exotica around me. Like other tribes I would meet in the next few years, walking a thin line between privilege and discrimination. Poor. "Lost" because reduced to being a historical fossil, little more than a genetic anomaly for whom no one wants to claim paternity. Too white for some. Too native for others. Their society a closed, incestuous microcosm.

I am conscious of the fact that if, a couple of hundred years ago, an ancestor of mine had decided to join the Dutch East India Company—as did many respectable Europeans in search of adventure, or simply intent on landing a good job as their counterparts today might opt for a British merchant bank—today I could have been that white boy in a sarong, a white Sri Lankan. And when, years later, I saw a photograph in Tim Page's great book *Sri Lanka* of a house dating from the Dutch colonial period, a pathetically dilapidated old house, I couldn't help thinking of it as the waiter's home.

The Dutch Burghers are not alone in their predicament. In Windhoek, in Namibia, I lined up to use the public telephone with a group of Baster builders whose green eyes regarded me with the look I had come to recognize. Their great-great-great-grandfathers belonged to the same generation of colonists as those who conquered Ceylon. The ships that berthed in Cape Town were, after all, the same ships that sailed to Colombo.

Many countries have left lost tribes of their own nationals in one-time colonies, and have now forgotten them. Napoleon's Poles in Haiti, the Blancs Matignon in Guadeloupe, the fair-haired Norman fishermen in Les Saintes, the Germans of Seaford Town in Jamaica, the last Confederates in Brazil's sugar-cane plantations. The list could go on. There are the Griquas of Griquatown in South Africa, to say nothing of the Souza, Theseriras, Alcantra and Monteiros families and a further forty-five hundred in Melaka, the Portuguese enclave in Malaysia formerly known as Malacca. There are the French in Pondicherry, in India, who cherish the memory of De Gaulle and have been French since 1664. I saw the German Mennonites in Belize, dressed like the Pennsylvanian Amish people but without the comforts of modern American life. The West, rightly concerned about the fate of Afghanistan, seldom remembers that the Gavurs, the last descendants of Alexander the Great and his armies, with Greek blood and white skin, still live there. And how could we forget, not least on account of their extreme geographical isolation, the Scottish and Genoese sailors who populated Tristan da Cunha, an island lying eighteen hundred nautical miles west by south of Cape Town. Or (even if too individualistic to constitute a tribe) the "insabbiati," the Italians who went native in Eritrea, Somalia and Ethiopia.

In some cases the lost tribe is white not because of old ties with Europe but for some genetic reason. The White Indios living in the forest of Darien, Panama, aroused the curiosity of travelers in the nineteenth century. And only recently an indigenous white-skinned tribe that uses parrots to sound the alarm when strangers are about was discovered in Irian Jaya (Indonesia). The tribe's home is the Bird's Head Peninsula.

Anomalous cases? Irrelevant? Perhaps. But all of us, beneath our apparent normality, belong to a lost tribe. We can all become minorities. We are all potentially irrelevant. The whites living among Jamaican banana plantations are not basically different from the Jamaican immigrants living on the outskirts of Western cities. Both are frequently outcasts. Both have the "wrong" skin color. Different.

The places I normally visit in the course of my work are those where events make news, if not history. The journeys described here went in the opposite direction: to the forgotten places, forgotten people.

1
Sri Lanka
Dutch Burghers of Ceylon

The men wore tweed, the women wore their best crinolines. After the races they would return to Ambalangoda, pick up the oysters "which we swallowed with wine if we lost or champagne if we won." Couples then paired off casually or with great complexity and danced in a halfhearted manner to the portable gramophone beside the cars. Ambalangoda was the centre for devil dances and exorcism rites, but this charmed group was part of another lost world.

—Michael Ondaatje, *Running in the Family*

Colombo, December 1998–January 1999

Negombo Road, 2:30 one afternoon shortly after Christmas. A sullen sky. Bungalows with wild banana trees sprouting from their roofs. Smell of warm rain descending from the tea plantations in the hills. A snaking line of tarmac dividing the Indian Ocean from the Salomon Bandaranaike Airport, so named in memory of the prime minister gunned down in 1959 by a Buddhist monk dressed in his best robes for the occasion, his head protected from the sun by an English umbrella. *Tuk-tuk*s, motorized rickshaws painted black and yellow, revving at full throttle and sounding like wheezy old Lambrettas, swerve to avoid the horns of roaming cows who wander out of the bushes and cross the road slowly, inexorably.

5

The *tuk-tu*ks heading toward town pretend to overtake each other on bends to earn a tip from the passenger sitting behind them, hidden by curtains and completely indifferent to any danger. Whenever a *tuk-tuk* accelerates, black exhaust fumes envelop the one nearest to it, provoking a three-wheel skid.

The name of Negombo evokes colonial Africa, but the latex-colored clouds overhead and the whiffs of coconut oil rising from the valley below belong unmistakably to the blessed land once trodden by the Buddha.

"Number 41?" the driver asked me with blatant skepticism as soon as the middleman had done the deal and left.

The tout had buttonholed me the moment I stepped through the sliding doors of the arrivals hall at the airport. He carried a mobile phone in his pocket and a wad of business cards.

"I'll hire one of your cars," I told him, "if you can assure me that the driver is very good. I don't just want a taxi. I need a guide. He must be able to speak English well and take me to the Burghers, tell me whom I should visit and where I should go." I knew I was asking a lot. "In return, I'll hire him for several days," I added.

"No problem," he replied. "The driver I have in mind is special, the best. And he knows all about the Dutch Burghers." At his summons, the first taxi in the rank rocketed toward us with a squeal of tires.

"Is this the one?" I asked uneasily.

He ignored me. A short, middle-aged man got out of the car and flung the boot open without even inquiring about my destination. The middleman gave him some instructions in Sinhalese, then repeated them loudly in English for my benefit: "My friend, this mister wants to meet the Dutch Burghers. You know them, don't you?"

By now an interested group of colleagues had gathered around the chosen driver, who, without replying to his boss, turned to them with a shrug of his shoulders. "The Burghers? OK. But he must give me their addresses."

The crowd responded with a chorus of approval. Yes, of course he must be given the addresses. The *sudu,* the white man, naturally knew where these other white people lived even if he claimed not to. Some mentioned acquaintances or friends of acquaintances with names like Fernando, De Silva and Ludowick who claimed to be Burghers. The driver said nothing, but waited for the decision, which his boss eventually translated: "So everything's settled. Standard fee, no credit cards. This driver speaks very good English and knows where you want to go. He's just a bit reserved."

The air-conditioning in the ancient Toyota was at full blast. "Negombo Road?" he asked gingerly, as if touching on a subject of great delicacy.

"Yes, Number 41," I repeated. "A small house. Home of a Professor Sapramady."

The driver set off rather tentatively, muttering the words "Negombo Road Number 41" under his breath as if reciting a mantra.

After a while he pulled up between scattering hens and the votive chapels of a Christian mission, a collection of small buildings pock-marked by humidity and grandiosely identified on a peeling tin placard as the "Mission of the Sacred Heart of the Immaculate Conception. God is the Saviour of the Oppressed who Believe in the Eternal Way. Negombo Road Branch, Colombo, Sri Lanka." A smaller placard announced that Mass was celebrated only on the first Sunday of the month, at 8:00 A.M.

There was an embarrassed silence before the driver finally asked, as if lifting a weight from his conscience: "But exactly *which* Number 41 do you want? There must be at least ten Number 41s in Negombo Road, one in each district."

"The professor did say something. Kandana? Bandana? . . ."

The driver turned a shocked face toward me. "Kandana? But that's in the other direction. So we need another Negombo Road."

"But this *is* Negombo Road, isn't it?"

"Yes, but you should have said you wanted Professor so-and-so in Kandana. That's his proper address," he replied irritably.

"You get to the district and then you ask. Just the name of the road and the number tells you nothing. I just hope," he continued bitterly, "you've got the right addresses for the other Burghers you want to visit."

Negombo Road leads eventually to the capital, Colombo, passing mile upon mile of Taiwanese factories and the clutter of half-finished houses dotted among palms and tropical jungle of an indeterminate green. The rows of little houses with verandahs, strung out along the road by English builders at the start of the twentieth century, still have an aura of gentility. Pick-ups are parked in the drives, school uniforms hang on the washing-lines. Piles of empty king coconuts, the orange, round-bellied fruit, sweeter and juicier than any other kind, lie at the corners of lanes leading to the beach.

It was on Negombo beach four hundred years ago that the Portuguese first set foot in the land of the Dancing Kings. The capital, Kandy, was far away, a village among the mountains. The Portuguese sailors built a fortress of stone and mud and departed, leaving a small garrison behind. Their number was insufficient to conquer the whole island and, anyway, they were after spices, not land. They had sailed from garrisons in Mombasa and on the Mozambique coast. Perhaps it was from there that the name Negombo derived. They were driven from Negombo by the Dutch, who replaced them with colonial administrators, fortune-hunters and tradesmen with a sprinkling of Sinhalese fishermen. When the Dutch left, many God-fearing English families moved in, dividing up the coconut plantations into tropical gardens for their bungalows.

Today Negombo is still a Christian enclave in a Buddhist, Hindu and Muslim Sri Lanka. But here God assumes the ingenuous forms of the folk paintings commissioned by Mediterranean towns to celebrate their patron saint. Plaster statuettes of Roman centurions, with gilded helmets and swords on their belts, stand on the altars of little votive chapels and greet the faithful with arm outstretched in a stern fascist salute; on the opposite side of the road, a voluptuously curvaceous Madonna swathed in hearts, canopies, ribbons and *ex voto* offerings wafts kisses to an imaginary crowd of devotees from lips covered with layers of scarlet lipstick.

Negombo's centurions and Madonnas compete with plaster statues of Buddha, sitting golden and rotund before his shrines, his lashes pomaded, his eyes heavily made-up like an old-style cabaret artiste, gazing over the woods toward the invisible horizon where Portuguese galleons first appeared.

The house belonging to Benny Sapramady, retired professor of English, really is at Number 41. Men are relaxing on the verandah, stretched out on chaises longues beneath the slowly revolving fans, chatting and sipping the fiery coconut-based arrack, diluting it with soda, which they say not only improves the taste but enables you to drink it all afternoon.

Their sari-clad women are gathered in another room. The children have been given the job of passing round canapés of spicy fish-balls.

Shortly before three the word goes round that lunch is about to be served, but nobody stirs. The nice thing about a casual Sunday gathering of friends is that everyone can relax as if they were at home and chew over family gossip. Food is placed on little tables on the verandah and eaten without benefit of cutlery, in accordance with the elaborate manners of an older generation, which dictate that you use the tips of your thumb and three fingers of the right hand only. The party, I learn, is to celebrate the engagement of a cousin.

The professor's house is hot and airless. Over Negombo Road the sun appears, peeping out from behind a kiosk stacked with exercise books and greeting cards. The island of Ceylon has been described as a teardrop falling off India. It could as well be a drop of sweat.

On the verandah someone inquires about my journey. I tell them about the party of Buddhist monks and novices on the Boeing from Madras, beautiful in their saffron robes, who had become very angry at being made to wait for their baggage when we landed while the tourists, on the contrary, had waited patiently and silently in the dry chill of the arrivals hall. When they left, the monks had taken a long and ceremonious farewell of their colleagues, pressing together the palms of their hands. The tourists had rushed to the exit.

Many years ago I arrived in Colombo in the middle of the night to the cries of the muezzin and the smell of rotting leaves. "It's Ramadan," the Tamil porters had explained with mild amusement. "The Moors fast and pray." The Moors are the descendants of Muslim merchants whose vessels plied the shipping lanes of the Indian Ocean between Oman, the Maldives and the Spice Islands. Still wealthy, people mutter, very wealthy indeed.

The smells today are the same as on that night in 1979, though now it is Christmas and the muezzins are silent. Along Negombo Road I recognize signs of a domestic life based on memories that have become more tenuous, more nostalgic with the passing of the years until all that remains is a *saudade* of sentimental fragments. That summer long ago I had been "adopted" by the De Silvas of Mount Lavinia, a suburb where fish-sellers with blood-smeared sarongs and panniers loaded with baby tuna go barefoot from door to door.

It was the year when the papers were full of the wedding of the Prince of Wales to a girl called Diana. Some in the De Silvas' circle of friends had ashtrays decorated with their smiling faces. The De Silvas had just bought a Toyota van and had just had a daughter. Nearly every night we were invited to a party in the garden of one acquaintance or another, but nobody could ever tell me what was being celebrated. The election of a new district governor of the Lions Club was the cause of much tongue-wagging, not always friendly. The De Silvas' eldest son was hoping to be selected for the Sri Lanka cricket team and had become secretly engaged to a girl who wore her hair in a plait: her father, however, had promised her to another.

That summer I had met Sri Lankans who were different from the others. White, and with the same strangely sad smile of so many on the island, their eyes, although blue, were almond-shaped. The De Silvas ignored them and pretended not to hear my questions about them. "Those folk?" they said eventually. "No, they're not foreigners. They're Burghers. Sri Lankans like us. But descended from the Dutch."

"You know what we call the Dutch Burghers?" asked Professor Sapramady. "In Sinhalese they're called *Landesi.* Or even *Lanzi,* which is rather derogatory." What a strange coincidence. The Italian for Dutch is *Olandesi.* And the *lanzi* (or *lanzichenecchi*) were wild, blond-haired mercenaries from northern Europe who roamed the peninsula in Renaissance times.

It was the Portuguese who first informed the islanders that these other whites, with their limited respect for the Madonna and possibly suspect faith, were called *Landesi.* Four centuries on, the name remains unchanged. "Today I'm a little busy with my guests," said Sapramady, hopping from one table to another in his anxiety to spend time equally with each and every one of his friends. "But tomorrow I'll have more time and will tell you about the dance of the Dutch Burghers. It's called *bailà*—at least, that's what the Portuguese called it." He removed his glasses and executed a few steps, watched by smiling university colleagues and girls in saris. I couldn't resist the thought that even where I then lived, seventy-five hundred miles away in the northern hemisphere, between the Alpine heights of the Adamello and the Po valley, teenagers went out on Saturday evening to *bailà.*

It was the last time I saw Professor Sapramady, Benny to his friends.

Just as I left the bungalow in Negombo Road, a thunderstorm broke.

Downtown in Galle Face the rain had sent the ice-cream sellers running for shelter. This coastal sand-flat has been the island's principal port for both passenger and mercantile ship-

ping for centuries, and two bronze cannon are still trained out to
sea, whence danger to Ceylon has historically always come.

Inside the Galle Face Hotel, a white elephant asleep on the
beach, there is a smell of polished wood and worn brasswork. A
uniformed doorman with the wrinkled face of an old soldier
salutes the guests in military style, something he learned as a
rifleman in an English regiment before Independence. The vel-
vet-lined lift creaks its way up the shaft beside the wide staircase,
attended by at least two barefoot "boys" in sarongs.

The driver waited outside the hotel, parked where instructed
by blasts on a whistle. I had agreed to a fee for five hours of
work; there were still two to go.

From Room 314 of the Galle Face Hotel the city seemed
uglier than I remembered it. Heavy drops of rain were now
falling. The sea lapped against the rocks of the Fort, the ancient
Dutch fortress. From behind a writing desk in reception, a lad in
white had promised me "the best hotel room in the world" as he
handed me the key, heavy, elegant and highly polished like everything else in the Galle Face. If not the best, the room was certainly the biggest. The sitting room alone, furnished with cane
and mahogany divans and colonial wardrobes of the kind known
as *almirah,* would hold the whole of my flat in Milan twice over.
Then there was a bedroom with two canopied beds, a smaller sitting room, and a bathroom the size of a parade-ground. The antique pot-bellied tub had English taps that dripped.

The floors were of dark wood waxed to perfection, and they
creaked. The smell was that of an old house. The TV didn't
work, but the shoe-shine service could not be faulted. The
sound of an orchestra wafted up from below. In the ballroom
where once the cream of Colombo society courted and celebrated Queen Victoria's birthday with dancing and bingo,
wealthy Sinhalese were celebrating a wedding.

The taxi driver greeted me with a grunt when I reappeared.

"Now I have to go to the old Dutch Burghers' rest home, St.
Nikolaas House."

"You're a bad man," he replied, looking straight ahead with an offended air.

"Why?"

"Heavy rain, can't you see? And it's very, very far outside the city. If we go there, I won't be able to get back by five-thirty when my shift ends. When I drive tourists round they don't ask to be taken so far away. And you don't have the exact address, yes?"

"No, but we can ask once we're in the area. Everyone knows the place. Don't worry. You said five hours and five hours it will be. If by any chance we overrun by half an hour, I'll pay you overtime. And don't forget that I shall need a driver tomorrow and the day after . . . "

"You are a bad man. And you give me little money."

"I'm paying what you asked."

"Yes, but I didn't know finding Burghers is so hard."

Colombo had been flooded by the monsoon and everything was gray, the streets transformed into rivers. There was no signboard outside St. Nikolaas House, which was in a narrow side street full of puddles. The residents, forty-seven elderly ladies, had decorated a fir tree with candles and red ribbons. The smell of resin mingled with the warm dampness of tropical plants.

The old ladies gaze into thin air, sitting in their deckchairs as they did on holiday in the cool freshness of the Nuwara Eliya hill station. One of them moves with the help of a walker.

"Ninety-four years old," says her roommate and inseparable companion proudly, herself a mere eighty-one. She wears slippers and a lavender-colored petticoat, her eyes scarcely dimmed by age, golden glints in her hair. She must have been a lovely girl at the time when life in Ceylon was easy for the Burghers and, perhaps, for everyone else too.

Near the entrance, between crucifixes and a notice-board proclaiming that "Jesus is the Master of this house," hangs a black and white photograph of one of the residents, taken half a century ago. Elegant in her high-heeled shoes and formal daywear, protected from the tropical sun only by a flowered parasol,

she looks as if she is on her way to some smart social function. It
could be the woman now playing the piano without looking at
the keys because she is nearly blind. Her name is Sonia Driberg.

"Life was good in those days. There was none of this mad
civil war and everyone knew their proper place; there was work
for all, and we went on picnics to the seaside. There were no lux-
uries, I agree, we only had what was necessary, and then the Second World War came along, but we were all so carefree, and
families were big and united and every now and then someone
would manage to go and study in London or Europe. They
always came back, though, because none of us can stand the
cold and all that grayness. Ah, I was forgetting the circuses and
horse racing and the juggling acts brought to the island by Mr.
Donovan Andree, a great man. Andree of the Andree family—
you must know them, surely?—best Dutch Burgher stock, any
amount of class. Ruined now. Even them. They tell me that old
Lorenz lives in a hovel, reduced to penury. But I bless the memory of old Donovan because he gave us such fun, the old devil.
And what an impresario! He even brought *Holiday on Ice* here,
and the whole of Colombo lined up to see it, rich and poor alike.
It only cost one rupee and fifty cents. Have you seen what the
country has come to now? It's a mess. But still the most beautiful place in the world. And then it's our homeland, the only one
we'll ever have. Yes, it's ours, even if we Dutch Burghers are
white and different from the Sinhalese, Tamils, Moors, Malays,
the other peoples of the island. We're all Sri Lankans, all children of the same island."

"Yes, all equal. But you should hear them quarrel in this
place!" Ruby Lucas, ninety-two years old, is the daughter of a
former accountant of the *Times of Ceylon,* the colony's daily
newspaper. "We have to find some way of passing the time and
staying alive. I don't have a problem, however. We've always been
middle class. But there are some here who give themselves airs."

She is referring to Doreen Henricus, with her flower-print
dress, German-style sandals and hair kept firmly in place by

large barrettes. Sitting stiff-backed on the edge of her armchair, she says that she does not encourage familiarity on the part of the other women because, "One shouldn't say this, but there are Burghers and Burghers. Some—we call them the Batticaloa Burghers—have gone native. They don't know how to eat with a knife and fork, hold a conversation or behave properly in society. I keep well away from them. I prefer the solitude of my room." Doreen has the severe expression of an old-fashioned schoolmistress. She considers some questions out of place, improper. But how can one tell if someone is a Batticaloa or not? She lifts her chin, looks straight ahead. "I haven't the nerve to ask certain people impudent questions. But you can tell immediately just by looking at them."

The Batticaloa Burghers are of Portuguese extraction, descendants of colonists from Lisbon who were the first to intermarry with the Tamils and Sinhalese in the sixteenth and seventeenth centuries. Under British rule they worked on the railways, or set up shop as butchers or mechanics. They were the half-caste, poor Burghers, speaking English peppered with a few words of ancient maritime Portuguese, and were never invited to the balls given by the Bartolomeusz or Graetian families. They were religious and heavy drinkers. "Always quarreling, always in love, not proud, not toffee-nosed, quite without airs and graces," is how Carl Muller saw them. They called January "the month of bottles" because after the excesses of Christmas, which they usually spent cursing, cooking and attending Mass, returning the empties was the only way a poor Burgher family could survive.

"But you know there are some people here who say, 'She's nice, what a shame she's a brownie!'" Sonia Driberg's family were sugar planters. She went to the most exclusive schools. Today she is penniless. When she goes into town she shares a *tuk-tuk* with a friend. She and Doreen Henricus hardly ever exchange a word.

The women argue about who is more Dutch Burgher than

the others, about who comes of "good stock" and who doesn't. Or about who used to have the best connections or whose husband held a higher rank in the colonial administration or had the best position in the social echelons of the Dutch Burgher Union, the club restricted to those of Dutch descent, once a powerful secret society but now only a gloomy billiard-hall near Buller Road, draped in dust and cobwebs.

On good days, the old ladies talk endlessly about the weather. "It's cooler today," says one. "Yes, rain freshens the air," adds another. Many have children and grandchildren who emigrated to Australia and Canada after 1956, the year when Sinhalese became the official language and the Dutch Burghers—an English-speaking minority—were marginalized after dominating the press, the public sector, hospitals, legal institutions and business. Indeed, in St. Nikolaas House the very fact of having a large number of emigrant relatives is a proof in itself of belonging to the Burgher elite. Before embarking on ships bound for Sydney or Vancouver, citizens of postcolonial Ceylon had to provide proof that they came of "good stock," implying European blood. Australia welcomed immigrants—but only if they were white.

Christine, the matron in charge of the home, is younger than the others, and her oval face suggests Sinhalese blood even if she talks about "we Burghers." Part nurse, part caring daughter, she tries to settle the little disputes and jealousies and soothe the bouts of nostalgia. At five-thirty in the evening she gives orders for the tables to be laid ready for supper. The Burgher women start to cross themselves so that they will be ready when the bell rings.

"Come back tomorrow, and I'll see you get to know them better," Christine tells me. "They're busy now."

Back at the Galle Face Hotel, I try to find the telephone number of my friend Dilsham De Silva.

There are hundreds of De Silvas listed in the Colombo phone book. Four hundred years ago the Portuguese sent only male colonists to the Indies, so their blood—and names—spread like wildfire. With the arrival of the Dutch, many Tamils and Sinhalese rushed to Europeanize their own surnames.

I find a Dilsham listed. His wife answers the phone. Her voice is cold. First she tells me that he's having dinner, later that he's gone out. Finally she says, "I'll give him a message when he returns. But he's never spoken to me about any Italian friend." I ask if he has a brother called Rohan. "Indeed," she replies. And a younger sister? "Yes, married, now, and with children." A rapid calculation tells me that the little girl I saw being shown how to use her fingers to eat grated coconut flavored with hot chilies must now be about twenty-five. They could well be one and the same. "And his father, Mr. Sriyan De Silva?" I ask. "He's been dead these four years," she says crisply. "But how come? He was so young," I protest. She responds to the observation with a short laugh, as if to say, "It happens."

After a few phone calls the mystery is solved. This Dilsham De Silva is sixty-five, and despite the fact that he does indeed have a brother called Rohan, he is nothing to do with my old companion in mischief, the cricket-playing lad who secretly taught me a coded English in which, for instance, instead of saying "going to bed with a girl" you said "going to town." So you could announce your intentions even in the presence of your parents before disappearing for the afternoon, and they would be none the wiser.

Down in the ballroom of the Galle Face the feasting and dancing are over and the wedding celebrations are coming to an end. As they leave, each guest places a gift beside a register. A member of the hotel staff makes a hand-written entry: Mr. and Mrs. Fernando, two bottles of Scotch whisky and a crystal candleholder; Police Inspector Nishante Weidyasekare, two silver trays. The car-park "boys" whistle the drivers to the entrance. It is a night of full moon. The rain has stopped. The smell of wet vegetation mingled with the scent of the ocean wafts up to the verandah.

❦

As you come out of the Galle Face Hotel, the road facing you leads
to a rotunda lined by buildings in early nineteenth-century English
style. These were once the offices of the colonial administration. At
the end of the road, beyond the Holiday Inn, is a sort of church,
now abandoned. An inscription carved in relief identifies it as having been a Masonic lodge. *Tuk-tuk* drivers, sarongs tucked round
their waists, flip-flop sandals on their feet, sit inside waiting.

"Are you alone?"

"Yes."

"Do you want a *tuk-tuk?*"

"No thank you, I'm walking."

"Want girls? For tonight?"

"No."

"Boys? I've got some very young ones."

"For heaven's sake, not in a million years."

"So I'll get you some girls. Very beautiful. Russian. Only arrived in Ceylon a few weeks ago."

"Very kind of you, but no."

"Sinhalese, then, genuine local girls. Very clean."

"Did you say local? No, no, no girls."

"Wait, don't go away. It's not safe to walk alone in the evening.
I was saying, my girls are Sinhalese, yes, but their skin is whiter
than yours. We call them Burghers. Trust me."

"No."

"But look, they really are white."

"Yes, I know."

"I see. You're English? Ah, Italian. So you'll want a Thai girl.
I'll take you in the *tuk-tuk* to a bungalow near here where there
are six Sinhalese and three Thais. Choose whichever you like, no
obligation. You only pay if you decide to go ahead."

"No thank you. Another time, perhaps."

"If you don't believe me, I'll show you. Look. This is a Thai
girl. Look at the photo."

"But this photo has been cut out of a fashion magazine. And she doesn't look much like a Thai to me."

"So, if you don't believe me, come and see her for yourself. In a room on the second floor of this building which was once offices. I promise I'll show you the very girl in the photo."

"On the second floor? Didn't you say something about going in your *tuk-tuk* to a bungalow some distance away?"

"Ah, this is different place. This girl only cost three thousand rupees, but is better."

"Just to look . . ."

"Put three thousand rupees here in this envelope. Keep it in your pocket if you don't trust me. Then if you like the girl you give us the envelope. If you don't, you keep it."

"No thank you. The system strikes me as rather weird."

"So how about a Russian? I'll give you Sergei's mobile number."

"What sort of name's that? A new Sinhalese name?"

"No, Russian. He is a friend of the girls. There are many like him here in Colombo. He works at the Russian Embassy during the day and goes round with the girls at night. They come and go with their women. I know an Ivan, too, if you'd rather."

"Interesting, but no, thank you."

"Now I understand. You're not a tourist. You're here on business, right? Then I think you need a Burgher. I'll bring you one tomorrow evening. I promise you, very pale-skinned."

By the middle of the sixteenth century Venice's ancient monopoly of trade with the East had been broken forever. Portuguese ships sailing around Africa called in at the East Indies in ever greater numbers. The route was longer, but the profits immense. They had realized the possibilities after buying the most sophisticated *mappa mundi* ever produced from Fra' Mauro, cartographer of the Monastery of San Michele at Murano, in the Venetian lagoon. Thus the Portuguese trade also became a monopoly. Without the map, considered a state secret, no one

would risk sailing around the Cape of Good Hope. And almost
no one but the Portuguese sailors had the map. At the end of the
sixteenth century, however, they, like the Venetians before them,
lost their supremacy due to maps produced this time by the
Dutch cartographer Petrus Plancius, disciple of the great Ger-
hardus Mercator.

Armed with these new maps, a growing number of European
merchant vessels could now anchor at the Cape before confronting the wide stretch of ocean to be crossed, with the help of
monsoon winds, before reaching India and then the Spice
Islands further east.

Pepper, cloves and nutmeg were the most prized and the
costliest of all commodities at the time. In 1602 a group of Dutch
merchants signaled the end of absolute Portuguese supremacy on
the spice routes by forming the Vereenigde Oost-Indische Compagnie, also known by the initials VOC. By 1670 it was already
the richest company the world had ever seen, with fifty thousand
employees, a private army of thirty thousand soldiers and a fleet
of two hundred ocean-going ships. Cape Town now became the
company's fortress on the sea. The VOC regularly paid its share-
holders—among whom were many great Rotterdam families—an
annual dividend equal to 40 percent of their investment. Two
hundred years would pass before it failed, in 1799, with the arrival of a new commercial superpower: England.

Because of the immense value of spices, no holds were barred
in the war to control the trade. One famous governor-general of
the VOC, Jan Pieterszoon Coen, enlisted an army of Japanese
mercenaries to torture, disembowel and decapitate all the males
of the Banda archipelago in the Moluccas. The archipelago, considered the nutmeg capital of the world, was governed by fierce
Muslims who had always managed to resist attacks by the Spanish and Portuguese. Before the VOC arrived the population of
the Banda Islands was fifteen thousand. Fifteen years later it had
shrunk to six hundred.

Throughout the Spice Islands (now part of the territory of

Indonesia and Malaysia) the Dutch imposed the death penalty for anyone found growing, selling, buying, stealing or in unauthorized possession of nutmegs, cinnamon or cloves. When the English recaptured Run, the principal island of Banda, covered with magnificent forests of nutmeg trees, the VOC sent in a fleet of twenty-five ships. The English retaliated by occupying a Dutch possession in the Americas called New Amsterdam.

The diplomats were now called in, and to resolve the quarrel with England over the Banda archipelago the VOC's all-powerful administrative council proposed an exchange of territory. In return for England's renouncing all claims upon Run, it offered to let the English keep New Amsterdam, a young and promising colony. The island is now known as Manhattan.

One of the first Dutch captains to sail the warm seas around the East Indies was Joris van Spilbergen. A native of Antwerp, he was the second sailor to circumnavigate the globe. He died in 1620 aged fifty-two.

Spilbergen began his most important voyage on 5 May 1601 (before the VOC existed), with three destinations in mind: Bantam, Achin in what is now Sumatra, and Ceylon. After a brief stop in the Comoros Islands he arrived in 1602 with three ships at Batticaloa, a port on the eastern seaboard of Ceylon. He and his party were greeted by a local ruler who at first suspected him of being Portuguese. Once reassured that this white man was of a different race, the lord of Batticaloa told Spilbergen that he was only one of many vassals of the great king of Kandy, capital of the Sinhalese empire, and offered to accompany the visitors to meet his legendary sovereign.

The king was a Sinhalese nobleman, Vimala Dharma Surya. The Portuguese *conquistadores,* who had been colonizing parts of the coast since 1505 and now alternated between war and peace with the Kandyan kingdom, had baptized him with the name of Don Joan de Austria, even though Vimala had no idea what or where Austria might be.

An engraving now preserved in what used to be a Portuguese

convent, in the Pettah district among the narrow streets of the old city of Colombo, shows Spilbergen's long cortège winding up the mountain paths toward Kandy. It comprises twenty-two elephants, a band of musicians, bearers laden with gifts for the king, trumpeters in gaudy liveries, a safe-box containing a letter from Balthasar de Moucheron, the merchant adventurer who had financed Spilbergen's ships, to the ruler, whoever he might be, of Zeilan (one of the many names by which the island was known in the West), an armed escort of soldiers who called themselves *singalés* (the name by which the people of Batticaloa had introduced themselves to the Dutch) and also a foreign legion of Turks, Moors, Portuguese deserters and *cafferos* (black Africans). At the very end of the procession we see Spilbergen, with his white goatee beard, puffed breeches, saber at his side and—despite the heat—his neck enveloped in a lace ruff.

As soon as he arrived in Kandy, the Dutchman wanted to talk business, discuss trading and spices. But Vimala had other things on his mind. He asked for military aid against the hated Portuguese and appointed the captain his ambassador to the court of Maurice, Count of Nassau, ruler of the Netherlands, who, Spilbergen avowed, was the enemy of the white people he already knew.

As a gesture of good will Vimala agreed to name his island New Flanders. He then showed his visitor the sights of Kandy. The captain, impressed, wrote in his diary: "Indeed their pagodas far surpass the Popish churches in architecture." The king asked him if pagodas in the Netherlands were filled, like the Portuguese ones, with images of strange beings called "Maria, Petro and Paulo," to which Spilbergen replied, "We are true Christians in faith and not Popish Roman Catholics like the Portuguese." Spilbergen left for his next destination, Achin on the island of Sumatra, laden with precious stones, which he listed in his diary as *robijn, toupas, saffieren* and *olias de guattes,* "cat's-eyes," semiprecious stones abundant in Sri Lanka. He also had pepper and cinnamon worth three thousand Flemish pounds:

not a vast amount, but enough to make his employer, the merchant and shipowner Balthasar de Moucheron of the province of Zeeland, dream of colossal profits from future dealings. The king also gave him a few slaves for his personal use and one very special object, a battle trophy captured from the Portuguese, which he referred to as a *somberero.* It was an umbrella.

This was the start of what would come to be called the Hollandse Tijul, the period of Dutch rule in Ceylon. In 1644 Negombo, having resisted a previous siege, fell into Dutch hands. In 1656 it was the turn of Colombo, and in 1658 the Portuguese also lost Jaffna, in the north of the island. From all the possessions under the control of the VOC, and from the motherland itself, Dutch colonists began to arrive in their hundreds. The law gave them the exclusive right to carry on business, open shops, possess land. Butchers, bakers and shoemakers all had to be Burghers. Marriages with local women were only permissible if the women concerned were Portuguese Christians of mixed blood who undertook that their children would marry Burghers so that, as Governor Rijcklof van Goens said in the second half of the seventeenth century, "Our race will degenerate as little as possible."

The Hollandse Tijul was to last for nearly two centuries, until January 1796, just before the Dutch East India Company was declared bankrupt and immediately after the Netherlands, rechristened the Batavian Republic, was absorbed into the French sphere of influence as a French protectorate.

The Netherlands had by this time ceased to be a world power, and the white, blue and orange flag that had flown over the fort in Colombo was hauled down for the last time in 1802 when the British East India Company took control of all the Dutch colonies. Thirteen years later English troops stormed Kandy, putting an end to a kingdom that had survived, in name at least, because the thirty-one governors sent by the VOC had never seen the necessity of conquering it, preferring to have it as an ally.

The family of Sri Wickrama, the last king of Ceylon, was

exiled to India. English and Scottish settlers began to colonize the highlands, clearing the forests to cultivate tea, the "green gold" of Ceylon. Many Dutch families emigrated to other Asian colonies or returned home. About nine hundred families decided to stay on because after the collapse of the Dutch East India Company there was no certainty of employment in Batavia, now known as Jakarta.

After centuries in the tropics the Dutch were fully acclimatized. The English regarded them as an indigenous people even though their origins were patently European, and to begin with preferred to keep them at arm's length. "The first years under English rule were hard," recalls Barbara Sansoni. "They put taxes on jewelry, taxes on the size of your verandah, we had no rights of citizenship and became, overnight, stateless persons."

Then the English decided to conquer the kingdom of Kandy too, and with much more territory to administer found their numbers insufficient to do all the work, so the colonial authorities began to employ Burghers. As the years passed, the Burghers became Anglicized. The census of 1871 revealed that there were 15,335 of them. By 1901 the number had grown to 23,482, while the true Europeans numbered only 6,300. But, still in 1871, the Colombo Club, preserve of the English, did not yet accept members from either the Sinhalese or Dutch Burgher communities.

In 1844 the Reverend James Selkirk of the London Missionary Society published a book of memoirs about his experiences as a missionary in Ceylon between 1826 and 1840. A passage in his *Recollections* describes the Burghers as follows:

> The Dutch, who, together with the Portuguese, are called the "Burghers," form but a small portion of the inhabitants of Ceylon. Most of them are descendants of officers and others who belonged to the military and civil establishments of the Dutch East India Company, while in possession of the island. Though much reduced in circumstances since their island was ceded to the English, they continue to

keep up the appearance of great respectability. In general they partake of the listlessness that characterizes the native population, but they are in great measure free from those vices which are so degrading to some of the other classes. Their own language is not much used among them, except it be among the old ladies. The common language used in their families is Portuguese. They have filled situations of importance and respectability under the English government. They are employed in the Courts of Justice, where some act in the capacity of magistrates, and others as secretaries to the courts, or clerks in government offices, and have been found, by the experience of nearly half a century, to be trustworthy. The dress of the young people is precisely the same as that of the English, though perhaps they are more fond of gaudiness and display in their dress than becomes their station in society, or can well be borne by their incomes. The dress of an old Dutch lady approaches to that of English ladies in the middle of the last century, and high-heeled shoes are still in vogue among them. In passing through the streets in the middle of the day, the face of a Dutch lady is not to be seen. In the evening they make their appearance, either leaning over the half-doors of their own houses, or walking through the streets, or in the public walks, or driving in their carriages. Their evenings are often spent in gaiety and dancing, to which they are much attached. They do not mix much with the English society, but on all public occasions they attend the "Queen's House" and add not a little to the display at such times. Within the last few years, the hauteur, formerly shown by the English to all except those of their own nation, has been wearing away, and the intercourse between them and the Dutch, which at one time was formal, and only on public occasions, has become more frequent, and intermarriages have taken place between them. Whether this will tend to draw the bonds of union closer between the two nations in Ceylon, time alone can show.

His was the warmest voice on that glorious Radio Ceylon, when the whole island listened on short wave to his radio plays in English, the obligatory language of the time. He was a young star, Chris Greet, even though few people knew his face. He was lionized at parties in the best houses in Colombo, that madman Chris, that joker who pretended to be studying at university but had the soul of an artist. And to think that his father, Martin Greet, was an important inspector of railways, ranking fifth in the administrative hierarchy. And his mother was a Paynter, a family that had provided equerries to the British royal family itself and had amassed a tidy fortune dealing in fine wines. One grandfather had been a general in the English army.

Then one day Chris Greet disappeared. He vanished into thin air like many of the Burghers. Radio plays were now transmitted in Sinhalese. The country had decided to cut itself adrift from its colonial past and had even changed its name. Ceylon had become Sri Lanka. While Chris was standing in a bus queue, he heard a hostile voice shouting at him, "Hey you, white boy, why don't you bugger off to Australia?" The man had no idea that the skinny youth he was speaking to was the great Chris Greet. But "bugger off" is exactly what the actor did. He became a refugee, a stateless person. Ceylon now belonged to those he still refers to, "with no derogatory intent," as the indigenous population.

After a long silence, Chris Greet has recently started to return intermittently to Colombo. Among the Burghers who have stayed on, unable to find the money for the journey or the courage to abandon the old life, every now and then the rumor circulates that "old Chris Greet's in town." They meet him in some house where he is staying, garbed like a down-at-heel count, his nose sharper than before, still uttering his famous operettalike exclamations of "Honey! Dearest! What an incredible pleasure to see you again!" or "Darling, wonderful! Now come with me because I absolutely must introduce you to a simply divine person! He's a great . . . how shall I put it . . . friend of mine."

Nowadays Chris Greet earns his living acting in the theater and appearing in brilliant cameo roles in English films where he only has to be himself, witty and melancholic. He lives in a part of London where there is a large proportion of Caribbean immigrants. They take him for an elderly, courteous gentleman who has lived there all his life. He, however, still remembers where he was that day in 1956 when the government headed by Salomon Bandaranaike abolished English, eight years after the declaration of independence.

"We were coming out of the Radio Ceylon studios, a friend and I, when we bumped into someone who had just heard the news that from that day Sinhalese would be obligatory in schools, offices, on the radio, everywhere. Tamil and English had been abolished. My friend and I looked at each other and knew that this was the beginning of the end. But who could speak or write classical Sinhalese? Hardly anyone! A stupendous language, incidentally. Did you know it was developed from Sanskrit? That day the exodus began. All the Sinhalese that we, the Burghers, knew were the few phrases necessary to communicate with our servants. Our language was English, but for heaven's sake, we thought of ourselves as Sinhalese, not English! Take me, for example. I have some Scottish blood in me of the Campbell clan, besides Dutch, French and Portuguese. What race am I? Caucasian, I'd say. Or, to be more precise, Dutch Burgher. Ceylon has always been inhabited by a mixture of European races, besides the various indigenous peoples. In our families everything, from food to music, was influenced by Europe, but we felt we belonged to the island. Then came the moment when they told us we were no longer welcome. Formerly first-class citizens, we now had to compete with the indigenous people. The politicians deceived them, promising them the earth. They launched the slogan 'Sinhalese only' as if it were the solution to every problem, to poverty, to discrimination. But have a look at this photo. That's Arthur Paynter, my maternal grandfather, in his Indian period. Turban, bare feet. He had renounced his family inheritance to join the Salvation Army. He became commander in chief for the whole of Southeast Asia, with the rank of colonel. My father, too, was the son of a parson who devoted himself to the care of Eurasian orphans.

They were the children of English planters, for the most part owners of tea plantations, who had fraternized rather too much with the 'darkies,' the girls from the hills. Their sons became rent-boys, their daughters concubines. Very few landowners dared leave their farms and plantations to these unfortunates because they knew they had nowhere to go, that they would never be accepted into either community, European or indigenous. No, we didn't just take; we gave a lot. But now they started hurling insults at us. My dear chap, just think. They called us *polkuddu suddah,* literally white coconut powder: it means white trash. They called us other names you can't even imagine. So we all left, or nearly all. We weren't like the Dutch in South Africa, who held out. The Boers—God bless 'em—are country people, tough and lots of them. We Burghers are townies, as the word itself implies. We were a tiny minority. And we had no isolated farmhouses to escape to. The life of the rural colonial has never appealed to us. We prefer theaters, salons and libraries, working as lawyers or businessmen, to farm life. Sure, a few stayed on. Like my friend Carl Muller, who a few people, including my wife, don't like very much because he has written books that appear to denigrate the Burghers. Then Muller doesn't altogether belong. Lower-class, if you know what I mean. One of the people, a working-class Burgher. His protagonists are railway workers and so on. Very intelligent man, however. Used to work in the gutter press until *The Jam Fruit Tree* made his name as a writer. In Colombo there's also Barbara Sansoni, my dear, dear friend Barbara, in better form than ever. Aristocratic family, fine old name. Go and see her. She'll tell you about the old times."

Colombo's *Sunday Observer* now described him affectionately as "that wonderful chap whose voice we all used to recognize on Radio Ceylon. Chris had a rich, undulating timbre perfectly suited for radio." The affection, the kind we show to an elderly and harmless relative, is genuine because, deep down, everyone yearns to some degree for the good old days, and now that white skin is no longer a threat the affection can be openly displayed.

This year, which was long after he left Radio Ceylon, Chris had returned to Colombo shortly before Christmas and the word had spread quickly that he was staying in a hotel paid for by the theater that had engaged him for their Christmas show.

Dominic Sansoni heard about his arrival as he sat in the courtyard of his workshop *cum* office *cum* shop *cum* art gallery, the "Barefoot," which opens onto Galle Road and, having no shop window, looks like the entrance to a private flat. He heard the news from someone who dropped in to cast an eye over the paintings and the latest batik-dyed materials en route to an apéritif at the bar, then dinner at a house in Colombo 5, the most elegant part of town.

To outsiders "Barefoot" is simply the best shop in Colombo, packed with ethnic goods, multicolored materials, well-cut tropical clothes, curios and art books. To friends it is a parlor, always open, old-fashioned but easygoing, where they can exchange the latest gossip.

Barbara sweeps into "Barefoot" without warning and, as always, in a hurry because she is late for her next appointment, being simultaneously architect, designer, writer and publisher besides owning cotton mills. "Mother, I've heard that old Chris Greet's in town. He's to play Father Christmas at the Lionel Wendt Theatre," Dominic informs her, grinning, as soon as he sees her alighting breathlessly from a *tuk-tuk* in her ample cotton dress. "Can you imagine it? Father Christmas complete with beard, moustache and red hood!"

There's another subject of gossip today at "Barefoot." During the Dutch Burgher Union's Christmas dinner a few days ago, the president, old Harold Speldewinde, solemnly ordered everyone to stand and sing the hymn "Het Lieve Vaderland," "Dear Fatherland." In English, naturally, because—apart from these three words—no one speaks Dutch anymore. The one exception is Sam Mottan, a scholarly archivist from Nuwara Eliya, who has stubbornly refused to forget it.

Dominic was sent the text of the anthem by a friend with a

sense of humor who had rushed to the nearest fax machine. "It read like a Nazi rallying-cry. Ridiculously xenophobic," he said with a derisive smile. "What idiots! What small minds! And then Speldewinde wonders why I always 'forget' to fill in the application for Union membership! He keeps saying, 'Dominic, you're the first male Sansoni not to be a member. Fill in the form.' And I reply in all innocence, 'Forgive me, but I must have left the last form you gave me at home.' I've got five of them in the drawer." Then he turned to me sharply: "And don't turn us into a bunch of eccentrics by equating us with those fanatics. We've been the most cosmopolitan, the most open-minded, the most nonconformist of anyone in the country. Slightly anarchic, even."

The first Sansoni was Giuseppe, captain of the *Livorno,* which sailed into Colombo—no one remembers why—in the first half of the eighteenth century, at the height of the Hollandse Tijul. A Tuscan, Sansoni had enrolled in the VOC in search of adventure knowing that it was a kind of foreign legion in which Germans, Spaniards, Scandinavians and even renegade Portuguese all found employment. A few years later he changed his name to Joseph Sansoni. His son Joseph, born in 1770, became army surgeon to a Dutch garrison and married a certain Wilhelmina Schorer in Wolfendaal, at the Dutch Protestant church where the Burghers gathered every Sunday morning. His other son, Louis, enjoyed a successful career in the VOC's public administration, becoming chief excise officer in Galle and Matara. And so the line continued, with a succession of doctors, lawyers, businessmen and several gentlemen of leisure who, when asked their profession, replied simply "of independent means."

Today the name Sansoni ranks among the highest in Dutch Burgher noblesse. Barbara Sansoni, now seventy-one, is the daughter of eccentrics, mother of eccentrics, an eccentric herself and proud of it. Gray hair surrounds a pale face sculpted by generations of ancestors who married within their own caste and spent their lives drinking champagne and reading good literature.

"My mother was a Van Langerberg. She was ostracized throughout her life by the Burgher elite because she married a man who was not one of them. . . . No, she did not marry a Sinhalese!" Barbara Sansoni laughs, amused by my naïveté. "That would have been unthinkable, even though we were on friendly terms with certain good families of the Sinhalese upper class such as the Jayawardenes and the Bandaranaikes. No, my mother married an Englishman, a colonial administrator called Reginald Young Daniel. A man with a good job, regular hours, sense of duty, a country of his own. An adorable character, you know. But in my mother's family he was considered lacking in elegance, in glamor. In short, he wasn't good enough. The Van Langerbergs were art collectors, socialites, progressive thinkers for their time, people who even rather enjoyed causing the odd scandal in society. A bit like my husband's family, the Sansonis."

Early every morning, Barbara Daniel Sansoni sits on the patio of her old house. The patio, open to the heavens, is surrounded with climbing plants and parrots in cages, ancient masks of Sinhalese deities and English prints. Her son Dominic, besides running "Barefoot," is a photographer, and has photographed some of the loveliest landscapes in Sri Lanka. His wife is a Tamil, slim and elegant and with the dark skin and chiseled features typical of old Tamil families. She speaks with an American accent like many Sri Lankans who have studied abroad. Their children's toys lie around the house, which is furnished with heirlooms, some of which are the stuff of legend, such as the famous rosewood table.

This table was traditionally presented to whichever young Sansoni was expected to be the next to marry. "When the Sansonis celebrated a wedding," Barbara explains, "there was a sort of ritual handing-down of heirlooms. Fathers, uncles, cousins, all got together and carried this enormous inlaid table in procession to the door of the young Sansoni bachelor. The poor chap would cringe with terror as he heard his relatives approaching with the famous table. He knew that his life was about to change forever. The clan was demanding an engagement."

Today the processions are usually of a different kind. "During the last few months two old ladies, widows, have died, both from elite Dutch Burgher families. They lived in our road in two houses like those of a bygone age, filled with books and common sense. I've spent many an enjoyable evening with them, listening to the gramophone and talking. But because they were alone, with no living relatives, who would carry their coffins? I asked Dominic to do it. He grumbled a bit. 'Mother,' he said, 'I'm tired of all these funerals. There are so few of us left that I seem to have become official pallbearer to the Dutch Burghers.' But he did his duty. I told him, 'Remember what your father said, Dominic, that when a neighbor dies without relatives, it's up to you.' At one of these funerals a little old lady came up to me and said, 'Barbara, how nice to see the coffin carried on the shoulders of two of our men from Negombo, just like old times.' Because the Sansonis, like many old Burgher families, come from Negombo."

Two men from Negombo? There are hundreds of them living along the road from the airport. Perhaps, I said provocatively, she meant two *white* men from Negombo? Barbara gave me a hard look, sipped her tea and munched her traditional Dutch Christmas cake in silence for a while. Then she said pityingly, "Yes, of course white men. But we never use the word white. Dominic never uses it. Nowadays it would make no sense to describe oneself in such a way in this country."

The following day she resumed the conversation. "We Burghers have become strangers in our own land. We have given so much, created so much. And now that I'm old, it sometimes happens at a reception that someone will ask me where I come from and how long have I lived in their beautiful country. They

take me for a tourist, or a missionary. I tell them that my ancestors have probably been here longer than theirs. But the old
times are gone forever. My parents and their friends would go
horse-racing, then on to dinner, then dance until dawn. Then
they would jump in their cars and dash down to the beach for a
swim. Fresh as daisies, they would all go together to the Mount
Lavinia Hotel, one of the grandest colonial buildings on the
island, for breakfast. After a short rest they would be at the racetrack again, placing their bets. And in the summer they would
go to Nuwara Eliya, in the hill country, because it wasn't so hot
there, and indulge in sport and play golf, and those who had
them would cast an eye over their tea plantations. They were all
related to each other, the De Heers, the Gratiaes, the Ondaatjes,
the De Voos, the Muellers, the Sansonis, the van Langerbergs.
Religious, often Catholics, but having nothing in common with
the obscurantism of the Catholic Church today."

A manservant answered the phone and, with a slightly
reproving glance, called her. She took the call, arranged another
appointment. "For us true Dutch Burghers our domestics are
part of the family. We love and respect them from childhood.
You will never find a domestic badly treated in any of our families. We all grew up with a Tamil *ayah,* sleeping in her bed and
being spoon-fed by her. You used to spend much more time
with your *ayah* and her family than with your mother, who
would always be busy with going to cocktail parties, meeting
friends, attending functions. Who rocked you to sleep at night
when you were ill? The *ayah.*"

These were the parties I had heard so much about from Marilyn Andree. I met her in a rest home run by a religious organization in the dreary suburbs of Milan. She made her entrance
into the television room, which smelled of bleach and Formica-
topped tables, dressed as if for a ball, with makeup that was too
thick, heels that were too high, long nails and a slinky satin
dress.

I had first heard about her from a Sinhalese decorator. Nosing among my books, he had noticed and remarked on Tim Page's classic, *Sri Lanka*. I asked him if he knew of any Burghers living in Italy. A few days later he rang me up. "I've got the phone number of a lady called Marilyn. She married one of us, a Sinhalese. Give her a call."

Marilyn arrived in Italy by mistake. For five years she had been living in London, where many other Andrees live, and she wanted to go to Switzerland, to her brother. She fancied a holiday in Italy first, went there, missed her next flight, stayed, and has been in Italy for seventeen years. To begin with she tried to get work as a cleaning lady, despite being the niece of the famous Donovan Andree, the impresario who had had such success with horses, circuses and *Holiday on Ice*. The agency arranged some appointments for her, but the ladies of Milan rejected her because she did not look Sinhalese. She was white. "I tried to explain that I really did come from Sri Lanka, but they thought I was having them on."

She could hardly tell them that her father was born in a big house in Talangama with a swimming pool and servants. And that one member of the family married a Canadian tennis champion, another was involved in litigation with the Bank of England over certain numbered accounts that his grandfather forgot to declare in his will, and that yet another was a femme fatale, an exotic singer passionately courted by millionaires old enough to be her father, who had performed for George VI at Windsor Castle and, in 1943, sang for Lord Mountbatten. Another relative had three wives, fathered a bevy of children of mixed race and was declared "the most famous person in Ceylon" every year in a competition sponsored by the *Times of Ceylon*. "Here in the religious institute they think I'm Brazilian," Marilyn joked. "They say, 'You're a *mulatta,* aren't you?'"

In Colombo I met Marilyn's father, the Lorenz that everyone says, with a sad shake of the head, is now all but destitute. At sixty-eight, he already has the wrinkled face of an old man: his voice is weak, his blue eyes slightly misted over. He lives in a small, run-down apartment block on the outskirts of Colombo. Neighbors point out his flat. "The white man? Up there, the flat with the open door." Donovan Lorenz Andree, son of the great Donovan Andree, married a Tamil girl who was only seventeen when they met. Marriage seemed out of the question because he was white and, furthermore, an Andree. So she, being a good Catholic, went to church and prayed. "God, I don't know what to do. You must help me. Give me a sign. I've always gone to church; now You must tell me what to do." And she got her sign, for his courtship of her never wavered even though it made him the target of cruel gossip among the Burghers.

They lived modestly. No family money came to them. Relying on nothing but his father's name, he made a living as a clandestine bookmaker at the old Colombo racetrack until it closed down. Horse-racing has always been an obsession in old Ceylon. Michael Ondaatje writes that "in Ceylon the bankers and limeburners and fishmongers and the leisured class would spend their afternoons, shoulder to shoulder, betting compulsively. The ruler of the country believed that betting eliminated strikes; men had to work in order to gamble." When the racing was over, the so-called "leisured classes" would change and be off to dine and dance. Semi-respectable women slept with jockeys to get closer to "the horse's mouth."

Of all the people in the island, the Dutch Burghers were second to none in their love for horses. During the war all the officers of the Ceylon Light Cavalry, the regiment favored by the young Burgher men, spent every afternoon at the racetrack. Most of them only started to take the war seriously when English regiments requisitioned the thoroughbreds.

Lorenz Andree's sitting room is full of photographs. Photographs of the cups won by his father's horses, photographs of big, curvaceous automobiles of the 1930s, photographs of his daughter, Marilyn's sister, coming third in the national "Miss Working Girl" contest when she was secretary to the chief of staff in the Sri Lankan Navy, an admiral who was killed in a bomb attack by the Tamil Tigers one day when she happened not to be with him because she had stayed behind in the office to catch up with a backlog of work.

The door of the tiny flat is left open to admit light and air. On the stairs, the cement has been eroded by rain. At ten o'clock in the morning a plastic model of Big Ben on the table strikes the hour with the Westminster chimes. Lorenz is confusedly recalling lawsuits, wills that were never drawn up, avaricious mothers-in-law, deceiving accountants, big old houses still owned by other members of the family. His wife gently nods agreement and corrects quietly when necessary. "Dearest, when your father married his third wife, Binnie, she was seventeen, not nineteen. They were married in England, remember?" He mutters, "True, she was seventeen. Like Marilyn when she left home. We don't often hear from her now. She married a Sinhalese in Milan, so they tell me. My son, though, works in Berne, in the hotel industry. He's done well for himself. He comes out here every now and then so we can see how the grandchildren are growing up." His wife nods. "Yes, he works in tourism. Well, in a hotel. He converted to Presbyterianism and married a Swiss girl. A Hofer." She drops this very common name as casually as the Andree brothers would once have referred to a friend at the Dutch Burgher Union by saying, "He married one of the young Clementi-Smiths. You know, the girl who tries to dance like Isadora Duncan."

The Union building resembles the wealthy merchants' houses that line the canals in Amsterdam, but there are palm trees in the garden and the society's badge adorns the walls, proclaiming "Hollandsche Burgher Vereeniging van Ceylon." The motto reads "Eendracht Maakt Macht," unity is strength. High up in one corner you can still see the coat of arms of the Dutch East India Company, with the letters V, O and C intertwined. Perhaps this is the last coat of arms in the world still bearing the name once powerful enough to start a war. The shield shows a caravel, a palm tree and an axe surrounded by fasces identical to those of the Fascist symbol. Officially this last represents a bundle of cinnamon branches.

In the bar, which is only open to the public once a week, the billiard table is shrouded in a dust-sheet. The number of beers consumed is noted in a book. A poster, handwritten in elegant calligraphy, reads: "Members are kindly Requested to Refrain from Attempting to Repair the Telephone. The Telephone is Out of Order. Please lodge your Complaints in the Complaints book so that Appropriate Action can be taken. Thank you. The Treasurer." A few balloons—orange, blue and white, the colors of the Dutch flag—have been left over from the last function. A notice gives information about the latest charity event: "Treats for the Poor."

The extraordinary vocabulary of definitions, insults and epithets, many of which are still used today in everyday speech in Sri Lanka, is the result of centuries of obsession with racial classification. In their three main languages—English, Sinhalese and Tamil—Sri Lankans of every ethnic group and social level have shown remarkable imagination in developing dozens of derisory, ironic or just funny definitions of the "others."

Black bugger is the term of affection used by Carl Muller's characters and their real-life counterparts—working-class Burghers—for their neighbors. The Sinhalese reciprocate by calling the Burghers *karapotta,* the word for beetle. One of the most imaginative epithets to describe poor, uneducated Burghers, mostly of Portuguese descent, is *mikos.* Literally the abbreviation of "mechanics" because that is what they were originally, the insulting word is still used by non-Burghers and Burghers alike. The original "victims" were white or mixed-race Burghers, considered inferior because they had to use their hands and loved technology, a degrading interest in traditional Sinhalese culture. Another epithet still in common currency is *pratikal,* used for laborers. In marked contrast to *natumarayo,* "the people who dance," as the Sinhalese call higher-class Burghers.

Poor whites are also known as *casados,* or "settled ones." These were originally Portuguese soldiers, mostly poor and illiterate, who married local girls in Ceylon in the sixteenth and seventeenth centuries and became permanent residents, producing children of mixed race. Derived from *casa* or home, the term implies a degree of stability, the status of emigrant rather than colonial.

In old Ceylon the Persian word *parangi,* which literally means "ugly, disfiguring infection of the skin," was used for Burghers in general and, at the same time, for illnesses such as syphilis and yaws. In 1953 it caused a famous public row: Dr. R. L. Brohier, then president of the Dutch Burgher Union, had tried to mount a campaign against these racist insults and took great exception to the translation of *"parangi"* as "Burgher" in a bilingual government document.

Sometimes the game of insults is played inside the Burgher community, where to define different shades of skin color is essential for denoting social status. So low-class Burghers are *tea bushes* in the eyes of many high-class Burghers. They are also *tupass* or *tupaz,* a stone that in Ceylon is almost always one color: brown.

F ollowing is the result of a census taken by officers of the VOC in 1694, referring to "Male Household Heads living in Colombo Castle and Town":

European	223
Castizo	None
Mestizo	16
Topass	6
Portuguese	34

Sinhalese	9
Parawar	5
Chettiyar	27
Muslim	1
Javanese	1
Total	322

This is the result of a census of male inhabitants of Colombo, limited to those of European descent or affiliation, taken by the Dutch administration in 1798:

	Adult males	Male children under 16
European or of European extraction either on the maternal or paternal side without distinction	432	805
Malabar and Cingalese descendants that earn their bread in the same manner as the Europeans	96	310
Descendants of freed slaves that earn their bread in the same manner as the Europeans	35	106
Total	563	1,221

These are the results of the 1871 census "with special reference to the city of Colombo and the coffee estates":

1. Of Non-Indigenous Race

Afghans	6
Africans	11

Anglo-Swiss	2
Celts	22
Italians	27
Maori	1
Normans	3
Prussians	6
Siamese	7
Swedish	11
Teutonic	1

2. Of Indigenous Race

Malays	6,839
Moors	163,516
Sinhalese	1,669,998
Tamils	534,339

The general source for these census returns was *People in Between,* published by Sarvoday Book Publishing Services, Colombo, 1989.

Question: What was a Maori fisherman doing in the coffee plantations of Ceylon in 1871? And who were the six Afghans and three Normans?

Donovan Andree died on 4 July 1959. On his deathbed, as the Ceylon papers reported on their front pages, he was attended by "three medical experts who came expressly from London, Doctors Tanner, Owen and Clark." Their articles stressed the fact that an Air Ceylon plane had delayed its departure from the English capital for two hours for the doctors' benefit. The previous day Colombo General Hospital had appealed to the public to donate twenty pints of blood for Donovan Andree. Queues of donors had immediately formed outside the clinic.

His funeral was attended by the governor-general of Ceylon, Sir Oliver Goonetilleke, the prime minister, the ambassadors of major countries, the cream of the Burgher elite, private citizens, bettors from the three national racecourses and hundreds of unknown people to whom Andree had given money or jobs not because he owed them any favors but simply because they asked him. There was also a large contingent of teachers and headteachers from schools to which he had donated money for their carnivals. The directors of all the most important sporting organizations were also present, particularly those from the worlds of hockey and cricket and naturally that of soccer, a sport he adored and to which he had been a generous, if secret, benefactor.

In his eulogy, the Right Rev. Lakdasa de Mel recalled how, thanks to Donovan Andree, Ceylon had experienced the delights of the San Francisco Ballet, the Westminster Cathedral choir, dancers from Paris, acrobats from Japan, black trapeze artists and, of course, the skaters of *Holiday On Ice.* Over the following days, the papers published obituaries and memorial articles under headlines such as "A King is Dead" and "End of a Fairytale." One of these same papers had elected him "Personality of the Year" in 1955 by a margin of 9,641 votes over his nearest rival, Sir John Kotelawala, and awarded him the readers' prize, a silver cup worth one thousand rupees. The personalities who had the honor of bearing the coffin were enumerated in the press with meticulous care.

Journalists working for his own paper, a publication devoted to horse-racing, wept openly at his funeral. This was the paper whose front page carried the famous slogan "Without fear, without favoritism, without prejudice." Someone once said that of these three aims, only the third was legitimately open to doubt.

At midnight on 4 July, five minutes after the coffin had been nailed down, Donovan's wife, Binnie Marcelline Charmaine Augustine Andree, aged twenty-one, gave birth to a girl, Donna Andree.

Years later the Ceylon press reported a lawsuit brought by

Lorenz Andree, eldest son of Donovan, against the young widow, his own brother Donovan Jerome and other members of the family for the return of valuables that had, he asserted, been removed from his father's safe boxes before the will was opened. In a note passed to the judge Lorenz maintained that Binnie, "being only 21 and having been married to my father for only ten months before his death, was not qualified to manage his estate, in particular the Stadium Sports Club, which is a night club." The case was dropped the following year with no decision being reached. Of the precious stones and jewels reputedly deposited in various European banks, including the Bank of England, no less, nothing was ever heard again.

Donovan Andree's second wife was Erin de Silfa, a well-known singer and femme fatale. A Burgher girl from a poor background, her dark silky skin, sensual lips and turbulent life brought her fame. Andree discovered her when she was only nine years old. The pianist Walter Rodrigo had suggested her as a backing vocalist for Donovan's new group, the Red Tail Minstrels, and while skeptical at first ("At nine years old?" he exclaimed. "Impossible!"), he changed his mind as soon as he heard her sing. He married her a few years later, making the marriage conditional on her quitting the stage. Erin had agreed to this, despite her newly acquired status as a star thanks to the six hundred concerts she had given during and after the Second World War for English troops stationed in Southeast Asia. In those days of patriotic fervor she only had to sing "God Save the King" to send shivers up the spines of an audience in uniform. A complete break was impossible.

Even after her marriage to Andree, Erin was still known as "The Girl with the Voice." One day that voice failed. At his own expense, Andree summoned a famous Harley Street specialist. He operated on her. The first time Erin tried to sing after convalescing, she found her voice had changed. It had become more special than ever. She was now a contralto.

Then Erin met a man still older and richer than Donovan, the theater impresario Jack Hylton. Her marriage to Andree was failing. Hylton knew this. He courted her, flattered her and finally convinced her to take over Vera Lynn's role in his production of *London Laughs* at the Adelphi Theatre in London's West End. In 1950 she sang for the royal family at Windsor Castle and was paid the supreme compliment of being invited to supper with them after the concert.

Further marriages and further divorces followed. In 1965 a court order obliged her to pay damages to one ex-husband for "prolonged adulterous behaviour." Londoners continued to rave about this exotic colonial who was every inch a Mayfair socialite.

Erin knew her power over men. In 1963 she gave an interview to the *Daily Mirror* in which she was quoted as saying: "I can walk into a room full of men and know I can get anything I want from them. The biggest difference between us and Western women lies in our mystery. Men are entranced by mystery and by shyness. Even in the intimacy of marriage it is necessary to be mysterious. In all the years of my two marriages neither of my husbands ever saw me in the nude nor saw me undressing."

Meanwhile, in Colombo, her ex-husband Donovan Andree had hit on a great publicity stunt, employing beautiful girls to take the place of mannequins and pose—titillatingly but never *too* scantily dressed of course—in shop windows.

There may have been an especially dark chapter in Erin de Silfa's past, but when she told the story no one knew whether she was unburdening her soul or glamorizing her image. She said that when she was eight years old her father had sold her for an unspecified sum to a man who made a habit of "collecting" young girls with the excuse of training them as singers. Carl Schmidt, the man in question, was a millionaire Burgher with a dubious reputation who drove around Colombo in a Fiat convertible, always had a bevy of women in tow and was a close friend of the bishop.

One of Erin's friends was the model Nina Dyer. Another Burgher of Ceylon, Nina married Baron Henry von Thyssen in Colombo in the summer of 1954. When they were divorced in

Lugano a few years later, the judge ordered Thyssen to settle a million pounds sterling—an enormous sum at the time—on Nina, who went to live in Versailles surrounded by exotic birds, rare animals and, most spectacularly, with the black panther that had been Thyssen's wedding present to her.

In Ceylon, marriages tended to be more short-lived than illicit affairs, which, by contrast, seemed eternal and passionate, uniting high-society families or dividing them in picturesque and sometimes violent feuds. During that magic interval between the two world wars, everything seemed possible. Fortunes could be won or lost at the gaming tables, fashion was as closely followed as if Ceylon were the center of the civilized world, responsibility was nonexistent. Men celebrated their fortieth birthday in exactly the same way they had celebrated their coming-of-age in college at an English university where no one knew their origins nor the source of their wealth or carefree high spirits. By the age of forty their curriculum vitae had progressed no further than a register of parties, balls, motor races, fads, fancies and extravagant financial ventures destined to failure.

In the hot months the best Burgher families escaped to the Nuwara Eliya hill station with its golf course, racetrack and English club where billiards was played every morning at eleven o'clock. Everyone was related more or less. And marriage partners were swapped in the knowledge that this was a forgivable sin. In the evening they danced to gramophone records. Fires burned on the hearths, not for their quite unnecessary warmth but to create the delicious fantasy of living à la English Home Counties.

All were of mixed Dutch, Tamil, Sinhalese and English blood. Willy Gratiaen collected snakes, Philip Ondaatje wine glasses. Lyn Ludowyck (whose family, originally Ludovici, was of Italian origin) sang obscure ballads from operas of which no one had ever heard. Wilfred Bartolomeusz was accidentally shot by friends during a hunting expedition (they had mistaken him for a wild boar), while Jessica Cantley was very nearly killed by person or persons unknown (a rejected lover, possibly, or maybe the wife of a lover she had failed to reject) firing 113 shotgun pellets at her during a game of croquet. On the Gasanawa rubber plantation there was a big flat rock standing high among the frangipani, almond trees and rice fields, where they tangoed till they dropped.

At the end of the war, Queen Wilhelmina's sixty-fifth birthday and the liberation of the Dutch East Indies from Japanese occupation were both celebrated at the Dutch Burgher Union. A committee of ladies organized a Variety Entertainment and a so-called "Dutch Tea" with cakes and pastries such as Broeder, Poffertje, Fougetti and Bolo de Amor, the "ball of love" made from a recipe inherited from the Portuguese. The Broeder were prepared according to instructions given to the daughters of the Woutersz family by a maiden aunt who remarked with some asperity that, "When good Burghers make Broeders the raisins don't sink to the bottom."

At Colombo's Havelock racecourse, a water buffalo grazing in one of the fields around the lake apparently went off its head and charged the starting lineup at the precise moment when the signal was given for the "off." The horses took fright and in the silence of what was described by a Dutch Burgher Union reporter as the "indigenous crowd," several jockeys were thrown, while the Band of the Ceylon Fusiliers struck up a patriotic march to relieve the general embarrassment.

At Christmastime, a few elderly Burghers with long memories exchanged greetings in the Portuguese-based dialect once spoken all along Main Street in Pettah: "Bon entragu de Natal." None of them had ever been in Holland or Portugal. Inside the fortress of Galle, in the labyrinth of narrow streets lying beyond the great gate crowned by the protective talisman of the VOC coat of arms carved in marble, a handful of Burghers were still speaking Portuguese, just out of habit, in the 1920s. In Batticaloa on the east coast a community of Portuguese Burghers, despite being completely forgotten by the Lisbon authorities, once enjoyed a degree of autonomy and even used to elect their own headman. A few, possibly about fifty, still survive. But even in their heyday when their numbers were more substantial, no one in Galle or Colombo would ever have dreamed of associating with these mulatto *mikos* who became, in effect, a tribe within a tribe.

In church most Burghers sang the old hymns surviving from the sixteenth century, such as "Alleluia per nosse Senhor / Jesus tem nascide / Grande Redemptor / Jesus tem nascido," but there was no faith except in the easy life that seemed guaranteed to last forever, and no patriotism, only dedication to their own eccentricity.

To an English governor who inquired about his nationality, the Burgher bon vivant Emil Daniel famously replied, "God alone knows, sir." Emil, like many of his friends, never felt himself to be either Dutch or English, nor, perhaps, entirely "Ceylonese," unlike old Ondaatje, who pretended to be Tamil although his ancestor emigrated from Holland to Ceylon in the seventeenth century. Others felt close to the South African Boers, among whom they had friends and relatives.

The first Boers made their appearance at the start of the twentieth century as prisoners of war captured during the Boer War. Dutch Burghers had fought in this war, naturally on the English side, but had found themselves confronting an enemy that spoke a language that was vaguely familiar and ate biscuits baked from their own recipes.

There are those who still remember the story about an old, robust peasant from the Transvaal captured by the English in the Boer War and deported to Ceylon. After the war, many of his fellow POWs had married Burgher women—and been surprised to find them preparing the Christmas fare according to the familiar Dutch tradition and reading Bibles written in the language of the old motherland. They had either remained, becoming Burghers and British subjects, or had taken their Burgher wives back with them to South Africa. The man from the Transvaal did something quite different. He went to live alone in a log cabin near Hambantota, preferring the forests of his new country to his native Africa. He became famous for his stubborn refusal to swear allegiance to the British crown, as was required of every naturalized subject.

The ex-POW's name was Engelbrecht. He lived by killing the leopards that were a threat to the local people, and this was probably why they tolerated him. They even gave him a job, as first game warden of the Yala National Park. One day the English governor-general encountered him on the road between Badulla and Hambantota. Ordering his driver to stop, he spoke severely to Engelbrecht: "They tell me that you are the Boer prisoner of war. Tell me, why won't you swear the oath of allegiance?" To which Engelbrecht replied: "I hear you are the governor of Ceylon. So I prefer to keep your friendship and not lose it by answering your question." The governor proceeded on his way puzzling over a problem he was unable to solve.

Much later Engelbrecht recounted the episode to R. L. Brohier, the Burgher construction engineer who built Ceylon's irrigation system and whose manuals are still sold in the Colombo bookshops. Engelbrecht explained, "Mr. Brohier, I was a scout rider for General De Wet. Before I set out with one of his messages we took an oath together, namely, that neither would surrender to the English enemy. I have only kept my word." Engelbrecht died happy in the forests of Ceylon, where elephants drag away the trunks of felled trees and antelopes sip water from rice fields with dainty grace.

Barbara Sansoni recalls that the Dutch Burgher elite always regarded the South African Boers as blood brothers. "There were families who went to and fro between Ceylon and South Africa. We felt close, even though racism has never been a problem here."

One day in 1982, Barbara was revisiting the Fort in Jaffna, one of the earliest built by the Dutch but long off-limits due to

Tamil occupation of the city, when a thunderstorm broke out and she sought shelter in a small stone-built church inside the Fort. There she encountered a French missionary who took her to his study where she introduced herself. "Sansoni!" he exclaimed, leaping out of his chair. "Yes, I'm a Sansoni," she repeated, thinking that the priest must have heard of the noble lineage founded by the Italian captain. He interrupted her brusquely. "You should be ashamed of yourself!" he scolded, then forcibly escorted her on a brief tour of the Fort, home for centuries to the families of the Dutch East India Company and later to English civil servants with their Tamil and Sinhalese counterparts. Even to that day, the little community in the Fort was still isolated, a city within a city. "See that boy with blue eyes?" asked the priest. "Sansoni! . . . And the other one over there? Same blue eyes . . . And that one further away? Can you see his eyes?" Every time he pointed out a boy he exclaimed bitterly, "Sansoni, all Sansoni! All Sansoni's doing!"

They were the famously blue eyes of Louis, one of Captain Giuseppe's two sons who, in the course of a successful career with the VOC, had been posted to Jaffna. Here a libertine lifestyle resulted in his genes becoming so liberally scattered that by the end of the eighteenth century he had become the involuntary founder of a strange tribe with eyes identical to those of certain Tuscan fishermen. Then his children intermarried, because if you lived in the Fort in Jaffna you trusted nobody in the world outside.

At St. Nikolaas House, in the Dehiwala district, the octogenarian Christobelle Oorloff (once a pupil at Wesley College in Colombo and Trinity College in Kandy) often reminisces about the narrow streets inside the Jaffna Fort. Cobbled. Smelling of the sea. White buildings, thick walls, fans always whirring. From the inside you can see the sea, and you delude yourself that you can control it.

"It was 1941. Singapore had just fallen to the Japs and we knew that Ceylon was next on the list. My husband had been posted to Jaffna to organize food rationing. We were assigned a place called King's House for our living quarters, one of those old houses with the kitchen miles away from the dining room, a verandah and enormous *punkahs* to keep it cool in the evening. I remember the Dutch tombs with names carved in relief, the tennis club with its two courts where everyone went in the evening to play a game or two and chat endlessly. Before we went, they warned us about the ghost of a Dutch girl in a red dress who walked through the house at night. Those were the happiest months of my life. But Ceylon was never invaded and we were posted back to Colombo. I didn't have time to see the ghost."

The specter was that of the daughter of a governor of the Dutch East India Company who had lived in the Jaffna Fort. Michael Ondaatje tells the story of how she committed suicide in 1734 by throwing herself down a well when her father refused to allow her to marry the man she loved. Perhaps he was a Sinhalese.

Honking of *tuk-tuk*s. Smell of petrol. Heavy Chinese "boneshaker" bicycles with coconut-shell helmets dangling from their rear wheels. Traffic jam on the road leading from Colombo to Mount Lavinia and on toward the beaches in the south. Buddhist temples where people leave offerings to ward off the dangers of travel. Elephants with tufted ears dragging tree trunks to a builders' yard. Their great feet, chained together, pad softly on the tarmac. Cars slow down respectfully. American music blasts from a car radio. Water buffalo drawing tanks of bitumen that is sold by the bucketful; the buckets dangle from the tanks. Old English school. Humidity. Placard on the wall of a Protestant mission promising "Jesus is coming very soon." You can see that the words "very soon" are a recent addition. The original "Jesus is coming" didn't have enough punch.

❦

The first Brohier, a Huguenot captain from Normandy, arrived in Colombo in 1777 and the family stayed on in Ceylon even after the Dutch were driven out. The family has now lived for generations in a bungalow close to the beach beside Galle Road in Colombo.

You can see the sea at the end of the road. The railway line that runs parallel to the beach has carried no train in years. There is a hint of sickly sweet languor in the air, of tropical idleness tempered with solid sobriety. Inside the Brohiers' house silence reigns. Old photographs on the walls have been left just as they were when the old engineer was alive. A bare-footed maidservant serves ginger beer. Deloraine Brohier, the engineer's daughter, has never married and is now an aging spinster with her hair in a bun and a touch of lipstick on her pale lips. The man in her life is still her father, the hydro-engineer and historian of the Burgher community. "Everything here was collected by him," she whispers as if confiding a family secret.

One wall of the sitting room is adorned with blue and white porcelain plates. The easy chairs are of wicker-work and old, dark tropical woods. In this rarefied atmosphere, talk of race makes Deloraine uneasy. "Of course, when I was young the adults wanted to keep our race pure. Mixed marriages with Sinhalese or Tamils were taboo. But we Burghers have always mixed very easily with the people of the island. We have never been racist. My father was a man of the people. No time for luxury. But nowadays everyone wants everything and wants it immediately. Shortcuts are all that matter. Some time ago I went to a village of straw huts. A boy noticed my gold bracelet and ring and rounded on me angrily saying, 'You have everything, we have nothing. Give me that bracelet.' I told him that if he wanted a bracelet like mine, he had to earn it first. We Burghers were not the privileged heirs of anybody. We were loyal to the British. We worked hard. Our lives were always based on the principle of duty, on the Victorian values."

Outside, the daylight is waning. The furniture in the Brohier house has become as dark as the eighteenth-century furniture stacked in the organ loft of Wolfendaal church. "You mustn't believe all you read in Michael Ondaatje's books. They deal with a very small proportion of Burgher society. We were not all social butterflies like his characters. You mustn't believe what Carl Muller says in his books, either. We were not railway workers, drunkards, uneducated boors. We were somewhere in between. Ordinary people. We lived in the Tropics as we would have lived in Europe. We were taught to respect others, to work and to study. In Sri Lanka today they are in the process of forgetting we exist. I act as an adviser to the tourist board. I go to meetings and conferences. I too, like many of us, find Sri Lankans asking me, 'And what country do *you* come from? Have you been in Colombo for several months?'"

Barbara Sansoni: "When I was a girl, I remember the pastors in the Dutch Reformed Church of Ceylon saying that colored people couldn't be saved. I belonged to that stratum of Burgher families that eventually left the Reformed Church and went over to the Roman Catholic, which has always been much more open-minded here. We didn't want to be associated with any kind of racism. Just imagine! We were related to the Bandaranaikes, one of the very best Sinhalese families."

Deloraine Brohier: "In my time people were still talking a lot about Sir Richard Francis Morgan, a legal luminary who became vice-procurator general of the colony and later a member of the legislative council, a barrister and a judge noted for his fairness. There was a scandal when Sir Richard was turned down for membership of the Colombo Club. The English members said he was

Sinhalese, a native. His sin was to come from an old Burgher family. Shortly afterward the governor offered him the post of procurator general. He refused, for health reasons he said. A great man."

Barbara Sansoni: "In his book *Running in the Family* Michael Ondaatje describes his parents' engagement. That memorable event took place in my father's house; his father and mine were friends. I remember his grandmother, too, the famous Lalla Gratiaen. Always wore skirts down to her feet. She led a madcap existence. In the purest Dutch Burgher tradition."

Deloraine Brohier: "Ondaatje. A good writer. But, if I may say so, not exactly one of us. His family claims to be of Tamil origin. No harm in that, of course!"

Barbara Sansoni: "With my name, I've often found myself involved in misunderstandings. Once, when we were living in Boston because my husband was teaching at the university, I went into a pharmacy run by Italians. When they saw my name on the prescription, the Sicilian assistant kissed me on both cheeks. As soon as I began to speak, however, they were confused. I heard them saying to each other: 'She's not one of us. She comes from the North.' They obviously meant the North of Italy."

Deloraine Brohier: "The glue holding our community together was always the English language. Despite differences of class and shades of skin color, the Burghers all recognized each other by that."

Barbara Sansoni: "My family, the Van Langerbergs, was German."

Deloraine Brohier: "The Dutch East India Company employed huge numbers of Poles, Hungarians, Scandinavians, Flemings, French Huguenots like my own ancestor, and Germans too. They came to seek their fortunes in the East. In those days they said, 'Go East, young man.'"

Barbara Sansoni: "Deloraine's a sweetie. Rather too straight-laced, perhaps."

Deloraine Brohier: "Barbara's a sweetie. Rather too much of a social butterfly, perhaps."

❦

The office, furnished 1950s-style, is sealed off from the outside world by floor-length orange curtains and lit by strip-lights. No chink of daylight enters, even though the sun blazes outside. The desk is dotted with heavy brass lamps with green glass shades. On the walls are photographs of cargo ships and good-conduct diplomas awarded by Mexican and Ukrainian port authorities. The air-conditioning roars like a diesel truck.

The shipping agency run by Harold Speldewinde, president of the Dutch Burgher Union, consists of a reception area where Sinhalese secretaries with long lacquered fingernails answer telephones, and the closed office where he sits in his dark orange jacket and dark orange shirt.

Speldewinde is seventy-one. He is descended from a Speldewinde of Amsterdam who found employment in the legal department of the VOC in the eighteenth century and was assigned to the colony of Ceylon. His father worked for Ceylon Customs and Excise. His brothers are all ship-owners, in the mercantile spirit of the country he insists upon calling the Dutch "motherland." Speldewinde lists his own merits as being an elder of the Dutch Burgher Union, having replaced the roof of St. Nikolaas House, having revitalized the Burgher Union and having organized a party for 450 guests at which the colonists' anthem was sung. He concludes by saying, "In every field I always reached the top and became the best. And I made the right choice when I decided not to emigrate to Australia as did many Burghers. If I were in Sydney now, I would be a clerk, a humble employee. Here I am the managing director of five companies and represent eight shipping lines. Now all I want is to see my grandson play cricket for Sri Lanka. And to receive an application for membership of the Dutch Burgher Union from that crazy Dominic Sansoni, who has told me five times that he left the form at home."

THE DUTCH BURGHER ANTHEM

Fair realm, they from the ocean won
The cradle of our race,
Where all their noblest deeds were done
The theme of song and praise—
We subjects of great England's King
From Ceylon's distant strand,
To thee our loving tribute bring—
Het Lieve Vaderland!

May we who here, mid toil and strife,
With diverse class and creed,
Need courage in our race of life,
Our fathers' virtues heed.
They, when by sore oppression tried,
True to themselves remained,
Their watchword still may be our guide—
Het Lieve Vaderland!

Along Negombo Road pale sunlight falls on banana bushes and plaster Roman centurions. Word has got round that the army liberated a city from the Tamil Tigers last night. Professor Sapramady's verandah is empty today. At the Burgher Union a Sinhalese employee in a white tunic has handed me photocopies of a pamphlet printed in gothic script. It contains the family trees of the Colin-Thome, Muller, Ohlmus and Speldewinde families and an essay by John Capper published in London in 1878.

The room on the second floor of the Union is empty but for the flags, the marble tablet inscribed with the names of Dutch Burghers who fell fighting in British uniform, and the association's crest of palm tree, caravel and bundles of cinnamon.

Capper writes that during Dutch rule, two ships a year sailed to Europe from Colombo. The fashionable dance in town was the "Caffreina," a kind of tropical can-can. The widow of a man called Plaats and the Van Graafs sisters (all spinsters) organized Christmas celebrations.

Tomorrow evening the Sansonis are entertaining at home. Chris Greet, the actor, will be among the guests. The Madonnas of Negombo Road are already shimmering with light.

2
Jamaica
German Slaves

If you know your history
Then you would know where you coming from
Then you wouldn't have to ask me
Who the heck do I think I am
— "Buffalo Soldier," Bob Marley

Seaford Town, August 1996

Extract from a letter written in 1836 by Karoline Wulf, emigrant, to a German newspaper:

> My fellow-countrymen, under no circumstances must you come to this land called Jamaica. The temperature here is extremely hot and five crowns will only buy five potatoes. Everything else, too, is incredibly expensive. For ten days after my arrival I felt so ill that I could not walk. We live surrounded by wild beasts. Let no one deceive you, do not let yourselves be persuaded to emigrate to this place unless you want to starve to death and be dragged down, like us, forever. I felt that I had to write to warn you because we, unlike you, had no choice. The emigration contract was given to us on the ship, when we had already left port. And what could we do, in those circumstances, except sign it?

The following is an extract from an anonymous letter published on 13 May 1835 in Issue No. 38 of the magazine *Der*

Sprecher—Rheinisch-Westfälicher Anzeiger ("The Announcer—
Rhineland-Westphalia Advertiser"). The paper's motto was
"Truth, Justice, the Common Good":

> At the beginning, when we first arrived in this distant land,
> we were very happy. The natives welcomed us very warmly.
> Then we were taken to the place appointed for us, and we
> immediately saw that the firewood was unusable and the
> water undrinkable. Over the following weeks we realized
> that it would be impossible to grow food on these moun-
> tains, but we were ordered, nevertheless, to build our huts
> on that poor, infertile soil. Now we never have enough food
> to eat. And we continue to suffer.

"I was eighteen when I went to Germany for the first time. I'll
tell you what happened."

In the sitting room of the Wedemeyers' house on the outskirts of a Jamaican village—christened Seaford Town by
founders who dreamed of a city dedicated to the beneficent (if
distant) Lord Seaford—the light, tinged green by the wild banana trees covering the surrounding hills, barely penetrated the
heavily embroidered curtains. It was tea time on Sunday, hot
outside, and Tony was not feeling talkative. Seen from the
Wedemeyers' sitting room, Jamaica was a motionless forest dripping with sun and moisture.

"Always the same old questions," Tony grumbled. "Look,
who do you think is going to be interested in the history of a few
Germans who happened to end up here God knows how long
ago? All Jamaicans are descended from people who arrived in the
Caribbean by chance. And too much attention is paid already to
skin color, race and nonsense of that kind. We must be the most
ethnically diverse nation in the world. For centuries we've been a
mixture of white, black, Chinese, Arab. Yet class distinctions still
persist, and how! All based on the color of your skin. If you're Indian or Chinese, your class is defined automatically. Do you know

we have seventeen different definitions for at least twelve different shades of skin, from white white to black black? Each shade has its own name: Quadroon, Quintroon, Octoroon etcetera. And the destiny of each is predetermined. But if you really think someone will be interested, I've got a story for you."

Tony Wedemeyer shook his Rasta-style dreadlocks. Once blond, they have now faded to a strange shade of yellowish-gray. To look at him, you might take him for one of those aging hippies still to be seen on the beach in Goa and Hikkaduwa with their sandals, their ethnic necklaces so fashionable in the 1970s, and their hand-rolled cigarettes. He could easily be an American or Scandinavian flower-child adrift in the Tropics. But Tony Wedemeyer is no imitation Rasta; he is genuine, born in the Tropics as were his parents and grandparents before him. His great-great-grandfather, however, was a shoemaker in the Duchy of Saxony who one day—motivated by a spirit of adventure, financial necessity, ingenuousness or perhaps a combination of all three—boarded a ship with many others like himself and disembarked under the blinding Jamaican sun. A reluctant colonist, a settler by default.

Outside the church a few hours earlier, Tony's mother, Ines Wedemeyer, had greeted us like old friends. "So you are Riccardo and Pia! From what you said during Mass I understand you come from Italy or England or somewhere like that."

Pia and I had introduced ourselves to the congregation of fifty or so at a church in whose adjoining cemetery all the tombstones are inscribed in Gothic script with names like Wilhelmina Kameka, Gertrude Teresa Brown and William Somers. We had been told that all strangers visiting Seaford Town on a Sunday were expected to introduce themselves.

"Today we are happy to have visitors with us. From Canada we welcome back some we already know well, relatives of our dear Annetta Kameka. From Europe . . . well, I think it's best if our visitors from Europe introduce themselves." Deacon Vince's pronouncement took his flock by surprise, but this small man with a deeply tanned face gave the impression of one unused to contradiction. He beckoned me energetically to his side. So, trying to conceal my embarrassment, I mounted the altar steps, something I had not done since serving Mass as an altar boy at our local church. There, facing the silent stares of the congregation, I explained why I and the blonde girl in the T-shirt sitting in the third row (everyone turned to glance at Pia) were going to spend a few days in Seaford Town. When I finished, the audience nodded silently. The explanation had gone down well.

"Mr. Vince, the deacon, says Mass every Sunday despite not being ordained, because the parish priest spends all his time in Montego Bay," Ines Wedemeyer told us as we stood outside the church. "Vince asked me to give you a hand. If you're interested in our folk here in Seaford Town, come to my house. I'd like you to meet someone who would certainly interest you, the one person who can still speak the tongue of our forefathers. My son Tony." Ines paused for a moment, watching us carefully to see the effect of the sensational revelation she was about to make. "He actually lived in Germany for years!"

Ines broke off, removed her straw hat and greeted an elderly friend, Hilde, as she appeared in the church doorway draped in an embroidered, lace-trimmed shawl. The two women exchanged polite phrases in a strange, guttural English before Hilde pulled the shawl around her pale face and set off for home, a farm some distance away.

She disappeared along a footpath hidden behind a stall. From the stall, roughly cobbled together from planks of wood, a black mother surrounded by numerous children was selling mangoes, kerosene and corn-cobs, lifting the steaming cobs from a large black pot bubbling on the fire.

Hilde's gait as she set off was that of a feeble old woman, yet in church we had noticed her sitting in the pew next to ours with her back as ramrod-straight as a Prussian soldier's. At one point, when the deacon intoned the opening of the hymn, the slight porcelain-doll figure seemed to be galvanized as by an electric shock. Silent until that moment, Hilde followed Vince's lead with unexpected enthusiasm. From the prim mouth hitherto pursed into a disapproving sneer came, loud and clear, an old church hymn transformed into negro gospel music. Hilde sang at the top of her voice with unassailable solemnity, staring straight in front of her while beating time (in our direction) with a beautiful lace handkerchief, inherited perhaps from an ancestress who arrived on the same ship as Tony Wedemeyer's great-great-grandfather.

"Well," Tony Wedemeyer began, "it all started when I won a scholarship to the faculty of modern languages. I was one of 230 students from developing countries. There were Africans, Orientals, South Americans, some from eastern Europe, of every color under the sun. There were three of us from Jamaica. I didn't know the other two, they were city types. To begin with, I kept myself to myself. They came from the capital, Kingston, while I was country born and bred and knew only the mountains of my patch in what you would call the provinces, the parish of Westmoreland. It's what you can see from the window, nothing but banana plantations and dripping woodland and a few poor souls who try to make a living from farming.

"Anyway, when we got to the foreigners' university in Saarbrucken, we three Jamaicans immediately became bosom pals. It was inevitable. In Germany we felt like fish out of water, so we found ourselves clinging to each other for encouragement, comforting ourselves with Jamaican music, joints and food—especially pork ribs with jerk sauce. Everything was going fine until one day one of the German teachers took me aside and said in a very paternal way, 'Listen, Wedemeyer, I don't want to interfere with your private life, but why are those two blacks always dogging your heels? You can speak quite freely to me. . . . Are they making nuisances of themselves? Do they bother you?' I didn't understand what he was driving at to begin with. Then I thought maybe he was getting at me for not socializing enough with the South Americans or—how should I know—with the Bulgarians, perhaps. So I said, 'No, sir, there's nothing wrong. It's just that we're all a bit homesick for Jamaica. You know how it is, we stick together because we miss our home.' The teacher's eyebrows shot up. 'What home are you talking about, Wedemeyer? Are you having me on?' And then he stammered, incredulously, 'Do you mean that all three of you come from the same place?'

"It was then that I looked at my white skin and realized, for the first time in my life, that I was different from the other two Jamaicans. I believe that that was the day when I stopped being a child. Just imagine losing one's innocence in the dark corridor of a university college in Saarbrucken!"

Tony Wedemeyer laughed, reveling in the pleasure of speaking about Germany, his ancestral homeland, above all when pretending to speak ill of it. But a wave of his hand signaled that he had not finished yet. He tried to find the right facial expression, somewhere between horror and surprise, and when he had found it, raised prophetic hands to heaven. "And when I told the other two about what had happened, we stared at each other and burst out laughing. One was called Chow; he was a 'Chinaman,' half Chinese, half Syrian, Lebanese in fact, but we call all Arab traders Syrians. The other chap, Schroeder, was as black as coal. His great-grandparents came from Africa."

At last we felt that we, too, could laugh, we foreigners who had invaded his house on his mother's say-so and were now providing him with his Sunday afternoon audience.

Introductions had been hasty. "Pia's my wife. We've only just been married. She's English. I'm Italian. She's a doctor. I write. We came here in search of the last Germans in Jamaica. We arrived in Seaford Town this morning." That was all I managed to say before Tony launched into his monologue.

Every time he shook his head, the gray-blond hair worked loose and he had to redo his ponytail. It was more than a bunch of fluffed-out dreadlocks. It was a symbol.

"Do you remember the great Bob Marley that memorable July afternoon in Battersea Park on the banks of the Thames?"

Who could forget it? It was 1977 and Bob, whose greatest passion—after poetry—was soccer, had decided to indulge himself. It was a fine afternoon and he had planned a little family match between his Wailers and a team from Island Records for a workout before the concert.

Some old photographs bore witness to the occasion. They hung in a tiny study awash with paper between the kitchen and the sitting room in the Wedemeyers' home. A map of Ethiopia was almost hidden by an ancient black and white television.

"Isn't that where we all came from and where we're going back to? And that's no mere figure of speech. Some actually did it for real. Twenty-six families, Rastafarian religious pioneers, went back many years ago following the route of the slave ships in reverse, presented themselves before His Majesty the Emperor Haile Selassie, and never returned to Jamaica. They stuck it out through thick and thin, through war, famine, revolution, dictatorship. Nothing beat them. Today they farm the same lands that were given to them by the Negus personally, at a place called Shashamane. They cultivate their 'African-ness' in the place where human civilization began. That's why there's a map of Ethiopia in the study.

"But that's another story, man. I was talking about the Wailers. They hated soccer. The Island Records people not only hated it but had no idea how to play. Still, to humor Bob they all finally agreed to have a go. The Jamaicans arrived at the pitch with their Rasta dreadlocks stuffed into great big woolen berets hanging down to their shoulders. The recording people pretended to play in earnest. And the Trenchtown prophet scored two great goals."

At that time Tony was still at the university of Saarbrucken. "I ended up staying on in Germany even after graduating. It was ghastly," he muttered. Then, thinking about it again, he admitted, "Well, it wasn't that bad to begin with. It was interesting getting to know the place my ancestors had come from. But after a while I couldn't wait to get away. Imagine, here was I, working for the Jamaican tourist office, advertising my own homeland, but in Germany!

"When I finally returned, I was elected to Parliament. It was the first time that anyone from Seaford Town, or in other words a German, had been elected. And I scandalized the ruling clique by appearing in Kingston dressed as a Rastafarian. Bob Marley hadn't been dead for very long. The men of Babylon—who are they? The rulers of the materialistic world of unbelievers and wheeler-dealers, in short the politicians—they pretended not to notice when they saw me. The only thing they were interested in, anyway, was my signature on certain bills of which I, unlike them, disapproved. Man, I'm not the compromising type. Listen to this, my friend. Six months after the election I resigned my seat and founded a party, the Jamaica Alliance Movement."

Tony Wedemeyer produced a business card embossed with three capital letters, JAM, against an African background. He had also included some Stars of David, because Haile Selassie, king of kings, Lion of Judah, in short the Messiah, was the 225th descendant of David and therefore related to Moses. There was also a hint of the American Dream. The name of the founder and president was written in the style of an aspirant governor: H. G. (Tony) Wedemire. An old ploy: initials to suggest importance, and nickname in brackets to inspire a sense of familiarity. Politics in Jamaica is not a game for amateurs.

On the electoral register, the name would appear as Wedemeyer, not Wedemire. But according to Tony his real name would have sounded too Teutonic. And *Jah* is a tolerant God who can allow a little lie in a good cause. *Jah* understands that, in the most litigious island in the world, the difference between an *i* and a *y* is a subtlety too far in the search for votes.

Bob Marley said as much himself, didn't he? "Emancipate yourself from mental slavery." Meaning mental slavery is worse than the physical kind. Man, if fate tries to tie your hands by giving you a German name but you feel the blood of Africa flowing in your veins like a true "Bongoman" or "Congoman"—remember the words of "Rastaman Live Up"?—then you have every right to break those mental chains.

And everything will be *eirie,* everything will be all right. Isn't that so?

Tony talked and talked, and the small blonde sitting beside him began to show signs of impatience and to puff out her cheeks. She had obviously heard all about Saarbrucken, JAM and "Congoman" more times than she could remember. He tried to soothe her by whispering something in her ear and handing her a hand-rolled cigarette.

The sweet smell of *ganja* filled the air. Officially, marijuana is illegal. Strictly prohibited. But eight million Jamaicans smoke it, cook with it, drink it, grow it, pass it to their friends, sell it to the tourists, praise it in music and in poetry. The Ethiopian Coptic Church of Zion holds *ganja* sacred as the herb of wisdom, to be eaten during the Mass like the Host. Reports suggest that there are eight thousand plantations and that it makes the single most important contribution to the economy after tourism. The government turns a blind eye.

Tony eventually relaxed, blowing little clouds of pale blue smoke out into the prim sitting room between the flowered curtains and the sofas with their sensible loose covers of printed cotton. He inhaled within cupped hands, his eyes turned to the ceiling, in silence.

"That's Michaela," Ines whispered proudly. "His current fiancée."

Ines—still wearing her Sunday best because the people in Westmoreland, praise be, are God-fearing and know how the Sabbath should be observed—looked the girl over from head to foot with an expert eye. "She's very young—and she's German. A proper German, from Germany. I don't know why, but all Tony's women come from Germany. I can't tell you how many he's had! They run after him like bees to a honey-pot and call him the white Rasta."

Ines's attention switched abruptly from Michaela as she turned adoring eyes on her son. He was gazing fixedly at the blank screen of the old television set. "I'll bet that he, my Tony, even thinks in German now. His grandfather would be so proud of that."

Clouds of marijuana filled the flowery room furnished like an advertisement from an old European magazine. Through the window we could see Tony's brother (his complete opposite, black-skinned, short-haired and with a hatred of politics) exercising a pair of horses. He had built a stable behind the Wedemeyer house, beside a road full of potholes in the middle of woods whose tallest trees are a few emaciated coconut palms.

This is a story about a letter stolen in a good cause. More precisely, it concerns a letter borrowed from a dusty library in a small blue-and-white painted house where the parish priests of Seaford Town lived for over a century.

Catholic missionaries came from Europe by somewhat mysterious routes. This was the one sign that the world had not forgotten the Germans who had, for whatever reason, established themselves in the mountains of Jamaica. The community, whose Protestant families had converted to Roman Catholicism, never knew exactly who sent the priests nor who financed their journey. They only knew that when the old priest died his place would be taken—after a long period of silence—by another who came, by ship as their own ancestors had done, to ensure that the little flock isolated in the Caribbean should not be without a shepherd.

The new priests came from Holland, Scotland or Austria. Sometimes they were Jesuits who arrived accompanied by teachests full of books. All were impeccably kitted out with riding boots and white pith helmets like officers of some nebulous papal army stationed in the Tropics. They were of strong faith and robust physique, their faces soon tanned by the sun and their hands calloused by the physical toil of repairing buildings flattened by hurricanes every two or three years. These devout men tended to avoid excessive familiarity, but if disease broke out in the banana, yam or ginger plantations, the farmers with German surnames would summon them to say a prayer in the fields and not hesitate to invite them—as they were to hand—to help spray the affected crops with DDT.

The Reverend Francis Kempel created quite a sensation in the 1930s by being the first priest to arrive from Kingston on a motorcycle instead of on horseback. As soon as it broke down for the first time, however, he had to abandon it for lack of spare parts and, like his predecessors, visit his flock on the mission's donkey or a horse lent by a charitable parishioner.

The wooden house built for him in the 1930s is still referred to in reverential tones as the "Rectory," the word often accompanied by an almost imperceptible inclination of the head, as if the Rev. Francis, with his strict schoolmaster's gaze, were still there. But the Seaford Town rectory now stands empty.

A few years ago another Father Francis, from Holland like the first, returned to Europe old and broken-winded. He was the last to live in the rectory. A few of his ex-parishioners, including Ines Wedemeyer, still keep in touch with the priest who christened everyone in the family and married most of them. Every now and then they get a reply, in handwriting that becomes ever more shaky as the years go by. Father Francis the younger retired to a village in Holland called Oosterhout. Word has it that he thinks of nothing else but the years he spent in Jamaica with "his" Germans.

The new priest, an Irishman, promptly moved to Montego Bay, 30 miles away, and lives in a single-story house only a few yards from the beach that figures so prominently in tourist brochures. The church in Montego Bay is a square, modern building. Every so often a Jaguar hired by one of the hotels drives through the gates and deposits some middle-aged, blushing Scandinavian woman swathed in lace on the newly mown lawn. All these women clutch enormous cellophane-wrapped bouquets. They are the brides who come by charter flight for an "all-inclusive" wedding in the sun. The hotel supplies everything: witnesses, reception, blessing. The bridegrooms perspire in their tight-fitting morning dress and joke nervously with the altar boys. The Jamaican photographer with his ancient Nikon strives to appear demanding and surly with the bridal couple: he has learned from watching foreign colleagues that this is the professional manner.

Mo' Bay—as all second-time holidaymakers call it—is growing all the time. Besides a Catholic priest it now boasts a McDonald's, intended by its promoters to attract tourists but usually packed with Jamaicans queuing demurely in front of doggedly slow-moving assistants.

By contrast, Seaford Town is dying. The pastel-colored rectory once occupied by the two Fathers Francis, with its verandah overlooking the hills and the roads that wind round them and upward to the coconut plantations, is only an abandoned house.

The Irish priest, Bobby Gilmore, makes infrequent appearances limited to baptisms and funerals. He never stops overnight. The roads are now surfaced, even if full of potholes, so after two hours of bumping down them in his station wagon he can be back home in Mo' Bay before nightfall. With a bit of luck he can make it in time for a few holes at the Montego Bay Golf Club before it closes for the night. His clubs came with him from Dublin, in a red bag that stands under the crucifix in his sitting room next to a pile of parish magazines waiting to be distributed.

The Seaford Town rectory is looked after by Mr. Spencer, a plumber by trade and Father Bobby's factotum. A big man with pale blue eyes and a square jaw, he invariably carries the rectory keys in his pocket as if expecting the priest to turn up at any moment requiring a bed and a study.

Every evening before dark, Spencer goes to the general store at the end of the high street for a bottle or two of Red Stripe. The emporium is run by a German couple in their sixties who make a point of being surly toward strangers and blacks. These

are the Kamekas; no one knows them by any other, more familiar, name. The husband wears a tight-fitting Panama hat reminiscent of those once worn by peasants of the Po valley when
they went into town. His wife is in charge of the American-style
fridge: she keeps it padlocked, and never opens or closes it without looking suspiciously over her shoulder. Most of the
Kamekas' trade is in cold drinks, seeds, dried fish and farming
tools, all lined up behind the counter according to brand and
color. At a given time they shut the shop, securing it with planks
and a heavy iron grille, and head homeward on foot through the
coconut palms and the herds of goats browsing among the flowers. They walk along the path silently, one in front of the other as
is the custom in the mountains. He has a pipe stuck in the corner of his mouth. She wears flip-flops.

Spencer, however, remains seated on the verandah. He's got
nothing else to do; besides, he hasn't finished his beer.

"If you intend to stay for a few days, you can sleep at the Rectory. It would mean some small contribution to the costs at least.
You wouldn't believe how much it costs to keep the place
together!" He sounded almost piqued, as if we were to blame
for the fact that bills have to be paid even in the absence of the
priest. And every time he has to go all the way to Montego Bay
to claim his money back from Father Bobby.

Inside the Rectory, the floorboards creak more loudly every
year and insects have taken over the big guest room. But no one
in the village will admit defeat and, in theory, the house of the
parish priest has never been shut up. All the everyday things—
books, cutlery, old English newspapers, enamel basins in the bathroom, mold-covered boots, a tablet of dried-up soap—are still in
their places, casually abandoned as in a weekend cottage, unused
for years, whose owners, expecting to be back the following week,
left everything ready for the return that never happened.

The library is like an archeological site where successive strata
lie exposed. The oldest layer consists of books belonging to past
priests, mostly on religion or history. The next layer contains

newspaper cuttings about the war in Normandy. The top layer reveals the odd novel by Ian Fleming, who dreamed up the adventures of 007 on the terrace of a Jamaican house called Goldeneye.

It was there, tucked into a James Bond book, that I found the letter I have yet to return, still in its envelope bearing a fifty-cent stamp depicting an aircraft in the red and yellow livery of Air Jamaica. The letter contains no secrets, no private communication. It is simply a little scholarly diatribe, low-key intellectual sparring that observes all the courtesies while making its point with all the requisite firmness. Without shedding any dramatically new light upon the subject, it summarizes some obscure chapters in the history of a Teutonic tribe in the Caribbean. It asks why hundreds of Germans who were not peasant farmers, and who knew nothing about working the land, found themselves in Jamaica in the winter of 1834 working as slaves in one of the harshest, most intractable woodland regions. Was it true that they intended to emigrate to America as free men and were tricked? By whom? Why should anyone have wanted to dump them in that godforsaken spot, isolated from all humanity? How did they manage to survive, trapped as they were by disease, hunger and fear? Why did other white people living on the island not come to their help? And what eventually happened to them?

All we know for certain is that many of them died only months after their arrival. Others managed to escape. Having cleared the trees, sown and raised some crops, they used the money from the sale of the first ginger harvest to pay for another passage on board ship. This time they made it to America. Some chose to stay behind because they now had homes in the forest and had, perhaps, acquired a taste for heat, lush vegetation and tropical fruit.

Spencer the plumber comes of this stock. It is written in his eyes and in his freckled skin, still white, still sensitive to the sun after eight generations.

So, to the letter. The envelope is addressed in meticulous handwriting to:

Padre Bobby Gilmore SSC
Mission of the Sacred Heart
Seaford Town
Poste restante Lambs River
Westmoreland

It runs:

Guava Ridge
P.A.
St Andrews
26th July 94

Dear Father Gilmore,

I thank you for your letter and pamphlet which I have just received which I have found most interesting; however there seem to me to be some statements made in your pamphlet which deserve examination. [. . .]

Indentured labour brought here since 1683 had always been found to be unsuitable since they either could not or would not work in the hot sun and so it seems improbable that [Dr. William] Lemonius would have brought Germans here for this reason and by 1834 indentured servants were no longer necessary. The only purpose it seems then is that they had skills necessary and needed by the owners of plantations.—Then the question must be asked: why at Seaford Town which is miles away from anywhere where their skills could have been of use.

The first migrants were landed at Port Royal in Dec. 1834 and so were required to walk or be taken from there to the other end of the island. In order to do so they had to pass through Cayamanas Estate which was then owned by the Ellis family who also owned Port St George. Now had they wished to help those people they could easily have allowed them to settle on the waste lands around Cayamanas and not have been obliged to walk so many miles.

The present Lord Howard de Walden and Seaford

has informed me that to the best of his knowledge the first Baron Seaford gave no land to anyone to settle and since Baron Seaford was named Charles Rose Ellis he could easily have given them a piece of Cayamanas Estate; they would then have been of use to him due to their skills and to the wider community as well as themselves.

Some consideration must now be paid to the ship *Olbers*. [. . .] The *Olbers* was owned by E and F Delius of Bremen. Now this firm did business in New Orleans in America and had as far as we know no connections in Jamaica. This leads me to believe that the migrants were told that they would be taken to America not Jamaica. This would then account for a number of facts. One: the migrants were dissatisfied with the conditions here. Two: that the second voyage landed them in Rio Bueno not Port Royal and that they were taken not to Seaford Town where the others were but to Ulster Spring and Montego Bay so that trouble with them could be avoided. [. . .]

Your pamphlet also states that at the end of their indenture they were given five acres of land. This would have contravened the existing laws since by the law of 1683 each servant was to be given forty shillings, and by the law of 1703 each was to receive thirty acres of land. Now laws made by Parliament in England have never been rescinded. So in 1840 the law would still remain. [. . .] It seems to me that they were either badly short-changed by Lemonius or else they were not indentured at all but brought under the pretext of being taken to America.

I have always had the deepest regard for the people of Seaford Town, and in fact all those brought here, as they have shown what hard work under frightful conditions can achieve. Yet Seaford Town is possibly the only town in Jamaica which I have never visited. One day I hope to correct this.

I would be most pleased to have any remarks or comments upon this letter which you may wish to make and any further information which you may have.

Awaiting your kind reply.

Yours sincerely

Alan R. Facey

When we arrived in Seaford Town for the first time, one sunny Saturday, we could still taste the chili prawns we had eaten in Black River, principal town of the parish of St. Elisabeth. Women with headscarves knotted over their foreheads sell them by the roadside, shoveling them into plastic bags as you watch, like the hot chestnuts sold on the streets of Milan in winter. You eat the prawns whole, spitting out only the tuft of whiskers and licking the saffron-colored oil from your fingers.

There are still crocodiles in the river from which the town takes its name and that flows into the sea a quarter of a mile away from the wooden Georgian-style houses owned until a century ago by merchants trading in sugar, timber and fustic dye. These were people who made fortunes by buying virgin land, clearing the trees, transporting the trunks by river to the town where they were loaded onto ships bound for Europe, and trading the valuable timber for the latest technology.

In 1893 Black River became the first city in Jamaica to be lit by electricity, and by 1903 motorcars were already driving along the elegant roads between the residential zone and the famous thermal spring.

Nowadays Black River has nothing but its prawn industry and a few shops with swing doors like those of the saloons in Westerns. From a distance the houses with their lattice-work verandahs and pastel-colored wood or plaster filigree decorations look like illustrations in a book of fairy stories, but their woodwork is crumbling, their gardens are neglected and overgrown. Long deserted by its clientele, the spa has shrunk to a trickle where only cattle go to drink.

To drive to Seaford Town you can start from Negril with its

four and a half miles of sand the color of talcum powder, crystal-clear sea, marijuana dealers and hotels that rent out surf. The road runs through Savanna-la-Mar, an area of plantations and slave rebellions, and skirts Bluefields Bay (an incredibly long, curving sweep seen from the hills above) before reaching Black River and then turning inland toward the heart of the island where the parishes of Westmoreland, St. James and St. Elisabeth converge.

When we first saw it, Seaford Town looked like any other village, if slightly more run-down and isolated than most. The winding road was full of potholes, some as deep as the wheels of the little runabout we had hired in Negril.

"Why do you keep sounding the horn? You know there's nobody coming round these bends," Pia protested from time to time.

To begin with, I insisted it was to warn traffic coming in the other direction. But in reality I knew that I was hooting, almost obsessively, at the holes in the road to punish them for being there. In the end, as we lurched in and out of yet another, I had to confess. "OK, OK, I'm hooting at the holes. Telling them what I think of them. That way they'll learn."

We were both on edge after visiting one of those magical villas the Jamaicans call "Great Houses": white-painted, enormous and standing way back from any road, at the far end of a plantation.

The word plantation slips easily off the tongue, but in Jamaica it has a bitter resonance. A sugar or spice plantation was light years away from any European or American farm. The plantation was a world apart, where thousands of human beings worked and suffered, sang and plotted, produced untold wealth and went hungry. A closed world where fear lived cheek by jowl with unimaginable luxury, where every individual knew that he might kill or be killed at any moment.

The "Great House" we had chosen to visit that day was even more imposing than the others. From a distance it looked perfect, standing on a hillside with magnificent views, its white paint bathed in brilliant sunshine. The fields we drove past had all been deserted, for no one wants sugarcane now, and no one wants to work under the hot sun, and even the owners—or their descendants—now live elsewhere, in Florida or some New York penthouse, working with the stocks and shares that are this century's equivalent of sugarcane.

Inside, the house was dirty and untidy, its old floorboards covered by tasteless carpet. A cook poked his head out from a tiny kitchen to explain that, as no bus was running that day, the hotel was empty. In fact, it was closed. We were free to look round the house if we wanted to, but that was all.

We found ourselves peering at second-hand reproductions of the original antique furniture, dispersed God knows where in the course of countless changes of ownership. Or perhaps it was burned after Independence, when the house was left empty and uninhabited for a long time waiting to see if anyone would dare buy it and install themselves as colonial overlords.

Many of the "Great Houses" of Jamaica are the same now, mirages that disappear on closer inspection. Mirages surrounded by expanses of long grass, waterless fountains, overgrown shrubs and scraggy trees that were once the proud landmarks of an estate producing ginger and allspice, sugarcane and cinnamon.

Seaford Town lies at one end of a plateau greener and more somber than the others, overshadowed by a chain of mountains. Every afternoon an old peasant walks up the road between wooden farmhouses built a century and a half ago in a mixture of styles—German chimneys, Caribbean verandahs.

There is no central square in the town, only a stone church at the highest point and a cemetery with tombstones inscribed with Gothic script.

Hanging out in front of the Rectory, Cleve Hacker and Odeen White always see the old man puffing up the hill with his basket toward the Kamekas' store where the boys only go to buy bags of luridly colored ice that they suck through a hole in the plastic wrapper.

The old peasant in the check shirt offers his avocados to passers-by, but there's no hard sell. He lowers his basket to show his wares and then continues to plod along the road, replacing the hooked machete in his belt. Words are unnecessary. He smiles and goes on his way, flicking the peak of his baseball cap down over pale-blue eyes and sucking in his cheeks until they almost disappear into the toothless mouth. Before him and behind, the village lies still, enveloped in sunshine. The stillness is interrupted only by a scooter ridden by a man with a fair moustache carrying a toddler gripped between the red fuel-tank and his own bare knees, appearing suddenly and raising a little dust.

The day we arrived in Seaford Town we immediately became inseparable: big Cleve, little Odeen and the two of us. Without wasting any words, they simply detached themselves from the low Rectory wall and attached themselves to us. And we, with a similar economy of words, adopted them as guides.

Cleve said, "Don't worry, we'll be good. And we'll tell you where to go. If you want to meet anyone, for example, we'll take you to them. I'm friends with everybody here." His tone was final.

I felt I had to probe a little, however. "Why do you call yourself Cleve? Isn't your real name Clive?"

"No. My name's written C, L, E,"—with a little puff of impatience—"Not C, L, I." Then, without wasting any more breath on explanations, he took charge of the situation. "OK. Tell us where you want to go and we'll take you."

Cleve was unsmiling, very much in earnest. He got into the car and gave orders, taking our compliance for granted. There was no danger but all the same he was our protector. Never asking a direct question, he watched us closely, trying to glean secret information about the world beyond the end of the road. He knew everything about the parish, about Spencer and about the Rectory. "I'm German, too. So's Odeen," he told us, and would have been shocked had we expressed any doubts about it.

The day we became friends, Cleve was barefoot and wearing a white woolen undershirt. On our way we had seen some mixed-race children with woolly blond hair. Pointing firmly at his own head, where a few golden hairs shone among the black curls, Cleve said: "Look at this." And in answer to the inevitable question adults put to a child, he said, "I don't know. I'd like to be a soldier, but maybe that won't be possible."

Sitting in the back of the car, he and Odeen chatted to each other. They were very keen to be seen by their friends, and when we came across groups of them sitting beside the shack the local black population uses as a bar, or perched on a farm fence, they would wave in leisurely fashion like presidents on a state visit. Every now and then Cleve commanded me to "Stop here!" As I braked to a halt, he opened the door, leaned out with great dignity and simply beckoned, saying "One," or sometimes "You and you." As soon as the chosen ones realized their good fortune, they rushed to the car and jumped onto the backseat with Cleve or into the luggage-space without so much as a glance at the two foreigners. Once or twice, when the number of passengers began to rival that of a school bus, I objected, saying there was no more room, they'd be uncomfortable. Cleve paid absolutely no attention. "Straight ahead, then take the first dirt track on the right after the post office with the yellow verandah," he said brusquely with a hint of exasperation. I drove on.

Cleve's composure was only ruffled once, the day Spencer took us in his minivan to visit Father Bobby in Montego Bay.

Sitting in the front, he found his way around the city like an old hand, waving to the woman selling papers in a kiosk near the church. Our visit to Father Bobby accomplished, Spencer announced that he needed to speak to his sister, married to a black baker. The bakery was shut. So we went to their home, in a peeling tenement block on which broken aerials and wet laundry were much in evidence. Cleve ignored the children hanging over balcony railings and shouting questions about his two white companions.

At lunchtime it occurred to me that the children might enjoy a visit to McDonald's. I asked Spencer if he agreed.

"Of course," replied the plumber-cum-sacristan, more morose than usual.

As we sat down beneath the big plastic umbrellas copied from American amusement parks, Cleve remarked casually, "My mother always brings me here." And Odeen immediately added, "So does mine."

Saying this was my treat, and without thinking too much about it, I asked Cleve what he and Odeen would like.

"Rice and peas," he replied unhesitatingly.

The one really safe answer, he thought. Rice and peas is the staple diet of poor people in Jamaica, the only food they can afford. The Germans of Seaford Town are no exception. He now learned that rice and peas were not on the McDonald's menu. And Cleve was embarrassed.

After toying with their burgers for half an hour, he and Odeen exchanged bemused glances. Odeen had discovered that he did not like this kind of food at all; Cleve had eaten the french fries but left the burger on his plate.

On our last day with them, having laughed at the tourists and gossiped about the whites of Seaford who secretly sleep with black women, Cleve and Odeen told us (as if answering a question, or perhaps judging that the moment had come to reveal a secret) that they were brothers.

"But that's not possible! I thought you were friends. In that case, why do you have different surnames?"

"Because we've got the same mother but different fathers."

"Do you live in the same house?"

"Of course. Come to our house this evening."

❦

The following is a shortened version of an article by Debra Anthony in a special "Jamaica Independence" supplement published with the *Sunday Observer,* 4 August 1996:

> To listen to many Jamaicans talk, this year's Independence Day is nothing to celebrate.
>
> "As a matter of fact, our Independence has been nothing to celebrate for about the last 15 years," says Alvin Brown, small time trader. Brown believes Jamaica lost its way on the path to Independence somewhere in the late 1970s and has been wandering in hostile territory since, searching in vain for a reliable signpost. "I don't expect everything to be perfect, it couldn't be, even old, old countries have problems, but when you start to make the majority of the population poorer and poorer instead of richer and richer, you know that something has gone wrong."
>
> When Jamaica became independent in August 1962 Brown was 15 years old, dirt poor and only "mildly excited" by the prospect. "It didn't mean much to me," he says. "I had my own priorities at the time." But he had somehow got the impression that with Independence there would be unlimited opportunities for "poor black people" to get a better life. "It didn't happen, not to me. But then I figured it was because I didn't have enough education. But over time, when I look at other people who had better education than me and I see that they're not going anywhere either, I realize, boy, that things [have] gone wrong and it is the politicians who screw it all up for everybody."
>
> Bruce Golding, founder of the National Democratic Movement (NDM), would agree with him, at least in part. He thinks that the experiment with socialism of the 1970s was a colossal mistake that disrupted the advances made in the 1960s and left the nation further impoverished, a prey to unemployment, social unrest and mindless apathy. He says: "We glorified poverty and indiscipline, telling people that it was wonderful to be poor and a crime to be rich. We led our people to believe that we were all aggrieved by slavery, colonialism and imperialism and that we had to be repaid for all this suffering. We didn't have to work or invest . . . we just had to sit back and reap our compensation. It was an awful period in the psyche of our people . . . and it left us carrying not a chip but a lightpole on our shoulders."

༄

Christopher Columbus landed in Jamaica on 5 May 1494, sailing from Cuba with an armed caravel, the *Niña,* and two other ships, the *San Juan* and the *Cadera.* He found an island inhabited by one hundred thousand Arawak Indians, a race of easygoing agriculturalists with mongoloid features and skin the color of bronze, led by chiefs called *caciques:* their home was an earthly paradise where hunger, illness and work were unknown. Columbus wrote in his diary that this was "the fairest isle that eyes have beheld, covered with valleys, fields and plains."

The Arawaks were neither artists nor warriors—even if their *caciques* chivvied them into numberless skirmishes with neighboring villages. Although capable of hunting and fishing, they were not particularly fond of either activity, and not even especially religious. Quite simply, they lived. Their world was confined to the Antilles, and the island of Jamaica, or Xaymaca (which Columbus tried—and failed—to rechristen Santiago in honor of the shrine at Compostela), was big enough, with its mountains, forests, rivers and shores, to provide them with all the food they required. They loved the sea and took to it in fifty-oar canoes made from hollowed-out trunks of cedar trees. They also loved stone, which they worked with some skill. Jamaica, in fact, had everything except the one commodity that Columbus immediately set his men to seek: gold.

There was no hidden treasure in Jamaica, only its fertile soil. So the Spaniards decided to use that, and from that moment everything that Jamaica could be made to produce—cassava, pigs, cows, dried fish, maize, fruit—was earmarked for victualing the armies fighting in other colonies of the New World. The conquistadores of Mexico, Peru and California now came to depend upon the goods exported from Sevilla la Nueva, a tiny port on what came to be called St. Ann's Bay. Sevilla was the capital city of Spanish and Christian Jamaica during the rule of

Diego Columbus, son of Christopher and the new governor of the Indies.

One hundred and fifty years later, on 10 May 1655, the Spanish were thrown out. One of the last governors was Francisco Ladròn. His name (meaning robber) was a fair reflection of the nature of Spanish rule on the island.

As so often in the history of Jamaica, a major event came about by pure chance. The English fleet of thirty-eight ships, sent by Oliver Cromwell, was under orders to take Santo Domingo, the much wealthier capital of Hispaniola. But the expedition had been badly prepared in a climate of scandal and theft, and things went wrong. So Admiral Penn, deciding that the only way to avoid Cromwell's wrath was by attacking another Spanish possession, looked at the map and ascertained that the nearest was a place of which hardly anyone had ever heard called Jamaica.

The Spanish fled to Cuba, taking with them everything of value except their slaves. Cromwell grumbled but decided to take possession of the place all the same. His first order was to dispatch a thousand Irish girls as wives for an equal number of soldiers. The second was to look to Africa for the muscle-power that would encourage English colonists to emigrate and open up the first large plantations.

On 28 September 1839, one year and two months after 311,000 Jamaican slaves had been declared free men, Father William Cotham, a forty-eight-year-old English missionary sent to the island by the Jesuits to teach and preach, was sitting at his desk in an old house in Spanish Town, twelve miles from Kingston. He shared the house, which he had transformed into a combination of rectory, chapel and school, with a French Jesuit, Father Dupeyron.

The mission to Spanish Town (the ex-capital of the island, known as Santiago de la Vega during Spanish rule) had failed.

The response from the Catholics had been cool, perhaps out of fear of retaliation on the part of the Protestant majority, and only a tiny handful had availed themselves of the chance to receive Communion and hear Mass. So the two Jesuits had decided that, come October, they would return to Kingston.

Father Cotham was turning these thoughts over in his mind when he heard the sound of a mule stopping outside the rectory door. Visitors were extremely rare in Spanish Town. This one turned out to be a robust man of twenty-eight who spoke reasonably good English.

"My name," he said, "is John Bierbusse, and I'm looking for a priest. I was on my way to Kingston, but they said to stop here because I would find what I was looking for."

"I'm Father Cotham. What can I do for you?"

"I've been sent as their messenger by the people of Seaford Town. There are three hundred of us there. Germans. Two hundred Catholics and one hundred Protestants. We came to the Americas some time ago, nearly four years in fact. When we first landed we met a priest who promised to come to us some day provided I undertook to write to him and tell him how we were getting on. I have written many times, but I have never received a reply."

"Did you say Germans?"

"Yes. We manage as best we can. We have no contact with other people, we are on our own and far away from everything. So far we have made do with the Bibles we brought with us from Germany. We have also built a school and a chapel. We have a Mass on Sunday, with Psalms, hymns, prayers, everything as the Lord would wish it. But we need a priest. People die, babies are born, marriages take place. I am only a Tertiary of the Franciscan Order. As a Catechist I am competent. I have also baptized twenty children, you know. But only when the parents have insisted. I can do no more. So I told my companions that I would go to find someone and tell them of our existence. Can you help us?"

Father Cotham was flabbergasted. How, given all the

Church's efforts to reach out to potential members, could it possibly have overlooked the existence of hundreds of good German Catholics?

"Do your people speak English?" asked the Jesuit, partly to gain time.

"No, hardly any of us. I'm the only one with a reasonable command of it."

"So you need a German missionary. But here in Jamaica not even I could help. I shall speak to Father Dupeyron. He should be back in a few days. He's on a pastoral mission, visiting the region. Where did you say you Germans live?"

The brief contact ended when the priests retreated to Kingston. Johannes Bierbusse returned to Seaford Town with the news that far away, beyond the mountains and the plantations, there were towns and cities, churches and even priests. Cotham, who had no overpowering urge to don riding breeches and travel to the other side of Jamaica, became contentedly absorbed by his duties in the city. But the French Jesuit James Dupeyron, having learned to drive a gig—terrorizing the streets of Kingston in the process—eventually felt free to set off on a lengthy visit to the large estates and the houses belonging to the proprietors of the sugar plantations, looking for the Scottish, Irish, Portuguese and German colonies that—so it was said— had remained isolated, cut off from all contact with their fellow human beings.

Advised (sensibly) against using his gig, he ventured out on foot or muleback under the tropical sun along mostly unmarked tracks. Every now and then he would come across a Great House buried among sugar plantations where he could stop for a night or two and receive a substantial meal and warm bed in exchange for a hurriedly performed baptism or marriage (long postponed due to the isolation of the plantations).

One of his last stops was at the home of a Scotsman, George MacDonald, who had first studied for the priesthood but then abandoned the seminary to marry and seek his fortune in

America. It had taken Father Dupeyron many days to reach the house, days when he had seen nobody, encountered nothing but heat and dust, eaten nothing but fruits and berries from the trees. Then, at last, he came to the fields of sugarcane, heard the rhythmic songs of the slaves, the hiss and crackle of machetes. A peasant had told him that the Scottish *massa* might be Catholic.

Over dinner in the MacDonalds' Great House, during which the proprietor and his young wife bombarded him with demands for the latest news of the city, it occurred to the priest that before returning to Kingston he might check out that strange story Father Cotham had heard about the existence of a village of Germans somewhere near, in the parish of Westmoreland but further inland.

"Don't know anything about it," said MacDonald, frankly skeptical. "Yes, I've heard about some white folk living many miles away, possibly on the Montpelier estate, but I've never seen any."

Much to the astonishment of all, the Abbé Dupeyron rode his mule into Seaford Town on 19 November 1839. He was greeted warmly by the three hundred Germans Bierbusse's story had led him to expect, and immediately performed two baptisms. Bierbusse invited him to stay on, but he left after three days. There were other scattered communities to visit, other neglected souls to save. Besides, there was no Great House, only a few farms run by people not only poor but in many cases illiterate. He also had to prepare a visit to British Honduras where, according to reports, a handful of Catholics in a mainly Anglican population were still waiting for the Church of Rome to acknowledge their existence.

The Germans arrived in Seaford Town in two waves. The first came at the instigation of a certain John Myers, a white Jamaican who came up with the idea—immediately dismissed as absurd by authoritative newspapers such as the *Jamaican Dispatch*—of countering the effects of the imminent abolition of slavery by importing European workers. They would be white, conscientious, God-fearing people who could be expected to set a good example and, if necessary, take up arms in defense of the English colonials should the slaves threaten a violent revolt.

Myers had gone personally to Germany and chosen—having felt their muscles and examined their teeth—eighteen healthy men, nineteen women, sixteen boys of sound constitution and twelve girls. He insisted on a well-balanced spread of skills. He could have been founding a Utopian city in Jamaica rather than a miserable outpost in the middle of a forest. The men included a gunsmith, a metal-worker, a cloth-weaver, a specialist in damask, a stone-carver and a miner, while the women were all experts in spinning and embroidery. There were even two acrobats, the brothers Christian and Frederick Meihaust. And because military service was obligatory in their native Duchy of Brunswick in the kingdom of Hanover, every man possessed a gun.

The first contingent arrived in May 1834. The agreement between the Germans and Myers stipulated that the emigrants would either pay for their passage in the normal way or hand over to him their earnings for the first three years in their new country.

Seven months later, on 27 December 1834, a second contingent, this time of 506 Germans, arrived on board the *Olbers,* registered in Bremen. They were welcomed by a reporter from the *Jamaican Dispatch,* who had to go on board to greet them as they were forbidden to leave the ship before being sorted into groups according to their eventual destination. He found the Germans in good health, full of optimism and already slightly sunburned. The House of Assembly (the Jamaican parliament) financed the voyage to the tune of £3,800, which incidentally left Myers £338 out of pocket.

On Christmas Day, with the scents of the Caribbean and the smell of damp earth already in their nostrils, the German emigrants dressed three little girls in the traditional costume of the Duchy of Brunswick and sent them to the captain with a letter signed by them all. It read:

To Captain Exter of the *Olbers* from Bremen

Had poverty not driven us into exile from our Fatherland, we would have given you a more valuable gift than these few lines. But given our circumstances, we can do no more than express the depth of our gratitude. We intend no empty form of words when we say that you, Captain, have gone beyond the call of duty during the voyage from Bremen to Jamaica. You have acted as father, friend and adviser. And your sweet wife has done no less with constant proofs of her humanity and her care for the sick.

We beg you to accept our gratitude, which can never repay you, but which will inspire us to pray to the Almighty every day that he may bless you.

We all wish you a speedy and safe return to our Fatherland.

With never-ending thanks,
The Passengers

Besides Myers, there was another individual very actively trading in white labor, one Dr. William Lemonius, previously employed as a doctor in a unit of the Austrian army commanded by the duke of Brunswick-Oels, who later served under the British. After several years as a ship's surgeon on vessels plying between England and the Caribbean, Lemonius was nominated a justice of the peace in Jamaica by His Grace the duke of Manchester. In 1831 he enrolled as a volunteer in special detachments mustered to quell the slaves' rebellion. During the second insurrection, the following year, Lemonius fought with such valor that the British regarded him as a hero. In 1835 the House of Assembly officially gave him the job of finding more German immigrants for the island, and over the next two years Lemonius managed to procure eight hundred, promising them a certain amount of land in return for five years' free labor.

The Germans brought over by Myers and Lemonius were dispersed all over Jamaica. Like the slaves from Africa and Haiti, they were allocated to the most isolated landowners. Two groups, 249 brought in by Myers and fifty-odd by Lemonius, ended up in a wild tract of land on the borders of Lord Seaford's property, an estate known as Montpelier. Lord Seaford assigned them five hundred acres of forest.

Bitter memories of the journey from Germany to Jamaica have haunted Seaford Town ever since. The inhabitants still refer to Lemonius as the devil and say that had he ever set foot in Seaford he would have been lynched. And there are still, despite the touching letter of thanks, unexplained feelings of resentment toward the captain of the *Olbers.*

Without John Bierbusse's initiative the Germans of Seaford Town would quite possibly have perished of hunger and general deprivation. It was he who set them the example of working the land they had been given. The annals of Seaford Town record that Bierbusse had 73 plots of yams, half an acre of cocoa and ginger, 100 plantains, 20 sugarcanes and 540 coffee bushes. As principal of the school, he persuaded his colleagues to teach both German and English.

Bierbusse stayed in Seaford Town where, like him, many succeeded in making the transition from trades and crafts to agriculture. By 1837, only a few years after the Germans' arrival and despite their being decimated by sickness, Seaford Town was producing eleven tons of ginger a year. Some families had achieved an annual income of £300, and between 1837 and 1841 as many as eighty-eight of them had saved enough for a ticket on a ship that, this time, would really take them to the United States. Their names can still be seen written with felt-tip pen on the walls of a wooden hut they call the Museum of Seaford Town, just beside the German church.

❧

We went to Cleve and Odeen's home that evening. It was a pale green bungalow, built on the top of a hill covered by the flat leaves of banana trees. Around the building there was nothing but green vegetation and a wire fence attached here and there to tree trunks. The verandah was partly covered by a sheet of plastic that could be lowered during hurricanes to stop the driving rain from flooding the house. A window hung crookedly on broken hinges. In one corner of the plot stood an American station-wagon of the 1950s, bulbous and rusty, its bonnet jammed open by a stick.

The mother of our two young friends had another child, the latest, in her arms. She smiled shyly at us. A black woman in shorts and sleeveless T-shirt, she stood outside her bungalow in the single immense garden that is the valley of Seaford Town.

"Cleve is so good," she told us. "He helps me very much."

Cleve, slightly embarrassed, interrupted her, saying, "Here come our fathers."

The two men walked side by side, returning from the fields beyond the wood. One was black, with a beard fringing a scholarly face. The other was white, a German with reddish hair, wearing a white T-shirt, faded jeans and no shoes. When he put his hand up to his face to feel the bristles, the muscles bulged on his thickly veined arms. The black man took the baby, his son, from its mother, who gave it to him without a word, and the two men sat down on a flat stone between a clump of fern and a wild pine in a space that served as an outdoor room.

Cleve, meanwhile, had greeted his father with a "Hallo," and got a gentle pat on the head.

In the distance we could see Mr. and Mrs. Kameka making their way home along a path after shutting up their shop for the night.

Cleve dismissed us, saying, "We're going to eat now."

The woman, the baby, the two children and the two men disappeared together into the green bungalow that was home to all of them.

TO BE SOLD & LET
BY PUBLIC AUCTION
On MONDAY the 18th of MAY, 1829,
UNDER THE TREES

FOR SALE,
THE THREE FOLLOWING

SLAVES,

viz.

HANNIBAL, about 30 Years old, an excellent House Servant, of Good Character.

WILLIAM, about 35 Years old, a Labourer.

NANCY, an excellent House Servant and Nurse.

The MEN belonging to 'LEECH'S' Estate, and the WOMAN to Mrs D. SMIT

TO BE LET,
On the usual conditions of the Hirer finding them in Food, Clothing and Medical Assistance,
THE FOLLOWING
MALE and FEMALE

SLAVES,
OF GOOD STANDING

ROBERT BAGLEY, about 20 Years old, a good House Servant.

WILLIAM BAGLEY, about 18 Years old, a Labourer.

JOHN ARMS, about 18 Years old.

JACK ANTONIA, about 40 Years old, a Labourer.

PHILIP, an Excellent Fisherman.

HARRY, about 27 Years old, a good House Servant.

LUCY, a Young Woman of good Character, used to House Work and the Nursery.

ELIZA, an Excellent Washerwoman.

CLARA, an Excellent Washerwoman.

FANNY, about 14 Years old, House Servant.

SARAH, about 14 Years old, House Servant.

Also for Sale, at Eleven o'Clock,
Fine Rice, Gram, Paddy, Books, Muslins, Needles, Pins, Ribbons, &C. &C.

AT ONE O'CLOCK, THAT CELEBRATED ENGLISH HORSE
B L U C H E R,

ADDISON, PRINTER, GOVERNMENT OFFICE   PRINTED IN GREAT BRITAIN

❦

In the early nineteenth century, just before dawn in a sugar plantation of two thousand acres, the first sound to break the silence comes from a big pink conch-shell blown by a slave. The long-drawn-out note awakens the sleeping occupants of wooden huts in a far corner of the plantation. As the sun rises, the slaves gather in front of a young man wearing (unlike them) a shirt and a straw hat. This is the English bookkeeper whose duty it is to sell the sugar and buy in the labor, keep the accounts and send the profits to London. The white *massa* gives orders to the black supervisor, who shouts at his companions, telling them where to go. The men who cut the cane walk ahead of the rest. These are the strongest or freshest men; after them come the girls who tie the cane into bundles for ease of handling, then the old or pregnant women, who pull up the weeds. Lastly come the children, under the guidance of a woman, to clear and clean the now bare rows.

Sugar, sugar, sugar. Nothing but sugar. Source of all wealth and all folly; magical plant that grows on the most valuable agricultural land in the world and makes possible the most exaggerated luxury. A power both sweet and brutal that enslaves nine men out of ten on the island of Jamaica. Nectar of the gods that drips from the crushed canes and dissolves every social division, sticking to all skins alike, whatever their color. Because everyone, in this Isle of the Blest, is a slave. Even the slave-owners, who are surrounded by slaves and think like slaves and talk about slaves and love the slaves even though they whip them and buy them and sell them. They refer to fairy tales as "Anansi stories," the same word used by Ghanaian storytellers, and the real name for mud is *putta-putta* as it is in Africa. "This is an immoral society. An island of adventurers," write travelers from London, horrified at so much sensuality, so much vulgarity, so much simple vitality.

Now the Great House, too, is waking up. The owner is far away, in London, where polite society considers him one of the richest and one of the most boorish of their number. "He comes from the West Indies," they mutter when he appears in their salons laden with effeminate jewelry, and deride his coarse speech and efforts to hide the drops of African blood that found their way into his veins. One of his carriages outshone that of the king a while ago, and rumor has it that he has been hated at court ever since.

His trusted estate manager, who lives in the white mansion on the hillside surrounded by liveried servants, sleeps with a different female slave every night even though he is believed, with reason, to be homosexual. All day long he plays *batos* with a ball of rolled-up leaves. Sometimes other white colonials come to dance the night away. Never during the harvest, however, when work and profit rule and everyone is exhausted by the end of the day.

The sun is already scorching hot this morning, and in the refinery the machines are rolling, producing sudden bursts of flame as they crush the cane. Workmen shout continually as they maneuver the wagons. The stench of stale alcohol is so strong it makes the gorge rise.

The cane-cutters sing as they work. Behind them, women tease a "Guineaman," so-called because he was born not in Jamaica but in Africa and has only just been bought at auction in Kingston. The boss calls him William. He has not yet learned how to use a machete; before the day is out he will have cut himself and the women will have had to bind the wound with herbs.

Everyone knows everything about the boss. Every detail of his life, even the most intimate, filters down from the Great House. His sex life, sure, and also his business affairs. There is a rumor, for instance, that he intends to sell the estate. A well-known Kingston notary has offered a vast sum of money on behalf of a client. With all the changes of ownership and quarrels about boundaries, they say the notary earns half a million pounds sterling every year, as much as the whole island's annual budget. Every potential buyer or seller of property goes to him.

In Kingston people are still discussing the extraordinary business deal entered into by French diplomats a few decades ago, exchanging the island of Grenada, which grows not only sugar but cocoa, tobacco and indigo, where the plantations are the most modern and the most profitable of all, for an empty, useless wasteland in the coldest part of America, called Canada.

The other day a white man presented himself at the Great House. He was different from the others, thin and poor. He looked ill, his eyes red with fatigue. He said he was looking for work, but spoke with a thick foreign accent that made communication difficult. He said he came from a distant village many days' walk away. He admitted that he knew nothing about work in the fields, only how to weave damask cloth, so the bookkeeper had said no, he could not send him to work in the fields with the Africans. He went away, his hat clutched in his hand.

Perhaps he was a spy from another plantation. Or a saboteur. Sugar is precious, it must be protected by every means at one's disposal because sugar brings in higher profits than anything else in the world.

Delaroy Hacker owns a farm near Seaford Town, a tropical orchard with mangoes and coconut trees, besides chickens, goats and a few cows. He has used bricks for a few low walls and a run for breeding rabbits, but all the rest is a tract of jungle just like the jungle his forebears found when they first arrived.

"Would you like one?" he asked, pointing to the coconuts growing on a palm. "I'll pick it and open it up for you. There's nothing like it for quenching your thirst."

Delaroy screwed up his eyes, blue in a strange Chinese face with old-fashioned drooping side-whiskers. Stretching out his bare, muscular arm and plucking a heavy green globe growing implausibly on a tiny palm-tree, he split it open with three crisp machete blows, right, left and center.

"My ancestors had a hard job surviving here. My father used to say that half the people who came with his great-grandfather died of malaria. Many fled at once. What fairy stories they told us about this place! Said it was a paradise. On the contrary, we had to work our hands to the bone just to survive. And because we were white, we were accused of exploiting the blacks, of being racist. One of our number who emigrated to Canada still has an old map of the fields. Handkerchief-sized plots, too poor to grow anything. And when I was a boy there was no made-up road here. Everyone's turned their backs on us in Jamaica, even though we've never given any trouble. And those who went to Toronto a hundred years later betrayed us for the second time."

In rubber boots, baseball cap and tattered T-shirt, Delaroy works in the fields all day. A machete hangs on his belt all the time, even when he's at table. He waited for Cleve, whom he did not entirely trust, to go away before he spoke. The two of them share the same surname, but not the color of their skin. "I know his father," he said. "He's taken up with a black woman. Well, what can you expect? I did it too at one time." And he pointed to a coffee-colored child, his son.

Life in the forest is still tough. The dark evenings become oppressive. "We work and work, and that's it. But I'd never work for anyone else. I'd rather be independent. They wouldn't understand." When he says "they" he means the blacks, the Jamaicans. "Still, I've never had a problem with them."

Among the people who stayed in Seaford Town, there are only a few like him. "About fifty real Germans," he reckons. "The others are a mixture. They all went to Toronto when Canada said it would take emigrants from Jamaica provided they were of European origin. The banana market is finished, and even the egg-producers' co-operative went bust. We used to sell seventeen-hundred dozen eggs a week. Not bad, huh? Then people stopped buying them."

The farm leaves him little time for brooding. A few tourists come over from Mo' Bay when rain keeps them away from the beaches. He calls them "those who come from Hanover," as if the kingdom his ancestors knew were still in existence. "We see them, the German girls. They come on holiday to Jamaica hoping to go to bed with a Rasta with dreadlocks." He shakes his head.

Once, Delaroy and the other fifty Germans became actors for a short time. Not in any B movie, either, but in an international hit, *Papillon,* starring Steve McQueen and Dustin Hoffman.

In Seaford Town they still remember the day when Father Francis, in his broad-brimmed hat and dusty cassock, told them there was an easy job going that would pay well. Money for old rope, in fact. All they had to do was act the part of inmates in a French prison, or something like that.

The film people came to fetch them in March 1973. They were looking for about thirty men who had to be white, thin and look as if they had suffered. A long search in the towns had produced no one suitable; then someone remembered the German village.

In fact, the Germans of Seaford Town only had to play themselves. They too were prisoners, prisoners of the Tropics, their bodies sculpted by disease and overwork, their eyes haunted with the sad expression of those who have lived too long away from home. There is one particular scene that shows them, disciplined and submissive, as in real life. This is the scene in the Cayenne courtyard where the French legionnaires, in their *kepis,* hang the poor devil who tried to escape. Father Kempel did not even have to change his clothes to administer the last rites under the blazing noonday sun, nor his expression, that of one who has done it many, many times.

"Of course I remember. We were acting all through March and April, but only learned later that it was for a film." We were on a different farm now. Cleve had said, "Come on. I'm taking you to see another German. But that's the lot." And without even a farewell to Delaroy he had walked to the car, parked at the far end of the lane.

Morris is in his forties and lives alone. "Where could I find a white woman?" he said. "We live as brothers, the Africans and us. But I don't want to marry one. I'd rather be alone." He has been building a little house for years, and living in it too, unworried by piles of cement beside his bed and bricks for a kitchen table. Morris went to Europe, then enrolled in the Jamaican army. He even spent some time in Toronto, working as a laborer. Eventually he returned to Seaford Town. In the evening, he told me, after working in the sun all day, he likes to watch television. "As you do in Europe, right?" The other evening he was watching the Olympics from Atlanta when the TV broke down.

As we were leaving, Cleve smiled one of his rare smiles. "Television? I'll tell you where he goes in the evening: to his girlfriends. He's got at least five." Then he made an obscene gesture and added: "All black."

Croydon in the Mountains. An unlikely name for a stretch of land baking gently in ninety degrees of Jamaican sun. Its English proprietors named it after the London suburb—which could not be more different from this lush green mountain perfumed by exotic flowers. We reached it by a mule track bordered by ferns still glistening with raindrops from the latest downpour. Croydon in the Mountains has been voted National Farm of the Year three times, in 1985, 1990 and 1991. The machinery gleams, the wells are properly maintained, the ancient millstones still function perfectly. The farm can boast of producing thirty-two different types of pineapple and various species of coconut, including the exquisite Malay variety with its yellow-gold flesh.

The farm lies well off the beaten track, but has its own little place in history as the birthplace of Samuel Sharpe, the slave destined to become the liberator of Jamaica's blacks.

Cleve and Odeen listened in silence to the elegant youth acting as our guide. Perhaps they envied him just a little for his easy manner and new Nikes.

"We also grow eight different types of banana, including the red, the black and the green," the boy said proudly. "Would you like to taste them?"

Cleve nodded, and pocketed a bunch of small plantains.

"This is the famous Cowboy pineapple that you can buy in Europe. But this is the variety we call "sugarloaf," because it is extremely sweet and shaped like a loaf of sugar. Would you like to taste some?"

Cleve stepped forward and accepted two pineapples, which he handed to Odeen. The black workmen laughed and whispered among themselves. They had guessed that these were half-caste children, "Germans" from Seaford Town.

"This is a red banana." Cleve put more fruit in his pocket.

The workmen came over to our little group and said something to Cleve. He and his brother followed them. "We'll wait for you in the car," said Cleve. "We're going with the men." We eventually left Croydon under the blue noonday sky. The children's T-shirts had been transformed into fruit baskets, bulging with slightly imperfect fruit given to them by farmhands working the land where the African slaves' revolt began. They ate none of it themselves. "We're taking it to our mother," said Cleve earnestly. "But these are for you." He gave us a handful of limes.

That evening, sitting on the Rectory verandah watching darkness descend upon the mountains, we squeezed the limes into our rum. Spencer the plumber had been to say goodbye. Mrs. Kameka's relatives were also leaving, returning to Toronto. Father Gilmore had promised that next Sunday, perhaps, he would return to Seaford Town.

3
Brazil
Confederates in the Deepest South

It is understood that you have armed Bastards, Fingos and Baralongs against us—in this you have committed an enormous act of wickedness. . . . Reconsider the matter, even if it cost you the loss of Mafeking. Disarm your blacks and thereby act the part of a white man in a white man's war.
—From a letter written in May 1900 by General Piet Cronje, leader of the Transvaal commandos during the Anglo-Boer War, to Colonel Robert Baden-Powell

In the recent battle of Port Hudson it is said that the black flag was raised defiantly by the Confederates. This was justifiable under the circumstances. Let it be understood that the black flag is to wave in every battle in which the negroes are made the tools of the cowardly Abolitionists.
—*The Spectator*, American newspaper, 23 June 1863

We have been informed by a gentleman who has lately returned from Winchester that the Yankees are enrolling all the able-bodied negroes in Jefferson and Berkley. Poor deluded African, he leaves his kind Master and comfortable home to be placed in the front ranks of the Yankee army to save the lives of those who never had any sympathy for him and to murder those whose every thought and act was for his comfort.
—*The Vindicator*, American newspaper, 29 January 1864

Estado de São Paulo, April 1999

"See all that land down there, right to the last hill on the horizon? That was once a single, big cotton plantation. The farm

96

belonged to my family, the Daniels of Alabama. Before the famous murder, naturally."

Halfway along the dirt track Francisco has braked to a halt and wound down the window. The whole world outside is green. Sugarcanes sway in unison, as disciplined as an army ready for action in battle fatigues, commanded by the sun. The sky is clear at last after days of rain; warm air, eerily still and laden with vaguely tropical smells, permeates the car.

An old beaten-up bus stands lopsidedly at the roadside, two wheels in the ditch. Its passengers, twenty or so muscular blacks brought in to harvest the sugarcane, sit in the shade of the wheels, their legs spread wide, their straw hats beside them on the grass. They stare at us.

Throughout the drive from Sorocaba, Francisco was firing a barrage of impossible questions at me nonstop in a mocking, or perhaps merely ingenuous, tone. "Do you believe in God? Why? . . . If that strange war you're fighting in Europe is between Muslims and Christians, why are the Americans on the side of the Muslims? . . . If the war is on your territory, why do you Europeans leave it to the Americans? . . . When was the last time you sinned? . . . Why has Inter ruined our great Ronaldo, who no longer plays like he used to and you only have to look at his face to see he's unhappy? You Italians, you don't love Ronaldo enough. Why? . . . And—forgive me for asking—but what do you think of our famous poet who wrote, '*Deus es brasileiro,*' 'God is Brazilian'? Do you agree with him?"

We were on one of the many three-lane highways that criss-cross the state of São Paulo and are all identical whichever direction they go in: filling stations, 1960s motels with crumbling cement balconies, McDonald's, factories, small towns whose names you would have difficulty finding on a map but which are surrounded by heavily publicized shopping centers. And, naturally, kiosks selling freshly squeezed cane juice. You see them every sixteen hundred feet, preceded by hand-written placards promising cane juice that is *"muy jelado,"* "very ice-cold." It isn't. But in Brazil, even on the humblest highways, it's never enough for a drink to be cold. It must be at least ice-cold, if not very ice-cold or super-ice-cold. It follows the Brazilian law of exaggeration, of expansion.

As you drive, even the horizon seems to expand at every bend. And while Francisco drove toward Santa Barbara d'Oeste asking impossible questions (which he expected his nephew Bruno to translate for me word for word), the territory that wavered before us seemed monotonous and inaccessible. This is what Brazilians refer to, with bored indifference, as the *Interior Paulista*. The term has come to indicate an attitude as much as a geographical location, because although the state of São Paulo has great natural diversity—from mountains to plains, alpine firs to banana palms— it is as if, beyond the skyscrapers of São Paulo's *avenidas,* beyond the illusion of this poor man's Manhattan, lay only a dreary wasteland, its towns and cities unworthy of being identified by name and hence anonymous. And they say that for a Brazilian anonymity is worse than prison.

The towns that are springing up along the highways are condemned by this anonymity despite having fifty thousand or one hundred thousand inhabitants apiece, and no one in nearby São Paulo even admits to having visited such conurbations as Sorocaba, Campinas, Piracicaba, Rio Claro, Itapetininga, Americana or Santa Barbara d'Oeste. They are lumped together as the *Interior Paulista.* And having said that, you've said it all.

"Santa Barbara d'Oeste?" My Brazilian friend had shrugged his shoulders when he heard where I was going. "Never met anyone who's been there. . . . But what can you expect, it's the Interior Paulista."

Yet these phantom cities continue to grow and even flourish in a modest way beside the featureless highways. They form the industrial heart of a country that still hopes to achieve the goal of *ordem e progresso* embroidered by its founders on the Brazilian flag a century and a half ago.

Order and progress. Not God, country, family, victory, redemption and justice, the heraldic dreams formulated by

other South American nations emerging from colonialism, but
ordem, the fundamental cosmic order of things (the flag's blue,
star-studded hemisphere), and *progresso,* the country's inex-
orable material progress rooted in its rich natural resources (a
yellow rhombus symbolizing gold on a green ground symbolizing the luxuriant forests and fertile soil).

A motto of the Enlightenment, almost a progressive slogan.
But then Dom Pedro, who succeeded his father John as prince
regent in 1821 and became emperor of Brazil the following year,
was not like other monarchs. From his father he had inherited
not only the throne but also the position of grand master of a
Masonic lodge in Rio de Janeiro, prosaically called Comércio e
Artes, Commerce and Crafts. Because in Dom Pedro's Brazil
everyone, even its monarchs, shared the American attitude to
new frontiers, that conquest is not by divine right.

Dom Pedro came from a royal line with revolutionary
instincts. Having dominated half the globe from the unlikely
power-base of a tiny country on the edge of Europe, and after
spending several centuries vainly attempting to convert the
Indies to Christianity, the Portuguese House of Braganza had
surprised the other European dynasties by announcing that it
was emigrating to the other side of the Atlantic. The imperial
court was transferred in 1808 from Lisbon to a small tropical
city called Rio de Janeiro, River of January, surrounded by
swamps and forests but with one of the loveliest bays in the
world. By making this move, the Braganzas turned the custom-
ary roles on their heads. Portugal—now weak and impoverished—became the distant colony of a motherland called Brazil,
where industry and agriculture were booming to the extent that
twenty thousand slaves had to be imported annually from places
like Mozambique. A new frontier whose resources seemed inex-
haustible and whose confines, whether geographical or moral,
were nonexistent.

Brazil became a kingdom in 1815 and then, in 1822, transformed itself into an *Impèrio Autocràtico*—at a time when

Autocracy was not a term of reproach. Finally, ignoring the apparent contradiction, it changed its name in 1831 to become an *Impèrio Democràtico.* This "democratic" empire was, moreover, entrusted to a child of six, Dom Pedro II, the same Dom Pedro who was still on the throne when the Daniel, MacKnight, Thomas and Steagall families began to arrive with all the other immigrants defeated by the Union forces and settle on the land surrounding Santa Barbara d'Oeste.

Today, parked on a dirt road in the *Interior Paulista,* Francisco Vieira Daniel, a cameraman who works for local television stations, still utters the name of the long-gone emperor of Brazil with fondness, as if recalling a favorite uncle recently deceased. In some ways, Dom Pedro was one of the family. On the walls of Francisco's tiny flat in Sorocaba—in a drab block with parking spaces occupied by small Fiats—hang five old sepia-colored photographs. In the middle of each one is a seated group of farm workers with wide-brimmed hats and bulldog jaws; their women stand around, gazing at them admiringly. These are the Daniels of Alabama—not to be confused with the Daniels of Texas—"Totally different stock and totally different story, as I shall tell you later"—when they were still the proprietors of that famous farm visible from the lane in the hot, late-summer sun of February.

"When they arrived at Rio de Janeiro from America in 1865, the emperor himself was on the quay to meet them and he shook hands with the senior member of every family!" Gratitude is still evident in Francisco's voice. This surprising gesture on the part of a foreign monarch had gone a long way toward restoring the self-respect of the Confederate immigrants still smarting over their defeat by the Yankees, fellow Americans become mortal enemies.

Francisco climbs out of his car and stands looking at the hills covered with sugarcane plants all waving compactly at the same height. He has brought his film camera because he cannot bear to be without it, even on holiday, and every so often raises it and films anything that catches his eye. You never know, it might come in useful. He shows me his business card: Dakar Video, Sorocaba. This has nothing to do with Senegal. "DA are the first letters of my surname, KAR those of my partner's. About Africa I know absolutely nothing," he admits. The card has the same shape and colors as the Confederate flag, red with a blue cross and the thirteen stars of the Confederation. Francisco still claims the flag as his own even though there can be few drops of Confederate blood left in his veins and the only word of English he knows is "yes." All the fault of that wretched murder that caused his ancestor's expulsion from the American community and all that followed from it.

His nephew Bruno, a student at the University of São Paulo, whose almond-shaped eyes give him an Oriental look, whispers a warning that this is not the right moment to press for details of that unfortunate episode. He will tell me in his own good time, but Francisco isn't a man you can force. The whole family knows what he's like.

Bruno begins every phrase with the words, "Chico says that . . ." Francisco is known to his friends as Chico. "Chico says that the first Confederate immigrants were led by Colonel William H. Norris, the Alabama deputy, Civil War veteran and Masonic grand master. Dom Pedro offered them land in the state of Espirito Santo, and they went to inspect it. At twenty-two cents an acre, the land was a bargain, but the quality was not as good as the land they had left behind in the southern United States." So many of these southern Americans asked the emperor's permission to look elsewhere.

"They came to this plain and realized that it was similar to Georgia, South Carolina and Mississippi. A few years later the forests had gone, replaced by cotton, which needs hot sun then rain then hot sun, alternately."

We've all left the car now and are looking at the fields. Buildings are exceedingly few and far between. Bruno has never been here before, but has come along to interpret as a favor to his

uncle and because he's curious about the foreigner. But he fails
to understand my interest in American immigrants to Brazil and
occasionally voices a protest. "In this country everyone comes
from somewhere else. There's nothing special in that. For
instance, I'm a mixture of Italian, Spanish, American, German,
even Japanese. And you've come just to write about a few North
American emigrants? Don't tell Chico what I'm saying, but
what's so special about these *Confederados?* In Brazil they're just
Brazilians like everyone else; nothing out of the ordinary."

A few days later, walking through a shopping center in jeans,
T-shirt and new Nikes, Bruno comes out with a statement—in
English with the flat vowels of an American accent—that he has
been polishing for days. It sounds like a political manifesto:
"Riccardo, I must inform you that I and all my friends at USP—
the University of São Paulo—are deeply opposed to the undue
influence of American lifestyle and are determined to defend
our Brazilian values, culture and language."

Standing here now, Francisco observes the farm that once
belonged to his ancestors and lets his mind dwell on the famous
murder before speaking of it in subdued tones, as if he were personally guilty. "It's our family secret. I only learned about it as an
adult, reading the book written by one of us, Judith MacKnight
Jones. It was still taboo in the family. I gather that Bob Daniel,
my great-grandfather who was slightly mad, killed his partner,
Zeke Baird, an American like him. They were co-owners of the
facenda over there, at the foot of the hill. It was 1890. Bob had
found out that Baird had gone out one night and harvested most
of his millet crop to get even with him for buying some cattle
from him that he never paid for."

They had been arguing about it for days, and he had threatened Baird in the presence of witnesses by saying, "If you cut my
millet I'll kill you." One morning they found Baird's body in a
ditch. He had been killed with an *espingarda,* a long-barreled
hunting gun. "There was a scandal. My great-grandfather had to
leave everything and emigrate to Itatui, far away from the other

Americans. The Tribunal in Piracicaba found him not guilty. But as far as the Americans of Santa Barbara d'Oeste were concerned, he was guilty and they ostracized him. The Daniels, you know, were related to Colonel Norris, the community's founder. They were members of the elite. They had to set a good example. So we lost the farm. Years later, under my own roof, the family honor was tarnished yet again, perhaps more unpardonably than the first time. But I'll tell you about that some other day."

A century ago, all the farms in the triangle formed by the little towns of Santa Barbara d'Oeste, Americana and Nova Odessa were owned by American farmers.

The Confederates, or *Confederados* in Portuguese, arrived between 1865 and 1885 from the southern states of the U.S.A., mainly Texas, Louisiana, South Carolina, Georgia, Mississippi and Alabama. In the aftermath of the war that had claimed 625,000 dead and destroyed the economy of the secessionist states, many families in the South found themselves facing extreme poverty, while many others were in a state of mental prostration. So the Confederates chose self-inflicted exile, rediscovering their pioneering instincts and setting out in search of a rural Eden even farther south than the South they knew, rather than become subject to those "damned Yankees."

A few eminent men of the South were entrusted with investigating the feasibility of living abroad. One of these was James McFadden Gaston, a doctor practicing in Chester, South Carolina. In 1865 he went to New Orleans to open negotiations with Brazilian emissaries who had come to America looking for prospective colonists. Invited to go and see the country for himself, Dr. Gaston went to Brazil that same September and returned to the United States two years later to give lectures and publish a book, *Hunting a Home in Brazil,* based on his experience of life in Xiririca, near Iguape.

As it happened, Dr. Gaston never realized his dream of owning a plantation in Brazil; back in Xiririca, events forced him to
remain as a medical practitioner in the small immigrant community until, in 1883, any lingering hopes disappeared and he
returned to the United States, settling in Atlanta, Georgia.

The seed of emigration had, however, been planted. And all
the evidence suggested that Brazil was the perfect place for new
beginnings. It was a land of abundance, of promise; it had cotton, sugarcane, coffee and slaves.

The voyage from New Orleans to Rio de Janeiro took a
month. The emigrants sailed with dollars issued by the mint of
the Confederate States of America still in their pockets and with
the iron plows that were as yet unknown in Brazil, eager to make
a new start in a country where they were free to follow the traditions of the Deep South so humiliated by the war with the
North. Their dream was to reshape a Dixieland far from modern
temptations. Far from Abolitionism too, for in Brazil slavery was
still allowed and would be for many years yet.

No one knows exactly how many Americans came to Brazil.
Perhaps ten thousand, possibly twenty thousand. At least six
separate communities were founded. In 1870 there were 350
American families living in the vicinity of Santa Barbara
d'Oeste. But from the start there were many defections, many
precipitate returns to base. The English explorer Richard Burton, a student of the Koran who had been the first European to
visit Mecca and had then sought for the source of the Nile
among the mythical Mountains of the Moon, eventually became
His Majesty's Consul in Brazil (much against his will, having
been refused a consulship in Africa or in the Arab world). Once
in Rio, the temptation to explore what he christened the "highlands of Brazil" proved too great. In his diaries, Burton men-
tions having counted about 2,700 American immigrants in 1867,
800 of whom lived in the State of São Paulo, 400 in Espirito
Santo, 200 in Parà, another 200 in Paranà, 200 in Rio, 100 in
Minas, a further 100 in Bahia and 70 or so in Pernambuco. Ten

years later many of these outposts had already failed. Only Americana and Santa Barbara d'Oeste continued to thrive.

And yet Brazil under Dom Pedro II was enjoying an economic boom and urgently needed skilled workers. One of the emigrants, Ilisa Shippey, wrote in her diary, published with the title of *When Americans Were Emigrants:*

> On May 16 (1865) we began to see the outlines of misty mountains, which grew distinct by the next day, and the captain believed we would be inside the famous safe harbor of Rio de Janeiro before sunset. But we arrived just after the evening gun flashed and boomed across the entrance from the fort which guarded it. Therefore the "Marmion" anchored as close in as possible and we had a fine view of thousands of lights in rows and double rows, in semi-circles and scattered up and down the hilly city of Rio.

On board the *Marmion* anchored off Rio on 27 December 1865 and enjoying the pretty spectacle of the Pão de Açucar (Sugar Loaf) were about one hundred emigrants. Each had paid 130 dollars for the passage. They were rebels twice over, firstly because they had refused to be subject to the North, secondly because they had disobeyed General Robert E. Lee, the commander of the Confederate army who, after its defeat, had refused those who wanted him to lead the great flight into exile and form a new Confederation in the virgin lands of South America. On the contrary, he had declared himself opposed to the exodus and implored them to stay and rebuild the South.

The Brazilian emperor had inspected the first contingent of immigrants like a general inspecting his own hand-picked body of men. It was part of his plan that these modern Americans, with their agricultural expertise and technological sophistication, should spearhead his country's economic progress.

Dr. John Keyes, a dentist from Montgomery in Alabama who decided to follow in the footsteps of the farmers and craftsmen who were founding a new southern, or *sulista,* colony, arrived two years later, in 1867, on one of the *Marmion*'s later trips. The emperor was again on the quayside in Rio welcoming "his" Americans. Dr. Keyes regarded him with devotion and later wrote: "After the manner of all distinguished people, who are, likewise, good, his appearance was modest and unostentatious." Dom Pedro visited the kitchens of the camps where the Americans were provisionally held, tried the bread baked by the women, "complimenting them on the taste" and "pronouncing it well done." The inspection was a success. One of those involved later told Keyes that the emperor "expressed himself as being much pleased with the appearance of the Americans."

Keyes's objective and that of his companions was to join up with an adventurous former army officer from North Carolina, Colonel Charles Grandison Gunter, who had installed himself on an estate close to the Rio Doce two years earlier and had written to his friends describing the wonders of lands "more fertile than those of Alabama," cheap and furthermore "one could pay off the whole amount in four years." Gunter, who was called *Coronel* not only because of his military rank but also because that was the title assumed by all the great landowners in Brazil, had become a Brazilian deputy. Records show that he fought for the rights of women to own land in his adoptive country.

At the start everyone faced enormous difficulties. Many had been soldiers and had emerged from the war physically and mentally exhausted. Others had simply been victims of the economic crisis. For those who settled around Santa Barbara d'Oeste, Colonel Norris organized courses teaching the latest techniques for growing cotton. Some, utterly dejected, their hearts weighed down by the feeling that history itself had humiliated and betrayed them, ventured into the depths of the country, into the Brazilian rain forests. Those who survived became pioneers.

Lawrence Hill, who came to the banks of the Rio Doce from South Carolina searching for a new country where camellias, magnolias and jasmine would abound, wrote: "At present there is no way of transporting anything up the rivers and the lake, except in canoes. At first we thought this a terrible thing, but as it is the only mode of traveling as yet, we have become accustomed to it. We are assured that we shall have steam navigation at no very distant day."

Naturally, the Brazilian government's promise to provide steamboats on the rivers whose banks were now home to the *Confederados*—as the American settlers were now beginning to be called to distinguish them from other immigrants who came from all over the world—remained illusory. Many were discovering that wilderness, disease and nostalgia were more potent enemies than the Yankees.

Those who sought their fortunes in the gold and diamond mines failed almost immediately. Those who went to Iguape discovered that the climate was impossible and the soil poor, so after a while the survivors went to Campinas. The two hundred who settled beside the river Tapajòs, in the locality of Santarem in the state of Parà, held out and their descendants live there to this day. The brave souls like Lawrence Hill who finished up along the Rio Doce left the state of Espirito Santo. Those who had initially opted for Santos de Bahia eventually moved to the village of Campinas, arriving by train in 1875 only a few days after the railway was inaugurated.

The most stable group of all was that around Santa Barbara d'Oeste—where a Masonic lodge had been founded and named after George Washington—and its neighboring localities Nova Odessa, Piricicaba and Capivari.

The railway, however, did not reach as far as Santa Barbara d'Oeste. Passengers had to alight at a station some miles away. This place became the center of American trade. People went there to buy and sell cotton and it was there that the first textile factories were founded. At first it was known as Vila dos Americanos. Now called Americana, it is a city of 250,000 inhabitants and its coat of arms still shows the battle flag of the Confederate army.

Soldato descansa! Tua luta acabou.
Dorme o sono eterno, onde nao ha
dias de fadiga, ou noites de vigilia.

Soldier rest! Thy warfare o'er,
Sleep the sleep that knows no breaking,
Days of toil or nights of waking.

In the countryside around Santa Barbara, surrounded by fields of sugarcane, is a place where the *Confederados* come once a year to celebrate the *epopèia norte americana,* the epic adventure that brought them here from North America. For hours, three hundred Americans strum banjos and blow trumpets while the children play, the boys dressed in gray uniforms with yellow stripes, the girls in pink and blue frocks with bows of the same color in their hair, looking like prettily wrapped sweets. The lads march up and down in front of an "officer" who yells, "left, right, left, right." The atmosphere is that of a victory celebration.

On the day of the festival, in late April, the barbecue is lit at daybreak. Women cook toffee apples, men pour beer. People dance. Someone strikes up "Oh, Susanna," then "Oh, When the Saints Come Marching In." A man with a false beard, representing General Lee, reads in Portuguese and with the utmost solemnity the letter of surrender signed at Appomattox in 1865: "When men are divided there is no justice . . ." The speech ended, the "General" collapses, wounded perhaps. His men help him to his feet and he wraps a Confederate flag around his neck. The people applaud.

Then the dancing starts again. Beauty contestants parade in front of the obelisk engraved with the names of all the immigrant families. The compère shouts "Arkansas!" and a smiling blonde in a bathing costume steps forward. Then he shouts

"Tennessee!" and a brunette makes her appearance.

Another General Lee, a life-size portrait in oils, watches the *festa confederada* from inside the little red-brick church overlooking the celebrations. This was the first non-Catholic church in Brazil. The building is empty apart from an altar and the portrait of Robert E. Lee bedecked with medals. Used as a store for plows and grass-cutters throughout the year, it is only cleaned for funerals, because wherever the *Confederados* live, the *Campo* is where they all want to be buried.

For these tears of nostalgia and drops of perspiration are shed on no ordinary field, warmed by the sun or drenched by the notorious storms of the *Interior Paulista:* the community's meeting place is a cemetery. They call it *Cemeterio do Campo,* and it is the spiritual focus of the *Confederados,* the stage on which they act out their determination to remain different from their fellow Brazilians. The choice of this place has surreal consequences. They are in the habit of saying, "See you next Sunday at the cemetery for the *Fraternidade.*" Anyone who didn't know might think they were an association of necrophiliacs.

The graves are laid out side by side in a field behind the church, which is built on an artificial mound. Pines and palms grow in close proximity. The air is clear and shimmering. On the horizon you see only hills with gashes of bare earth the color of red clay: these are the roads separating one farm from another. A tall Brazilian fig tree, a *figuera,* throws splashes of shade. The inscriptions on the pioneers' tombstones are in English. Many display the Masonic triangle and compass.

James Anderson, born Franklin, Alabama, 23 August 1847: "He was esteemed by all who knew him as an honest man."

John Henry Wheelock, born 1898 in the U.S.A., died 1961 in Brazil: "Beautiful Souls are those that show the spirit of Christ wherever they go." Even thousands of miles from Dixie.

William Mills has the star of Texas engraved on the marble protecting him. The inscription simply says: "Texan in life."

Colonel W. H. Norris, founder of Santa Barbara, was born in

Georgia in 1800, fought for Alabama and died on 13 July 1893 in a part of Brazil that reminded him of his beloved home in the South. His tombstone reads: "He was a Masonic Grand Master."

His son, Dr. Robert Norris, is buried not far away beneath a large marble compass and the inscription: "A Confederate Veteran."

Roberto Stell-Steagall, 3 September 1899, Brazil–31 January 1985, Brazil. He has everything summed up thus: "Once a rebel / Twice a rebel / And forever a rebel."

I met one of the younger generation of Steagalls among the skyscrapers of São Paulo. His ancestor Henry Farrar Steagall lived in Gonzales County, Texas, enrolled in a light cavalry regiment and was taken prisoner in 1863 by the Federal troops. Thomas, a computer programmer, is a man of stocky physique. Punctuating his phrases with a strangely metallic laugh, he explains the meaning of the words "forever a rebel" for the Steagall family thus: "The first time we rebelled was when we fought against the North, up there in the States. Then, when we emigrated to Brazil we rebelled for the second time by joining up with the *Paulistas* in the Brazilian civil war of 1932. The state of São Paulo refused to accept the dictatorship of President Getullio Vargas, thus breaking the *Pacto Federativo.* There was a revolution, for the same motives that caused the Confederate States to secede from the North. We've got nothing against anyone, not even the blacks. We're honest citizens. But we've got this history behind us and, in our hearts, we'll always be rebels."

Innovations introduced to Brazil by the Confederates:

    The iron plow
    Kerosene and kerosene lamps
    Eucalyptus
    Watermelons
    Georgia peanuts

Pecans
The concept of the model farm
Orders to the oxen drawing the plow: "Get up!" to start
    plowing, "Gee!" to turn left, "Haw!" to turn right
Presbyterian, Baptist and Methodist churches
The first non-Catholic cemetery
The first blood transfusion
Modern dentistry

Daniel Carr de Muzio is forty-five and has the thin, refined face of an aristocrat in the habit of overseeing the plantation from a chair, sitting silently in a white-painted house. And he might have ended his days doing just that. But then came the accursed war. And the accursed surrender. And a ship to be boarded in New Orleans to escape from it all. Albert Carr enlisted as a simple private in the 56th Alabama Partisan Rangers. Another Carr, who called himself George Washington, was a medical officer in the same regiment. When the war ended, both decided to leave the United States for a new life in Brazil. They were among the first to arrive, together with another veteran called Napoleon Bonaparte McAlpine—in homage, perhaps, to another military man destined for defeat. The Carrs succeeded in buying lands and farms, becoming prominent members of the Confederate community like the Pyles, MacKnights, Steagalls and Norrises.

Daniel is now head of translations at the Berlitz School in São Paulo. He is responsible for setting up the website for the *Fraternidade*. His speech is still typical of the South, with drawled vowels and a cordial vocabulary. His mother, the famous Lucinda Carr, she of the melancholy expression and cutting repartee, lives in a small flat in Santa Barbara and maintains the style of bygone years. A stout black maid pretends to bustle around the kitchen, making strong coffee and providing extra cushions to make her easy chair more comfortable. In the afternoon there is a set time for a rest, in the morning she reads the papers, every now and then she visits relations on their sugar plantations. She has always insisted on speaking English and taught it to Daniel and her other two sons, one of whom is now a doctor and the other an agronomist in Mato Grosso. When I mentioned Daniel, her face lit up. "If you're going to São Paulo tomorrow, give him my love. I haven't seen him for quite a while."

"The Civil War, as the Yankees call it, or the War between the States as we call it, was not a crusade against freedom. We don't say that slavery was not *an* issue: it was not *the* issue. They, our forefathers from the Confederacy, came here just because they wanted to rebuild their lives, not because they could own slaves here. Do you know how many slaves were registered in Santa Barbara by the Americans? Only twenty-six. There was no money to buy slaves. They had to enslave themselves.

"It all comes from what the Yankees call the reconstruction. It was a tragedy, actually. At the end of the war the South was totally destroyed. Properties were confiscated, money grabbed, farms stolen or forced to be put on the market at a ridiculously low price. And this is still a dark chapter in American history, something seldom talked about. Do you know how many people died in the so-called Civil War? 625,000. Many, many more than in the Vietnam War. By the way, we take pride in saying that three out of four casualties were from the Federal side!

"The Civil War was our own internal Vietnam, but nobody recognizes it as such. So, when my forefathers came here to Brazil they were relatively poor. And here they died working. Never had any kind of leisure. Work, don't spend, don't spend, work: this was their life. All the rebel business? Yeah, you can say 'rebel.' But we never rebelled against anybody. It was the Yankees who called us rebels for their own purposes. And some of us have accepted the label. But be careful! My great-grandfather started as a farm foreman, then managed to buy a small farm. My grandfather was at one and the same time an attorney, a dentist, a farmer and a county sheriff. Never saw a show, never had a holiday. Owned the same Ford his entire life. These are spartan, disciplined habits, not rebellious ones. None of them became a colonel, as the landowners are called in Brazil. Why? Be careful: how many crimes do you have to commit to became a colonel?

"Yeah, the ghosts of the past are still here. For our fathers, the Yankees were still the damned Yankees. My grandmother did not allow anybody to mention the Lincoln name in the house. And when she referred to him, she referred to 'that man.' We were not friendly with those we didn't know. Because some families came late. Too late. Some were—how can I put it?—scallywags. Enemy collaborators. Some were even Yankees. We are different, we think different. When the American consul in São Paolo is a southerner, he comes to our meetings and *festas*. When he's from the North, relations are a bit—may I say this?—chilly.

"I don't feel really American and I don't feel as Brazilian as I should. The first time I went to the States, when I landed at Kennedy Airport in New York—I had never been in America before—everything was different: the wallpaper, the cars, the smells, the buildings, but I could hear those people, different people, speaking my language, American English. And I nearly went berserk. Because I was feeling really at home although I had never been there before. It took me five or six hours to recover. It was like a dream. I'm used to life in a country that I call Belindia rather than Brazil because it's a mix of Belgium and India, shaken well and served hot.

"So I gather you've heard the story of the Crisps. But maybe you haven't heard the real story. They told you that they were expelled from the community because there had been a black woman among them. Yes, a former slave. People were still sometimes ostracized in those days. But the problem with the Crisps was that they had a special building tucked away on one of their farms for the secret distillation of *pinga,* the illegal liquor very much in demand among the blacks. You see, with the *Confederados* things are always more complicated than they seem."

Daniel Carr de Muzio lives in São Paulo, a city with twelve million immigrants. You have to do more than be a *Confederado* to get noticed. The Berlitz School is at the back of Avenida Paulista, a canyon overshadowed by skyscrapers that go on and up for ever. Now and then Daniel patronizes a restaurant in the Avenida where he can eat *fejoada* and drink beer mixed with *caiperinha.* Most of the waiters take him for a foreigner. At the door and before sitting down to crispy pork and black beans, the largely Brazilian-Japanese clientele pick up a free copy of *Nikkey Shimbun,* a magazine that devotes its front page to Sumo wrestlers and the next to karaoke shows. The waiters don't regard these patrons as foreigners but as Brazilians with almond-shaped eyes.

Daniel's wife is part-Italian, like millions of other residents of São Paulo. Their daughter has just returned from the States, where Daniel sent her to meet the southerners of today hoping that she would rediscover her own roots. They showed her a good time, this young Carr de Muzio, with barbecues, dances and visits to shopping centers. It was like being back home in Brazil, the new Dixieland.

Daniel talks about his discovery of a direct descendant of General Lee in Rio de Janeiro. He is a nephew of William Lee, the American consul in Rio in the 1920s and second son of the general. The Second World War broke out just as his term of office ended and the Lee family decided to stay in the Tropics. If he were a true Lee, the Confederates would have found a figure-head. Daniel mulls over the importance of his discovery while sipping a liqueur glass of the greasy juice—black as tar—strained off the *fejoada:* a great delicacy for the initiated. The waiters, now hearing him speak Portuguese, have decided that he is not a foreigner.

Old Henrique Smith, by contrast, has never been to São Paulo or to Rio. They are part of a different world, too remote from his. He lives in a tiny house in Santa Barbara that he has transformed into a small tropical forest with jacaranda, bananas and purple and pink flowers as big as the palm of your hand overflowing into the pastel-colored living room. The furniture consists of two chairs, an old divan, the Confederate flag and a bedsheet separating the living room from the bedroom.

He is now eighty-seven, Henrique Smith, a son of the soil clinging to nature even in the heart of the city. His nails and teeth are the same yellow as the butterflies who find refuge in his garden. His spectacles in their heavy frames are always slipping askew, but he wears them more out of habit than anything else. He describes himself as a *caipira,* a country bumpkin, a man to whom words don't come that easily after a lifetime of doing nothing else but work on the land. "Can anyone tell me," he asks, "what the real Americans living in the southern U.S.A. think of us?"

This is his story:

"My father's family comes from South Carolina: they were considered rebels by the Yankees. Yessir! Rebels because they refused to bow down to the North. They were very proud people, people with *fibra,* as we call backbone here in Brazil. And that's why they came here, enlisting in Frank McMullan's expedition. A big man, six feet four inches tall, he became a naturalized Brazilian in 1866 then went back to the States to find settlers for his new country. Found 'em, too. But on the way back to Rio, they were shipwrecked off Cuba. Lost most of the stuff they had with them, but they were rescued by a good man, a rancher who got them ashore, took them home and gave them food and drink and somewhere to sleep. He was a good, generous chap; didn't mind slaughtering a bull a week so they could eat meat. They were there two months before another ship came to fetch them.

"Father's family has a strange history. It's in the books. Their real surname wasn't Smith but Ferrer. All started with a Robert Ferrer, a Frenchman who fled the persecutions and stowed away on a ship bound for the States, hiding in a barrel of flour. Or so the legend goes. Once in America he went to Georgia and started over, joining in the fight for Independence. He owned a lot of slaves. He wasn't cruel. Firm, yes. His son, Robert Smith, lost everything.

"My mother is a Thomas from Arkansas. Her father was the famous Robert Porter Thomas, a patriot of the American Revolution. He had bought a property for twelve thousand dollars, a lot of money in those days. Still is, as far as I'm concerned. Anyway, Robert Porter Thomas fought with the Confederates. After the defeat he went back home. Then in 1871 the North ordered a census and his property was valued at only four thousand dollars. One-third of what he'd paid for it, you understand? Life had been good before the war, but now it was time to move on and get out. The family were good Baptists, folks with strong morals. So he sold the land and went down to Brazil, where he started to look like a patriarch, with a big bushy beard. Always hoped to go back and die in Arkansas. Instead he died in Brazil. But his life here was not too unhappy because the Americans were treated very well by the Brazilians. Like gods, indeed, by the government. Do you know that Dom Pedro himself, the emperor, welcomed us with open arms? We never became Catholics, though.

"Slaves? A very complicated business, really and truly. I remember talking to men who had been slaves and they told me they were treated very badly. Oh yeah, very very badly, it's true. But let me ask you something. Does the United States have the right to tell us what to do with the Negroes? Here in Brazil, slaves got their freedom in stages. First the women, then the children, then those who had been brought over from Africa more recently. Eventually all of them. In the States three and a half million blacks were freed on the same day. They had nothing to do. They didn't know what to do. There was crime. A lot of rapes. And the Ku Klux Klan was a reaction. Can a country that allows this claim to be the number-one country in the world?

"My real name is not Henrique, but Henry Lee Smith. Lee in honor of General Lee, of course, who my father greatly respected. My brother was Horace Roosevelt Smith. I speak English because I learned it growing up in the countryside with Mother and Father. She only spoke English. He could manage Portuguese too. I was born and bred in Brazil, but my blood is American. Really and truly, the battle flag of the Confederacy is my flag."

Henrique heaves himself up from the divan and goes to fetch a smeary glass. Inside it is a little Confederate flag made of paper, given to him the last time he went to the *Cemeterio do Campo*. In a trembling voice, he says, "I know that I'm crying. Forgive me. I love Brazil. I've never been anywhere else. But the flag . . . well . . . if they cut me open they'd find these colors in my heart."

Only Charlotte Lucina is older than Henrique. She keeps her age a secret, but is undoubtedly the only living *Confederada* who can claim that both parents were born in the United States. Traveling to Brazil on separate ships, they married and had two sons, baptizing one Lee and the other Isaac out of respect for the Confederacy and the Bible (which amount, after all, to the same thing). Charlotte's wrinkles deepen as she smiles. "Yes," she laughs, "of course I'm American. I've never been anything else. They can get a hammer and an axe and beat me all they like, but they won't beat the American out of me!"

A friend of Lucina's, Mirela Cullen, answers simply when asked about her family: "My grandfather was an Ohioan, and we were ashamed of that. We tried to keep it, you know, hidden. A secret."

Ohio did not side with the Confederacy.

❧

"**M**y name is Judith MacKnight Jones. I'm a third-generation descendant of southerners who came to Brazil after the Civil War. They spoke English and to communicate with them the slaves had to learn English. When settlers of my parents' generation got together, they talked about things that were happening at that moment. They didn't want to talk about the past: it hurt too much. I remember when I was at school, at primary school, the head came to my classroom one day and asked each child what nationality they were. I didn't know what my nationality was, but I knew that my grandparents were American. And that's what I told him. 'And where were you born?' he asked. I said, 'Here in Brazil, in Campinas.' 'So you're Brazilian, you fool,' he said. I grew up thinking of the United States as a wonderful place. Then I went to see it for myself. We sailed to New Orleans and visited several states, meeting a lot of relatives we still have up there. After a while I started to get homesick. Home seemed very far away. When it was time to come back, we went to board the ship in New Orleans and as I put my foot on the gangplank, I looked up and saw the Brazilian flag. . . . Ah, I knew then what I was!" Judith MacKnight Jones sighs in a resigned way. "Yeah, I'm Brazilian."

Nova Odessa lies midway between Santa Barbara d'Oeste and Americana, five miles from each. Motorcycles roar along the highway, ridden by the agro-boys, as Brazilians call the youths who sport the cowboy hats and studded belts that are all the rage in the *Interior Paulista*. The sun blazes down. Founded in 1906, Nova Odessa is laid out like a German village with a market place, farm co-operatives, two Lutheran churches, the Jacobitz cotton factory and little houses belonging to *os lettos,* descendants of Latvian immigrants. These people were brought here by Carlos Botelho, the Brazilian minister for agriculture, by means that became one of the most surreal episodes in the history of Brazilian immigration.

In actual fact, Dr. Botelho never wanted Latvians. He wanted Russians. The fertile lands north of Santa Barbara were ideal for growing cotton but labor was in short supply, so he decided to find a few hundred Europeans willing to colonize the area and had heard good things about the peasants of tsarist Russia.

Electing to go personally to Russia, the minister sailed to Odessa. On arrival, he liked the look of the city and even before signing any immigration contracts, decided that the new colony should be called after the Russian port on the Black Sea.

He failed to find any potential colonists in Odessa, however. The idea of emigrating to America aroused no enthusiasm in the more nationalist circles, and Odessa was in any case populated not by farm workers but by sailors, merchants and 'artists to whom the offer of cheap land in a hot and distant country held scant appeal.

The Russian authorities then suggested that he should take the train north, to Riga, stopping in Kiev on his way. In Kiev Botelho found several families of Ukrainian Jews whom he immediately despatched to Brazil as an advance party. But a few dozen immigrants were hardly sufficient to populate the territory Botelho had assigned to "the Russians," so he continued his journey to Riga. Once a city belonging to the Hanseatic League, Riga was a meeting place of three cultures and three languages, German, Latvian and Russian. Here the Brazilian emissary was finally able to persuade hundreds of farm workers to take ship for the New World.

Two hundred people still speak Latvian in Nova Odessa. Another four hundred have Latvian surnames and Latvian ancestry but no longer speak the language. The community is not unique as a *colonia letta.* The enlightened Brazilian government wanted more of them in the state of São Paulo, and they are still there.

Donalde Kliango is one of them, a big man with blue eyes, drooping cheeks and side-whiskers reaching down to his chin, as used to be fashionable in provincial Germany. "We've always had contacts with the Santa Barbara Americans," he says. "Marriages, even. It was quite usual for our farmers' daughters to marry into their farming families."

In the Lutheran church—a stark, unadorned block of white cement—services were conducted in Latvian until twenty years ago. They are now conducted in Portuguese. The newly arrived priest is tall and fair-haired, a German Brazilian with a square jaw and the physique of a pop singer. He looks more Latvian than the Latvians.

Despite the historical background, the *Confederados* of Santa Barbara and Americana are still convinced that the people of Nova Odessa are Russian. "The Russians of Nova Odessa have always been our friends," says Daniel Carr, commandant of the SCV Camp 1653, *Os Confederados*, the Brazilian branch of the Sons of Confederate Veterans. "And during the Cold War most people were amazed to see how well we got on with them. They didn't realize they were White Russians, not Communists. And that we were Confederates, not Yankees."

A pillar in the shady marketplace of Nova Odessa pays homage to Dr. Carlos Botelho and celebrates the first fifty years of the *Imigracao Letta*. Silence now hangs over Nova Odessa. The cotton market has slumped, but a Germanic discipline remains.

By contrast, a shop in nearby Americana sells "religious and esoteric articles." A sign specifies that inside, among the aphrodisiacs and statuettes of saints holding olive branches, one may purchase "gnomes, angels, magic stones, incense, *defumadores,* devils and every personage of the *candomblé* religion."

Seen on the T-shirt of a boy in Santa Barbara: "A rebel. And proud of it."

Thomas Steagall, adjutant and treasurer of SCV Camp 1653: "To be a rebel is to have no fear. You can call it courage, I suppose."

Cicero Carr (many *Confederados* are called Cicero): "To be a rebel is a way of life. We're rebels when we go to the Cemetery for a festival, but not in everyday life. How can you have the heart to rebel when, as things are now, you need to have at least five thousand acres to get by in farming, and millet, maize and sheep have been reduced to a *meza de poker,* a gamble."

João Padovesi, seventeen, fifth-generation *Confederado,* just returned from a trip to the U.S.A. with his twin brother: "Rebel, *rebelde* in Portuguese, is someone who doesn't accept what is not good for him. So he's a good rebel, not a bad rebel."

Nancy Carr, married to one of the Padovesi and mother of João: "My father was a Carr, my mother a Crisp. Two old Confederate families who fought against the North and came back humiliated. Our whole history, why we came here, how we lived, who we are, can be summed up in an anecdote that was always being told in our house when I was a girl. They said that when an elderly member of one of the two families, I can't remember whether it was Carr or Crisp, arrived in Brazil and saw this lush, fertile, free land, he picked up a handful of soil and said, 'I'll be no hungry any more.' Much later I was told that the very same phrase occurs in *Gone With the Wind,* to symbolize the southerners' love of the land. Is that so?"

It's an obscure story involving old tales of illegitimate children, farms bought and sold, racial prejudice; a secret that the Santa Barbara *Confederados* prefer not to talk about because it is embarrassing for everyone.

Nancy Carr calls it "the tale of the *negrina* Damiana." Damiana was an *esclava negra,* a black slave, and hers is the story of a love that survived ostracism, separation, pain. "Study my face," Nancy said one day, sitting in the living room of her house in Santa Barbara, "and you'll see that I too share the African blood of that *negrina,* poor Damiana. I shouldn't be telling you these things, but if you insist . . . I've nothing to hide. But these are delicate matters."

So delicate that when John Crisp, then the only doctor the Americans of Santa Barbara had apart from Dr. Johns, heard what had happened, he considered closing his surgery and returning to the United States, even though he was doing relatively well, since many of his patients paid him in kind with parcels of land, which one day he hoped to bring together into a big *facenda.*

What had happened was that one of his sons, sixteen-year-old Richard, had fallen in love with a slave who worked in the house, the pretty Damiana. When their love for each other became an embarrassment to the family, Dr. Crisp decided to return to the United States and take his three sons with him.

"But he had reckoned without Richard's determination," Nancy continued. "At the age of twenty-four he got on a ship and returned to these parts, alone. And he met up again with his *negrina.* Eight years had passed, but they still loved each other. They went off to live together and had nine children. They in turn produced three hundred Crisps of mixed race, grandchildren of a slave. An unforgivable sin in those days, as it might be even today to some *Confederados.*"

One of the nine children was Ernesto Crisp, father of Maria de Lourdes Crisp, Nancy's mother. She eventually married a Carr, but was never invited to the festivities at the *Cemeterio do Campo* because the genes she had visibly inherited from Damiana would have given offense.

"For many years do you know what happened? When I introduced myself as a Carr, I was welcome anywhere. But if I revealed that my mother was one of the Crisp family, people would be horrified and give me very strange looks. It happened. Then one day I said to myself: You're a *Confederada,* a Carr, you too have a right to go to the Cemetery. And no one said a thing. They have, at last, forgiven the *negrina* and her Richard."

꧁꧂

The outlines of hills at the end of the dirt track have been softly rounded by the heat-haze. Francisco Vieira Daniel gazes at his grandparents' farm, which has passed through God knows how many hands yet without losing its identity. Not one white building interrupts the green sea of swaying canes. The black cane-cutters have got to their feet and are picking up their machetes. Francisco opens the car door. "I told you that the Daniels had another secret, another stain on the family honor, one that really did cause their exclusion from the community. Do you want to know what it is? It's worse than the murder of Zeke Baird. This was a crime of betrayal. Bob's son, that's my father, married a woman from outside the community. A black? No. Even less excusable from the *Confederados'* point of view. She was a native Indian. From a primitive tribe."

4
Haiti
Papa Doc's Poles

A rich Black is a Mulatto.
A poor Mulatto is a Black.
—Haitian saying

Port-au-Prince, August 1996

"Are you believers? Then maybe I can help you. I'm a pastor in the Baptist Church and Christians are supposed to help one another. But do you really believe in God?"

The Reverend Joseph Luc eyed us suspiciously, then echoed our reply—"One of us is Catholic, the other Anglican . . ."—under his breath without conviction. The meeting was taking place in the Mexican-patio style hall of El Rancho Hotel in Pétionville, built on the steep hillside that until two years ago constituted the most fashionable area of Port-au-Prince. Although we had only met him a few minutes ago, Joseph already seemed to be our last best hope for organizing an expedition in search of the mysterious white tribe of Haitian Poles.

This unlikely sounding community was descended from soldiers sent from Poland by Napoleon's fearsome brother-in-law, General Leclerc, at the beginning of the nineteenth century to put down the slave rebellion in what was then the French colony

124

of Saint-Domingue. Legend has it that *les polonaises* deserted the French revolutionary army and joined that of Jean-Jacques Dessalines, the black "emperor" of Haiti, helping him to create the first ever black republic. According to some reports, the Poles never left the island but were still surviving on a mountain far from the beaten track somewhere in the north of the country.

Negotiations with the baby-faced pastor were slow. To be catechized on the tenets of one's faith in the sun-drenched hall of El Rancho was a situation that smacked of paradox. The Silvera family, who own the hotel, came originally (and in somewhat mysterious circumstances) from Argentina, settling in Haiti in its heyday at the beginning of the century. Albert, the original head of the family and the business, was an elegant playboy who sported a silk cravat. He has been dead for many years but still keeps an eye on the hotel from a black and white photograph above the reception desk. His smile is clearly Latin, evoking golden summers on the Côte d'Azur and the beau monde of the 1950s. The Argentinian's great passion—besides beautiful women—was driving around the streets of Port-au-Prince in his red Ferrari, dropping in on one party after another in what was then one of the most snobbish and sybaritic of all American capitals.

Today the lower-lying part of Port-au-Prince is a shambles. The streets in the center, having shed their European pretensions, have been invaded by the down-at-heel, who, like swarms of desperate but indomitable ants, have moved into the old buildings of the commercial sector, the abandoned villas of the mulatto middle class, the government offices, and the depots of the great retail stores. The colonial-style houses of the Francophile elite, with their latticework verandahs and seventeenth-century balconies, now stand empty, reduced to crumbling shells shrouded in detritus. The painted names of shops once owned by traders from Syria, Greece and Italy who flocked to this "pearl of the Antilles" to make their fortunes are now fading; names such as Grands Magazins Napoli, Supermarché

Athène or Bazar Alwalid give the impression of being the for-
lorn ghosts of past cargo manifests. On pavements awash with a
dense tide of humanity, street vendors sell sticks of sugarcane
and wizened bananas while some men and women simply sit,
either too weary to move or because they have nowhere to go.

The dun-colored Jeep Pia and I had rented for the not incon-
siderable sum of two hundred dollars a day struggled to thread
its way at walking pace through the crowded streets. I wondered
how the playboy's red Ferrari would have coped. The potholes,
moreover, are almost continuous and very deep, like craters in
the tarmac. Whenever a car stops, its air-conditioning at full
blast and windows shut tight, vendors tap on the glass, holding
up food or painted gewgaws. Crime is burgeoning in Port-au-
Prince; many people carry machine-guns, leftovers from the civil
war, while others are more modestly equipped with machetes. It
is not easy for *les blancs* to move around unnoticed.

"We'll never manage without a guide in this place," said Pia,
alarmed. "Let's find someone to help us, otherwise we're in
trouble."

I knew she was right, but I was aching to delve into the past
and find that famous Ferrari, which still represents incontrovert-
ible proof of past affluence to Haiti's elite. The most transient
visitor will be regaled by some mention of it. I was willing to bet
that it would be lurking in some lock-up nobody had thought of
opening for years. Maybe it had survived without a scratch from
the fall of the Duvalier dynasty, through General Avril's dictatorship, the election of President Aristide and the American inva-
sion. But there was also the possibility that it had fallen into the
hands of Duvalier's death-squads, the Tontons Macoutes, and
ended up in a voodoo ceremony as a sacrifice more valuable
than human life and redder than blood.

"Reverend," I persisted in the most devout tone I could
muster, "we are believers, yes, but first and foremost we need
your help. Would you be willing to accompany us on our journey around the country to search for the Poles? I've been told

that they live in a place called Casales. After all, they are also poor Christians who would welcome the visit of a priest."

Today, El Rancho is the hotel used by UN soldiers and the representatives of the numerous humanitarian organizations who flock to the troubled island. Time was, however, when it was a hill station for revelers, with its own casino where the Haiti jet set—sometimes accompanied by foreign VIPs such as Helmut Berger, Baron Thyssen, the Agnellis and Truman Capote—paraded their starched shirt-fronts and old-fashioned French. The roulette room is still there, but only visited by members of the criminal fraternity sporting heavy gold chains around their necks, exchanging wads of greasy banknotes unsmilingly and speaking a slang that mixes French Creole and Miami American. The atmosphere is glacial.

Change is also taking place outside El Rancho's Mexican-style interiors. The mass of wretched, indigent humanity, having overrun the center of Port-au-Prince, is creeping higher and higher into hills that were once the preserve of the wealthy. In Pétionville, the suburb that takes its name from Alexandre Pétion, the president of Haiti who financed Simon Bolivar's Venezuela campaign in 1816, there are still a few restaurants, a couple of private schools, the Arab-owned Jiha art gallery and some antique shops, relics of the phase of Haiti's history when the island not only had the largest proportion of black inhabitants in the Caribbean but was also the most Europeanized. But the poor, with their makeshift markets, have now taken over the streets where once they would not have dared to set foot. And the rich—those who have not resigned themselves to quitting Haiti altogether—have responded by moving ever higher into the hills. The Creole aristocracy has now withdrawn to the summits of ever-steeper hills, to Kenskoff or even higher, to Fermathe, to dazzling white villas that shimmer in the limpid, bracing air and from which the panoramas beyond the windows are breathtaking. One may be certain, however, that the pursuit is not over yet.

"My problem is that I need money," the pastor eventually confessed. A thin young man wearing a shirt buttoned up to his neck and clutching an imitation-leather briefcase, modest and somewhat formal in manner, he looked reassuringly like an Italian small-town seminarist. Added to which, Joseph spoke English and seemed generally very competent. The fact that he was a priest was a bonus, Pia and I agreed, congratulating ourselves on our good fortune. When we had first asked the receptionist if she knew of anyone who could accompany us to Casales—a service for which we would pay, naturally—she had said, "Casales? I don't even know where it is. Still, I have a cousin, or rather a distant relation, who might have some time to spare. If I can locate him, I'll ask him to pass by." And she had left us abruptly, with a smile that was alarmingly ironic.

"I need money to purchase religious books. As a Baptist pastor, I should like to set up my own Bible school one day, or even a seminary for training pastors. Seeing that we all belong to the Christian family I could, as a favor, come with you. I've done the same thing in the past for UN soldiers and also for parties of American religious teachers. It wouldn't be easy for you to find anyone else who speaks English and can translate from Creole."

"Good. We're really grateful," I said. "How much will you charge?"

"That's up to you. I throw myself on your generosity."

"Oh no, it's for you to say. It's difficult for us, in a foreign country so different from our own, to make a fair offer."

Joseph blurted out the figure that had been on his mind from the start. "Two hundred dollars a day plus expenses."

The figure left us flabbergasted. "Isn't that a bit steep?" I hazarded.

"It's what the Americans paid. Plus I'm a good, trustworthy guide."

"It's too much. Make us a more charitable offer. If you insist on such a high fee, the deal is off. We can't afford it."

The negotiations continued with many an embarrassed smile

and exchange of courtesy. We finally agreed on fifty dollars a day. Joseph was not in the least put out, indeed I had the impression that he was more than satisfied with the result. Our departure was fixed for the next day, at crack of dawn because the village of Casales, from what we could gather, was a very long way off, lost not only in the mists of time but in the obscurity of Haiti's hazy topography. The map seemed clear enough: we had to get onto the road north of Port-au-Prince heading toward the port of Gonaive. But how long it would take to get from one point to another, and the condition of the road itself, were imponderables. "It'll take us several hours, maybe a whole day," Joseph pronounced. (By this time we had dropped the title of "Reverend.") We trusted his judgment. After all, God was on his side.

At dawn the next day the Jeep was ready. Joseph arrived at El Rancho clutching a sports bag containing his pajamas and Bible. Around us Port-au-Prince was waking up, as tattered as ever, potholed roads straggling uphill and downhill, with small fires burning at the corners and old women with handkerchiefs knotted behind their heads selling fruit out of tin bowls. I was excited, impatient to be off. He was anxious to explain that he had had to find someone to take the service for him next day and that it had not been easy. I handed him the keys to the Jeep, assuming that he would want to take charge of the expedition and steer us through the labyrinth of the city.

"No, it's better if you drive. I don't feel like it," he said without a shred of embarrassment.

"Didn't you say you had a driving license?"

"Yes, I've got a license, but I've never driven. I just thought it was a good idea to have one."

"OK, I'll drive. So, which do you think is our best route for Casales?"

"First we must get to a place called Cabaret. I don't know the way after that."

"What do you mean, you don't know? How are we to find the Poles?"

"We'll ask the peasants on the way. They know everything, the peasants," he replied with a note of resentment in his voice.

We set off apprehensively. "I'm sorry you had to take a short break from your work on our account," I said in an attempt to warm up a relationship that was showing signs of becoming distinctly frosty.

Joseph was sitting in the front passenger seat, as stiffly upright as a monarch in a state Rolls. I had asked him to sit beside me in the hope that he would navigate, and he had accepted without a second's hesitation. But the miles passed and Joseph moved not a muscle. Of road signs there were none, and when we had to ask the way, I was the one who did it. Pia, sitting in the back, consulted the map, but not once did Joseph speak to her. "Oh well, I don't have much to do all day long. At present I'm studying the scriptures and taking the occasional Bible class. One day I shall have my own school, perhaps." I remembered the two hundred dollars a day he had demanded, more than the average annual income in Haiti. "Do you get paid by this school where you teach?" Joseph looked at me calmly before replying: "No, nothing at all." "Does the Church pay you?" "No. There's very little money in Haiti and everything gets done for free." Except for the *blancs,* naturally.

To avoid losing my temper I tried to introduce some distraction and wound down the window, sniffing the smells of Haiti and enjoying the wind in my face. Joseph, scandalized by this contact with the real world, first glared at me and then demanded that the air-conditioning be restored and the window shut immediately. He apparently considered it undignified for two white people and a man of the church to expose themselves to the open air rather than make full use of the comforts provided. Meanwhile, we were crawling through streets blocked solid by the crowds: vendors selling sugarcane in bite-sized chunks, donkeys, ancient American cars that had ground to a halt with their radiators hissing. The heat was suffocating. Cartloads of green bananas were jostled by hundreds of Tap-taps, the buses painted

Dutch Burgher
Union House,
Colombo, Sri Lanka.

Colombo, Sri Lanka.
A prominent Dutch
Burgher shows off her
collection of plates.

Seaford Town, Jamaica. Spencer the plumber (*left*) on the rector's verandah with Germans from the Jamaican community.

Seaford Town, Jamaica. Delaroy Hacker on his smallholding.

Confederate girls, Santa Barbara, Brazil. (© Claudio Rossi)

Confederate youngsters in the graveyard, Santa Barbara, Brazil. (© Claudio Rossi)

(*Above*) Young Confederate on the obelisk in the graveyard, Santa Barbara, Brazil. (© Claudio Rossi) (*Below*) Chapel interior, Santa Barbara, Brazil, with portrait of General Robert E. Lee. (© Claudio Rossi)

Still hoping for
the pope's return,
Casales, Haiti.

Casales, Haiti.
A "Polish" mother
proudly pushes
forward her two
white daughters.

Baster children,
Reheboth, Namibia.
(© Gerald Cubitt)

Baster couple
by their house,
Reheboth,
Namibia.
(© Gerald Cubitt)

(*Facing page*)
A Baster girl
with firewood,
Tsumis, Namibia.
(© Gerald Cubitt)

Les Saintes, Guadeloupe.
(*Left*) Just as in a French village, a fifth-generation Santois fisherman carries his baguette. (*Right*) A Santois works on the beach before setting out on a fishing expedition.
(*Below*) Running home through the village of white fishermen.

with colorful advertising slogans and religious symbols that are the only means of public transport throughout Haiti.

"Have you ever been to this part of the country before?" I asked Joseph, still sitting rigidly beside me.

"I've never set foot outside Port-au-Prince except for one occasion when I went to visit my mother," he said, as if nothing in the world could have been more natural than this reply.

"And what do you know about the Poles?"

"Nothing at all, hadn't even heard of them before. But don't worry, we'll find them. We'll ask the local people."

Steering the Jeep gingerly, zigzagging between potholes and perambulators, I tried to assess the situation. Joseph, the devout pastor engaged to act as our guide through this purgatory, had refused to drive the Jeep, did not know where Casales was, knew nothing about the Polish community and did not appear even remotely interested in the subject. Besides which, contact with his compatriots was evidently distasteful to him while for us it was the prime object of our expedition. Things were not looking good. And supposing that Casales was as far away as he had said, far, far away, impossibly far?

The teenage children of the concierge at the hotel had registered simple incredulity when we asked them for information. Some of them pronounced Casales in the Spanish way, sounding the final "e" and "s," others in the French way, but not one of them was certain that it even existed. The wife of the Italian consul had visited us at the hotel. She carried a walkie-talkie the size of a machete in her handbag so that she could keep in contact with her husband while she was up in the hills and he was working down in the port.

This elegant woman was a native of Genoa but now spoke Italian with a faint French accent, having come to Haiti some years previously to marry the son and heir of an Italian family, the De Matteis, who had lived there for generations. She gave us the address of an elderly French priest who, she said, might know something about the Polish community. "I know they're there, somewhere, but I've never seen them. Hardly surprising, when you remember that there has been a curfew until just recently and we have been living like prisoners for months. And I've never been to Casales. It's a long way from any main road and can only be reached by a mule-track, but no one knows where the track leads or how long it is. It'll be a leap in the dark for you, and you'll simply have to *prendre votre chance* as we say here."

"Casales . . . *Loin, très loin,* very far," muttered the Reverend Joseph moodily as we finally left Port-au-Prince behind us and found ourselves on a very pretty road bounded on one side by a brilliant blue sea and on the other by the almost vertical slopes of a range of green hills.

Not two hours later we were entering the village home of the Polish community, the first foreigners for many, many years to do so.

The following lines are quoted from a letter to General J. H. Dabrowski, general inspector of the Polish contingent, sent by Battalion Commander Bolesta of the 3rd Polish Half-Brigade, dated the second of Messidor (21 June 1802), at the port of Malaga:

> On the 24 of the month Floréal we embarked at Livorno; the Expedition had been organized with the greatest possible economy in mind, both as regards the number of transport vessels and their provisioning; the men were accommodated in extreme discomfort and packed together like sardines in a tin. Despite the discomfort, we were not spared the ill fortune of a vessel of the third battalion foundering. Captain Kastus and a handful of men were the only survivors. We ourselves encountered storm-force winds, contrary winds and dead calms so that it took us no less than 34 days to reach Malaga where, due

to adverse winds, we remained only four hours. Two men died on the voyage. Commander Wodzinski has fallen ill and instead of disembarking has remained on board; the Economic Advisor to the Expedition has dispatched a request for leave. . . . Our Commander is now a Frenchman, Bernard by name. . . . And although it is common knowledge that our final destination is the Antilles, they all amuse themselves by pretending that this is a great secret.

These lines are from a letter addressed to Lieutenant Josef Nowicki by Second Lieutenant Weygall and dated the nineteenth of Ventôse (10 March 1803) at Cap Français:

On our arrival at Cap Français the Negroes rebelled and welcomed us by setting fire to sugar and coffee plantations, advancing to within a thousand paces of the port, the area covering a distance of ten Italian leagues along the shoreline. . . . The business of waging war is completely different here from that in Europe. In the last three days we have procured 300 fighting dogs from the Spanish colonies; we hope to receive 400 more tomorrow. The cost of feeding a dog for one month amounts to 6 French crowns and one has to bear in mind that they have Spanish handlers. Each handler is in charge of two dogs which he leads into battle in front of the infantry for a salary of 20 crowns a month. The mastiffs are in action all day long against live Negroes, whom they seize pitilessly and devour immediately. Our orders today are to go to the little island of Forte with five companies of French soldiers and 500 men of the National Guard who have taken 25 dogs with them. The population of this islet rebelled on the 16th of this month. The whole cape has been destroyed and everything burned. It is there that the French have their headquarters, commanded by General

Rochambeau. Przebendowski is his second-in-command; Kamieski was the Brigadier-General's aide-de-camp; he was killed during an expedition against the blacks and his wife died soon afterwards in hospital. . . . We are awaiting impatiently the arrival of the first Polish *demi-brigade.*

From a letter written by Vicomte Thouvenet, commandant of the Napoleonic contingent in the West Indies, to the minister for naval and colonial affairs, dated 10 March 1803:

General Brunet and the platoon commanders complain incessantly about the Poles' lack of courage. These lumpish and apathetic men, whose ways and language are completely different to our own, having been transported a vast distance away from their homeland, seem to have lost all their energy; the effort of marching is too much for them and they are terrified at the idea of having to fight a war of a kind about which they know nothing. It is therefore impossible to deploy them except as sentinels and it would be extremely dangerous to rely upon them in the future.

From a letter to an unknown recipient from Lieutenant Josef Zadora, dated 30 Germinal (20 April 1803), at the island of Santo Domingo:

I am writing to you for what is probably the last time before my death, because all that remains of my Third Brigade is 300 men and some officers, namely Zditowiecki, the battalion commander Kobylonski, Bolesta, Captain Zabokrzycki and some others I do not even know. All the rest are dead. I am filled with despair as I write and much regret my decision to come to the Americas and would not recommend it now even to my worst enemy. Far better to be a beggar in Europe than to seek one's fortune in the Americas where a thousand sicknesses

can do for you. We should all like to quit the army, but the
French force us to continue to fight. . . . I should like to
return to Europe, at least for a few months, and think of it
day and night. Our commander is Rochambeau and our
friend Rose is his aide-de-camp, but he can do nothing to
aid me. . . . The First Battalion has just beaten the
Negroes, we go into battle the day after tomorrow. . . .
When they counterattack the Negroes are capable of acting with appalling cruelty. Persuade Teodor for the love of
God not to embark, so that at least one of us two may survive. Greet all our friends. Szylewics Michal and all the
others here send their greetings to you.

To Major-General Jan Henryk Dabrowski, Inspector of Cavalry for the Italian Army, from Second Lieutenant Jurkiewicz of
the 114th Half-Brigade, dated the eleventh day of the month
Germinal (1 April 1805):

Now freed from the English prison, I present my most
profound respects to my General and Benefactor. . . .
Having left for America after numerous military cam-
paigns, during the evacuation of the island of Saint
Domingue I was captured by the English and subsequently all my private effects were lost at sea. I then spent
eight miserable months in prison until I finally obtained a
medical certificate establishing the impossibility of my
remaining on the island of Jamaica. The English allowed
me to leave and I went to New York and the Consul has
only just sent me back to France with the order to present
myself here at Châlons sur Marne. . . . Not even my comrades are there any longer. Through the good offices of
the General they have been ordered to muster in Milan,
but I, although still young, am wasting my time and cannot even rejoin my family in Krakow, in the Grand Duchy
of Warsaw. I am therefore certain that, since you have

shown such favour to my comrades, you will not refuse to show it to me also.

From the oath of loyalty to France which every soldier, irrespective of nationality, was required to swear before fighting under the tricolor:

> *Je promets d'être fidèle au Gouvernement Français et de remplir mes fonctions avec exactitude et probité.* [I swear to be faithful to the government of France and to fulfill my obligations with exactitude and probity.]

From the national anthem of Haiti, known as the "Dessalinienne":

> *Pour le Pays,*
> *Pour les Ancêtres,*
> *Marchons unis!*
> *Pour le Drapeau,*
> *Pour la Patrie*
> *Mourir est beau!*
>
> For country,
> For our ancestors,
> March united!
> For flag,
> For homeland,
> Death is beautiful!

From the Haitian constitution of 1805:

Article No. 12—"No white person, of whatever nationality, may set foot upon this territory as a land owner or master, nor may such persons in future acquire any property whatsoever."

Article No. 13—"The preceding article does not apply to white women who have been naturalized by the government, nor to their eventual offspring. The provisions of this article also include those of Polish and German birth whom the government has naturalized."

Cabaret is a market town on Route National 1 where rubbish rots in the mud left by the latest downpour while a blazing sun melts the ice for sale on the stalls. Blocks of this ice are brought in early every morning; it is a short-lived luxury that dwindles as you look at it and needs to be consumed without delay. The small boy who is usually in charge breaks the precious merchandise into cubes with a pointed tool.

The market used to take place beneath the corrugated iron roof of an enclosed warehouse, but it has now overflowed onto the main street, where it brings all traffic to a halt. Peasants sell pigs and donkeys brought down from the hills, as well as radishes and potatoes. Bananas, still attached to branches, arrive on overloaded carts from the semiwild plantations in the vicinity.

In Papa Doc's time, Cabaret was known as Duvalierville and the dictator, who practiced as a doctor here until elected president in 1957, intended it to be his Brasilia. But Duvalierville, true to its original name, became a fantasy-capital. Funds intended for building a mausoleum to François Duvalier were plundered from the state coffers in the name of the revolution he instigated; when the contents of the coffers proved insufficient, the Tontons Macoutes started to patrol the road leading north and to rob from all and sundry, including foreign diplomats.

The order was to transform Cabaret-Duvalierville into "a center where it will always be pleasant to live, beneath an eternally blue sky . . . and where every Haitian will be master of his own destiny." During the 1960s, while El Rancho's Argentinian proprietor was still cutting a dash in his red Ferrari around the streets of Port-au-Prince, Duvalierville even boasted a *ciné-théâtre* and a stadium

for cock-fighting. Government buildings of concrete, now used as
stables or warehouses, had the letters DDD engraved on their por-
tals. The three Ds stood for one of the megalomaniac slogans that
Papa Doc used to love formulating: "*Dieu,* the great Workman of
the universe; *Dessalines,* the Supreme Artisan of Liberty; *Duvalier,*
Architect of the New Haiti."

In 1986, Duvalierville was sacked by the crowd celebrating
the end of the dynasty. Cabaret, now in ruins, assumed its original name once more.

To reach Casales from Cabaret, one turns off the main road
onto a narrower one diving to the right. For seven hundred feet
the surface is tarred and gives the impression that it will continue to be so, but then it suddenly narrows to a dirt track and
becomes steeper, climbing between modest farms (seemingly
uninhabited) and small sugarcane plantations. Streams cross the
track at regular intervals, strewing it with stones and mud. For
the tires to grip, you have to keep up the momentum, bouncing
in and out of the potholes and ruts created by the lorries that
transport the peasants to Cabaret. There are few trucks, and
people who cannot find a space on one make the journey by foot
or on donkeys, keeping a careful watch from under their hats on
the goats that represent the mountain-dwellers' only means of
livelihood and that must, therefore, arrive at market in one
piece.

The higher you climb, the clearer the air becomes and the
wider the horizon, revealing expanses of rock and tracts of land
completely devoid of trees. The forests have been hacked down
by generation after generation of Haitians in search of firewood,
in spite of the occasional faded sign beside the road leading out
of Port-au-Prince that admonishes: *"Non à charbon à bois. Haiti
a besoin de ses arbres."* [Do not cut for firewood. Haiti needs
these trees.]

The mountains now present an all but lunar landscape, but
when the Poles first came here over two centuries ago they were
covered with woods as dense as those of the mother country,

which could well have been one of the reasons why Napoleon's ex-soldiers, having deserted from his army, chose to settle here.

"It's beautiful here. Like being on the roof of Haiti. Open the window, Joseph," I said to our guide. Joseph reacted with an indignant silence. After a few miles I got out of the car to buy a cold drink from a peasant family that had set up a table beside the road. I asked for a tot of white rum—the liquor that still tastes of sugarcane and is strong without burning the tongue—in my Coca-Cola, but Joseph declined, proudly announcing that he never touched alcohol and would be quite satisfied with Coca-Cola on its own.

A few miles farther on there was a group of houses that I thought might be Casales. Braking hard, I skidded to a halt on the loose gravel. Few things can be more satisfying, I thought, than to drive like this on a dirt track surrounded by natural beauty, even if that beauty is scarred by the red-rawness of landslides and deforestation. "Casales? Farther on," I was told by a couple of old women sitting in front of a house. As I got back into the Jeep, Joseph exploded. "When you need to ask for directions," he opined in his polished, ingenuous English, "you must not get out of the car. It is quite sufficient to stop and put your question in a loud voice. The peasants, *campagnards,* will come running, you'll see."

A few bends later the reverend had an opportunity of demonstrating to Pia and myself how well his method worked. We stopped in front of another shack, he lowered the window about two inches, and through the microscopic fissure inquired flatly: "Casales?" Having received the expected reply, "Farther on," he turned to me, completely ignoring the peasant, and translated the words in all seriousness: "Farther on." Then he wound up the window and was ready to continue the journey.

❧

Haiti's "little lost Poland" is a village similar to hundreds of others on top of a bare mountain. The houses are dotted about at random because there is no road, and with their wall of dried mud or plaited straw and roofs of banana leaves they look like African huts and are known as *caille-pailles*. The oldest are brick-built and in a strange style more Tyrolean than Caribbean, with upper stories and little balconies. The only substantial building, a small stone church dedicated to St. Michael the Archangel built by the Polish legionaries shortly after their arrival, fell down a few months ago, very suddenly and rather mysteriously. The inhabitants of Casales can offer no explanation for this, but there are rumors of witchcraft. The stones simply slipped and the entire building collapsed. Another few minutes and the pews would have been crowded for the Sunday celebration of the Mass in Creole.

Two objects survived, modest in themselves but regarded by these blue-eyed, high-cheekboned peasants as their ancestral heritage: a fat-bellied orchestral instrument similar to a double bass, whose layer of varnish has long since worn away, still played in church on the big occasions as if it were an organ, and a painting depicting the Madonna and Child, reminiscent of the Black Madonna of Czestochowa. The bass leans against a wall of the corrugated-iron hut that now serves as a church. The painting is kept under lock and key in a dusty sacristy.

Where the village begins there is a thirty-foot-wide river straddling the road. There has never been a bridge here so the only way of crossing, for trucks as for the very occasional car, is for the driver to engage a low gear, keep his wheels carefully centered on the rounded stones and trust to the power of his engine to keep going. Terrifying to start with, this becomes fun.

It was certainly fun for the boys who were playing in the water when Pia decided to get out of the car and take photographs of the ford while wading knee-deep through the water. Joseph's eyes nearly popped out of his head. "Haven't they ever

seen a woman crossing the ford on foot before?" I teased, pointing to the spectators who were trying, rather ineffectually, to
conceal their merriment. Without realizing it, I had voiced the
precise thought that was crossing the mind of our divine. "You
could bet anything you like that they have never seen a white
woman, let alone one who chooses to walk through the river!"

When we reached the point where the mule track ended and
not even a four-wheel drive could go any further, Joseph
scowled. The idea of leaving the air-conditioned comfort of the
Jeep and exposing himself to the blazing heat of the midday sun
did not appeal to him in the least. "We can get to work at last,"
I said. There was no response.

Casales has no electricity, no phone, no running water, no
nurse, no cars, no school, and now no church. There are no
shops, nor is there a central square. Even the graveyard with all
Polish names on the headstones is semiabandoned: people are
buried near their homes, the grave marked by two sticks for a
cross. One wonders how on earth hundreds of European officers and men with origins in the sophisticated culture of early
eighteenth-century Poland were apparently incapable of forming a more advanced rural society. Every one of the few faces
around us was as dark as Haitians anywhere else. There was not
a breath of wind, and the children watched us in complete
silence as if taking part in a 1960s-style documentary on tribal
societies. Eventually a small girl stepped forward to ask the
question that was in everyone's mind. It was asked timidly, but
as if it were the only sensible question to put to a couple of white
people from far away descending on their isolated universe.
"Have you come from Poland?"

When we replied that we had come from Europe but had no
direct connection with Poland, the disappointment was severe.
Many years have passed since the "Mother Country" last sent an
emissary to these mountains, and the descendants of General
Leclerc's troops feel abandoned by a world that has, for them, become ever more distant and indifferent. Occasionally it happened

in the past that someone in Warsaw would remember about these fellow Poles referred to as "Papa Doc's white Negroes" and, out of curiosity, find the way to Casales. Little material aid has come from these visits, but they keep alive the hope that one day some generous white person, naturally a Pole, will just arrive out of the blue and rescue them from their predicament.

The miracle nearly happened some fifteen years ago, when an illiterate peasant from Casales became the first Haitian Pole to repeat his ancestors' journey in reverse and visit Poland, where he stayed for over a year. But when he returned, they told us, he did not want to tell them anything. He just picked up the threads of his old life as if he had never been away.

For all the others, *la Polonie* has been but a vague concept for generations. No one can even visualize what the real place might be like. The soldier-ancestors left no books, no documents, and in many cases not even mementoes or tales to be passed down through the family. All that remains is a dance they call the polka, and those Slav features (now slowly emerging from all sides) that seem so out of place among the banana plantations and African-style huts.

The explanation, given with a shrug of the shoulders, was that they were too poor. The fight for survival meant laboring on the mountain slopes from dawn until dusk. They forgot how to read or write. Fathers taught their children Creole, the language spoken all around them, rather than Polish, and at times they even had to conceal their Polish nationality. *Labas en Pologne,* "over there in Poland," is now, and has been for some time, a turn of phrase rather than a reference to a place on the map.

But Fate chose one man, Amon Frémon, to be a witness to what things were like, or had been at one point, *labas en Pologne.* In 1980, when the painful years of Duvalier's regime were drawing to a close in Port-au-Prince and communism was on its last legs in Warsaw, Casales received a visit from a man whose name still excites love and veneration. Things would never be quite the same afterward.

This man, a real Pole from Poland, appeared to the mountain-dwellers as the Messiah whose long-awaited coming would rescue *les Polonaises* from their miserable isolation and neglect by telling the world about their sufferings. To provide proof of the survival of a Polish community in an obscure corner of the Caribbean, he chose Amon Frémon and took him back to the Poland of General Jaruzelski on the very eve of the strikes in the Danzig shipyards.

The story of this adventure is Amon's pièce de résistance, and while in full flow he can forget the festering wound on his hand caused by a mishap with a machete, and that his little daughter's belly is swollen by malnutrition and infected matter oozes from her eyes.

"My grandfather was Polish; his name was Faon Frémon Beké. My father was Polish. I am Polish. And I went to Poland because I was invited to go by Jerzy Detopski. Who was he? *Un blanc* who had come to Casales to look for any surviving relatives and take them back to Poland to meet his family. Jerzy was an important man, *un grand blanc.* Well, he chose me. I went all over Poland, but they took me to France, to Paris, too. I don't know if Jerzy is still alive today, and I reckon there's no way I could find out. Take you and me, for example. Here we are chatting together today, and maybe you die tomorrow. Who can tell. As we say, birds come and go, eating the crumbs we scatter. What was Poland like? There was snow and lots of forests. No, I didn't stay there, because the curfew came along and the white man sent me back home. I'm still fond of Jerzy, because he did a lot of nice things for me and always saw that everything was just so. I still love him even though I don't know where he is now." Turning to the little crowd sitting around him hanging on his every word, he repeated: "When I was in Poland I didn't have to spend any money at all. The *blanc* paid for everything."

Amon's account of his adventure was a mixture of satisfaction and annoyance. He enjoyed being the center of attention, but was also evasive. Maybe it was pure chance, but the man chosen by the mysterious Polish benefactor to revive the ties between the lost tribe and the mother country was a *houngan,* a Voodoo priest or magic-man. "Jerzy chose me because he liked the way I lived. I'm a magic-man, I have special powers, everyone here loves me. And the *grand blanc* liked the idea of a Pole who knew about magic."

We egged him on with more questions and Amon sighed, obviously thinking us ignorant foreigners so unimaginative that every last thing had to be explained. "Look," he said, "Jerzy knew that I was the one man who could bring peace to Poland. The country was up in arms and needed someone with magic powers. Jerzy took me all over the place, to one city after another, and organized great festivals of magic. Every city we went to, we would take at least twenty-five white men with us into the forest and perform the rites together." He broke off suddenly, as if he had suddenly recollected an incident that would not bear the telling, and concluded by saying, "Ah no, mine is not an easy profession."

The story was quite bizarre. I tried to imagine this Polish man, this *grand blanc,* as Amon had called him, who could travel and do business abroad despite the pro-Soviet regime and was therefore one of the *nomenklatura,* the communist elite, yet who was also a secret supporter of Solidarity in the very year that saw the first of the strikes (the "war," as Amon called it). This powerful Pole, obsessed by accounts he had heard of his forgotten "brothers" in Haiti, must have imagined that with a bit of help from Voodoo magic even the mighty U.S.S.R. could be made to yield some part of its invincibility. Who Jerzy might have been, and why he ever came to Haiti, remained unclear. Amon vaguely mentioned shops, leading one to suppose that he was some kind of dealer. In what? There was no way of knowing.

It is possible that the Pole was simply a businessman who led Amon around the country exhibiting him for payment in the villages and organizing quasi-Voodoo ceremonies in the woods, carefully avoiding discovery by the police who could have arrested him for subversion.

For Amon, time stands still. One moment and one year are much the same thing. The arrival of Jerzy in Haiti had become confused with that other arrival, much earlier but equally incomprehensible, of hundreds of Polish soldiers in the Napoleonic army. "I don't know exactly when my ancestors got here," said Amon the magic-man, "I think it had something to do with Dessalines and Toussaint Louverture. At any rate, in the end they brought peace."

"But weren't they soldiers, part of an army?"

Amon lost his patience completely and rolled his watery eyes. These whites! Destroying the poetry of life and its true meaning with their banal logic. They, *les blancs,* see only the surface. "There are two kinds of soldiers," he exclaimed at last. "Those who make peace and those who make war. Look, *mo'sieur,* it is sometimes important to have arms to establish peace in a country. As the Americans do nowadays." And in one phrase he had ideologically united Dessalines and George Bush.

The magic-man was tired. The wound on his hand looked ugly and there was not a drop of water to cleanse it. Pia had already seen the danger of gangrene. But there has never been a doctor in Casales. And of late even the priest has ceased to make the uphill journey from Cabaret every Sunday, mounted on a donkey or in a borrowed car, to visit these compatriots of the pope. "He hasn't come for years," said a blue-eyed woman whose hair was streaked with blonde. "Since this new priest came along, we have to go to Cabaret if we want to see him. He says he can't come, that he hasn't got the time. He's even got a car now, but he keeps saying it won't go."

No doctor, no priest. Amon was resigned. The best years of his life were long gone. And now illness was darkening his skin. Or maybe old age or that implacable, crystalline sun.

"My father was whiter than your wife," he said, glancing at Pia. "But in Haiti a peasant always becomes black." It was impossible to tell whether this was a reference to the climate or to the subtle sociological distinction between a *grand blanc,* or urban white, and a *petit blanc,* or peasant. "If I spent a year in Poland I too would turn white. Now that I'm ill I'm black." His trip had given him the right to speak with the authority of an airport-lounge habitué. "You see, when I travel abroad I usually feel Polish, but here I'm Haitian. And now, at my age, with all the sun I've been exposed to, that is what I have become." He raised his arm to show it to us and laughed bitterly. "I'm Haitian even down to the color of my skin."

The conflict that was to bring the Poles to Haiti began in 1794 when the plantation owners in the French colony refused to accept the decision to abolish slavery in Saint-Domingue and the black slaves rebelled under the illusion that revolutionary Paris would be on their side. But Haiti was too important to France for her to risk losing it. Half of France's sea trade was with her colony of Saint-Domingue, and many ports depended for their very survival on the cargoes of coffee, indigo, cocoa, cotton and sugar that came from the "Pearl of the Antilles." There used to be a saying, "as rich as a Creole."

Between 17 May 1802 and the summer of the following year, the first batch of 2,570 Polish soldiers left the ports of Livorno and Genoa bound for the island, dreaming of a quick and easy campaign in a country where bananas would be as plentiful as potatoes in Poland, a land of parrots, angelfish and yams. The soldiers spoke no French and, naturally enough, no Creole either. Their uniforms were heavy and ill-suited to a tropical climate. Their military objectives were precise: they had to halt the advance of the black troops referred to in their dispatches as "brigands." But they had been issued with no maps to guide them from the coast to the mountains.

A second Polish contingent was even more unlucky. Ten days after disembarking in a country in total chaos, led by officers who often spoke no word of French, their numbers had already been decimated by yellow fever.

In all, nearly four thousand Polish volunteers arrived in Saint-Domingue as part of the colonial army.

On 17 June 1803, Major Lozinsky, commanding a body of about fifty Polish legionaries surrounded by two thousand black rebels, blew his brains out. Nearly all his soldiers were killed; the few survivors joined up with the rebel slaves. "We cannot accuse these foreigners of dereliction of duty," wrote the vicomte de Rochambeau, who had succeeded General Leclerc as commander of the French West Indian Army, "because they fall where they stand, without giving a foot of ground, remaining united even under attack from enemy musket fire without seeking to retreat out of range of the bullets. But they understand no French and it is impossible to send them into battle and give them the mobility essential in moments of crisis."

The Polish troops stumbled from one defeat to another, ever more demoralized but nonetheless determined not to surrender. Their pact with Napoleon had been cut and dried. In return for their assistance in restoring slavery to the Saint-Domingue colony, Bonaparte would restore the freedom of Poland, which was then under the double protectorate of Prussia and Russia. The Polish soldiers worshipped Napoleon. In *War and Peace* the lancers of one Polish regiment throw themselves into the River Njeman like men possessed in their efforts to greet the emperor, while he, standing on the far bank, never spares a glance in their direction.

On the island of Hispaniola, though, there was no Napoleon to die for. Under the tropical sun, these patriots with their fair skin and antiquated uniforms fought against the liberation of the black people while dreaming of the liberation of their own country. But it was not long before they realized how uncomfortably close the cause of the slaves under Toussaint Louverture and Dessalines was to their own. Black Haitian slaves and Polish nationalists were all fighting for the same ideals of liberty, independence and freedom from foreign tyranny.

Perhaps the forests that had seemed hostile at first eventually captivated them, as did the languorous climate. Perhaps they had little to lose and all that awaited them on their return to Poland was a life of service to some landowner. While their officers could pen appeals to the military headquarters in Warsaw requesting reintegration with the Italian Army (which had a Polish contingent in which they could continue to serve the Napoleonic dream of the conquest of Europe), the common soldiers, scattered or held prisoner by the rebels, had no one to write to and no means of escape from their plight. Many hundreds of them—the precise number is not known —decided to stay and side with the black people as citizens of the only state in the whole world to be brought into being by a slaves' revolt.

But the campaign, for the Poles, had been doomed from the start. On 7 April 1803 Toussaint Louverture, the Negro ex-slave whom Chateaubriand had ironically dubbed the "black Napoleon," was found dead after months of imprisonment by the French in a castle in the Swiss Alps. Liberally minded Europeans were shocked by what was seen as the assassination of a rebel leader for political motives, but every Western government, fearful of what damage the wind of rebellion might wreak in its own colonies, sided with France. Talleyrand thundered: "The existence of an armed black population occupying a land stained with the most horrendous crimes is a terrible sight for all white nations."

General Charles Leclerc, commanding the expedition charged with putting down the revolt, was ordered to deport all blacks and all rebel mulattos to Corsica and to arrest every white woman who had had sexual relations with a black man. Leclerc, who in the meantime had married Napoleon's sister, Pauline Bonaparte, failed. He fell victim to fever and tropical diseases on the island of Tortuga off the extreme northern tip of the country, and died. His brief military campaign had lasted less than a year.

When the French troops landed in Saint-Domingue they found the island in flames. In order to deny the French the use of the ports and barracks, and to cut off their supply routes, the rebelling slaves had set fire to the then capital city, Cap Français (now Cap-Haïtien), and—having attacked the homes of the white estate owners—to vast swathes of agricultural land.

The man who succeeded Leclerc as commander, the vicomte de Rochambeau, thought he could end the conflict quickly with a short, sharp shock. He invited ladies from the highest echelons of mixed-race society in Port-au-Prince to a sumptuous dinner one evening, and at midnight, declaring the party over, had them shown into a room hung with black velvet and decorated with human skulls. French soldiers dressed as priests were singing the Dies Irae in front of a row of coffins. The soldier-priests then threw open the lids of the coffins. Every lady present saw the corpse of one of her relatives. "You have just attended the funeral of your brothers and husbands," declared the vicomte triumphantly.

On the first of January 1804, despite the arrival of further contingents of foreign "volunteers," this time not only Polish but also including battalions of Danish and German troops, Toussaint Louverture's bloodthirsty successor, the rebel general Jean-Jacques Dessalines, succeeded in proclaiming the Republic of Haiti. It was the world's first black republic. For thousands of whites the declaration signaled the start of a massacre. Dessalines had promised that he would "write this act of independence using the skull of a white man as my inkwell, his blood as my ink and his skin as my blotting paper. And my pen shall be a bayonet."

He kept his promise. Almost all the whites were killed, with only a few managing to escape. Five months after Napoleon had proclaimed himself emperor in Paris, Dessalines also assumed the title of emperor, calling himself Jean-Jacques the First.

The defeat had far-reaching consequences for France. The loss of Saint-Domingue forced Napoleon to abandon Louisiana as well; he sold it to the United States. The dream of a Caribbean empire lay in ruins. And the history books tell us that Napoleon, in his exasperation, yelled: "Damned sugar, damned coffee, damned colonies!"

꧁

We left Casales early that first day, having decided against trying
to achieve too much too soon. Many of the inhabitants had hidden in their houses during our visit and we realized they needed
time to become used to the presence of strangers. I asked Joseph
to explain that we intended to return the following day and stay
longer. Driving back down the steep mountain road, recrossing
the ford and the streams, we found ourselves once more in
Cabaret, where the market was now finished.

It was late and we had to find somewhere for the night. At
Port-au-Prince we had been warned that it would be difficult.
Tourism has all but disappeared since the civil war, and all that
remains is a Club Méditerranée, much further on, that the
French keep open as a favor to the American forces of the UN
and representatives of the humanitarian organizations.

Along the Côte des Arcadins the sea is deep blue and very
calm. A succession of tiny bays lies spread out like a half moon.
Every now and then you can catch a glimpse of white villas
among the rocks. Three or four signposts point to the lidos
where middle-class Haitians once disported themselves at the
weekend. We chose the first, which boasted the rather grand
name of Wahoo Bay Beach Resort. The rooms in the hotel were
clean, there was a swimming pool facing the beach and an
African-style restaurant with a plaited straw roof. Pia and I went
for a swim while Joseph (who had insisted on personally inspecting his own room before accepting it) read the Bible. The water
was clear as crystal, and we floated about on a homemade raft
wide enough for three made of tin cans held together by jute
sacks. Near us, a couple were encouraging their children to use
snorkels. The husband, Haitian by birth, had emigrated to the
States many years previously; his wife was a white American.
They looked like university teachers, and were anxious that the
people around them should notice that they had brought their
children up to speak both French and English.

When it was time for dinner we decided to take the Jeep and look for the famous castle built in the eighteenth century near the coast at Montreuil, surrounded by plantations of coffee, walnut and coconut. It was already dark when we arrived, and the castle looked as gloomy as a medieval château with its crenellated towers and barred windows. The family of French landowners (since become mulattos) who built it when Haiti was still the richest of the American colonies still lives in part of the castle. The rooms are said to be lavishly furnished with antiques, brocaded hangings and old paintings, but uniformed custodians are quick to discourage any show of curiosity. However, one part has been converted into what is, perhaps, Haiti's best-known hotel and restaurant, the Moulin sur Mer. In what used to be the stables, bedrooms have been created for the few tourists who venture further than the Club Med.

The Castle of Montreuil is one of the last residences to retain the style of imperial Haiti. Haiti's mulatto elite has always affected a style of unbridled luxury, clinging to the trappings of privilege copied from eighteenth-century French aristocracy even when these were no longer fashionable in Europe. The island used to be dotted with Palladian villas, colonnaded universities and medieval castles, almost all of which have been reduced to rubble by tropical humidity or political vicissitude.

It may now seem incredible, but Haiti, thanks to the enormous wealth generated by sugarcane, long regarded itself as a powerful, developed nation. King Henri Christophe, who reigned over northern Haiti from 1806 to 1820, even set up a state-owned printing press, a judicial system, a navy, a faculty of medicine, a Royal Academy of Classical Studies and an immensely elegant citadel he called a "Palladium of Liberty and Independence." Such things existed—if they existed at all— only in rudimentary form in the neighboring United States.

The fortress, considered the eighth wonder of the world in its time, was built on the top of a mountain so high that its summit was always half-hidden by clouds. A little lower down was the royal palace, named Sans Souci after the palace of Frederick the

Great in Potsdam. This was to be the Versailles of the New World, embodying a degree of luxury never seen before in the Antilles. When appearing at court, the Haitian nobles, many of whom were descended from African chiefs, were obliged to observe to the letter an extremely complex protocol. There was a special uniform: shoes of red morocco leather with gold buckles, a hat with plumes (blue plumes for barons, red for counts, and so on), and a velvet tunic. The titles bestowed upon these nobles show a decided—perhaps involuntary—sense of humor. From the court lists we learn of the existence of a comte de Limonade and a duc de la Marmelade.

The royal residence of Sans Souci is now reduced to almost complete ruin. Many of the other palaces that in their time gave the mulattos of Saint-Domingue the impression of outdoing the European aristocracy in matters of style have vanished without trace. But the quasi-medieval castle on the Archahaie shore is still intact and holds many secrets. By night an official prevents your parking in front of the main entrance which is fitted with security lights. The restaurant is right beside the sea, some way from the main entrance to the castle. The clientele is almost exclusively foreign, and when we finally arrived Joseph was extremely uneasy. I reassured him, reminding him that we were picking up the tab.

"That's not what is worrying me," he replied. "But I don't know if I'll like the kind of food they serve here."

"It'll be much the same as in any other restaurant. They even say 'typical Haitian cuisine.'"

The loveliness of the calm evening failed to drive away visions of the Poles, neglected and left to fend for themselves on their treeless mountain. Joseph sat frowning in concentration over the simple menu. Pia and I ordered. Joseph could come to no decision, and the waiter, after his third failed attempt to take an order, began to show signs of fraying temper.

"I never eat fish," pronounced Joseph, "and as for chicken, I don't know how they cook it here."

"We could ask."

The waiter's lengthy explanation failed to convince him. Eventually he gave in and agreed to try the chicken, but specified no onions.

When the food arrived, Joseph became more glum than ever. "Beetroot makes me sick," he protested, and dumped a forkful on my plate. The waiter watched, scandalized. But that reaction had nothing to do with beetroot and everything to do with his disapproval of the idea of two *blancs* traveling with a black man of the church who was all the more suspect for speaking English.

Joseph brightened only when we asked him to tell us about Haiti and the people who had come to prominence in the last few years.

"Here things are very different from what they seem. The official version is the opposite to the truth. The representatives of Catholicism and Voodooism, which is the same thing, have never told the truth to the people. But now we are trying to bring the truth of the Bible to this country."

A fine sermon. I should have liked to take him up on some points, but that evening I had decided to discover something about Joseph himself, and I wanted to make him talk. He picked at his food, glaring at it disdainfully from time to time, and continued to develop his theory. This amounted to a precise exposition of the average Haitian's view of the world. As Max Beauvoir, a Voodoo priest with an IBM computer on his desk, explained to the English writer Ian Thomson, "God for the Haitian is more like Fate or Destiny, a sort of *Deus otiosus*. He conjures up no precise image, for he is *trop grand, trop lointain*—too great, too remote—to mean anything. Any natural disaster beyond the comprehension of ordinary folk, such as a hurricane or epidemic or disease, may be ascribed to the intervention of *Papa Bon Dieu*, but anything supernatural—a mysterious death, the appearance of a werewolf—will be directly accountable to the *loas,* or spirits."

"For example," said Joseph, "Duvalier *père,* Papa Doc, did not die of an illness as the history books say he did."

According to the books, when the president-for-life François Duvalier died in 1971, his funeral, complete with a Requiem in the cathedral of Port-au-Prince and a 101-gun salute, took place on 24 April, coincidentally the day dedicated to Baron Samedi, the god of death and chief divinity of the Voodoo afterlife. A crucifix had been placed in his hands together with a copy of his celebrated pamphlet, *Memoirs of a Third World Leader,* in which he had said "a doctor must sometimes take life in order to save it."

Duvalier was elected on 22 September 1957, and 22 was his lucky number. On 22 November 1963 he celebrated the assassination of his enemy John Kennedy with champagne, and wherever he went he was accompanied by 22 Tontons Macoutes (the militiamen in dark glasses who terrorized the people by claiming to be zombies with supernatural powers). After his death Papa Doc entered the Pantheon of Voodoo gods with the name "Loa 22 Os," meaning Good Spirit Number 22. The Catholic Church had excommunicated him officially in 1962, but even the African gods must have abandoned him eventually. Or so Joseph believed.

"Papa Doc was poisoned, slowly. One of his generals, a mulatto, after attempting a coup d'état that failed, went to the United States and returned to Haiti with an American submarine from which he fired on the presidential palace with a magic cannon at precisely the moment when Papa Doc was looking out over the sea. My mother, who knew the general, told me many times that he had made a pact with the Devil and possessed magic powers. Duvalier destroyed the submarine, but only three months later he was dead."

Pia and I stared at him open-mouthed and speechless.

"Are you Catholics?" Joseph asked for the umpteenth time.

"I am," I replied, "but Pia is an Anglican."

"Today, the Poles mentioned the visit of the pope to Port-au-Prince, but they didn't say anything about one of the visit's most important aspects."

"What is that?"

"Well, the pope is actually a great Voodoo priest. Like the ex-president, Brother Jean-Bertrand Aristide, who was officially a Catholic priest although we all know that he is a high-ranking priest of an important Voodoo sect. There's even a video going the rounds in town that shows him taking part in a big black magic ceremony, with sacrifices and all. Human sacrifices? Of course. Look, you may not see evidences of Voodoo, but it dominates the world. Papa Doc even changed the national flag of Haiti to express his devotion to the spirits. He abolished Dessalines' red and blue flag, which was basically the French tricolor without the white band, and chose red and black instead, the colors of Baron Samedi, the traditional colors of Voodooism. Now the pope practices magic in secret, and when he came to Haiti he sent out very clear messages that the Voodooists understood perfectly even though they were not picked up by the rest of the world."

That both Duvaliers and all their predecessors starting with Dessalines were involved with Voodoo is a well-documented fact. Haiti's first black emperor, seen in many paintings wearing the Napoleonic cocked hat and eighteenth-century-style waistcoat, is now a god in the Voodoo pantheon. His soldiers went into battle convinced that they would die and meet again in a paradise beyond the grave, in Guinea, the land of their forefathers. But a connection between the Polish pope and the animistic rites of Dahomey . . . ?

"Joseph, are you teasing, or do you really believe this? It's the last thing I would have expected from you. And what were these coded signals?"

"There were many. For example, when he arrived at the airport he kissed the ground twice. This is precisely what the wizards, or *hougan,* do when they want to bring war to a particular place. One kiss means peace, two kisses mean war. And in fact, only a few years later the country was in turmoil."

"Joseph, you're saying the most irrational things. You don't really expect me to believe you, do you?"

"I'm only telling you things that everyone here knows already. John Paul the Second, I repeat, has made a pact with Lucifer and with the spirits of Voodoo. All the powerful men in the world have to do it. Otherwise they would go under because evil, or the Devil if you prefer it, is stronger than them. All the popes have made pacts with the Devil. All except one, John Paul's predecessor, who died suddenly and in mysterious circumstances. It was bound to happen. They killed him because he refused to strike out certain verses of the Scriptures, the verses that speak of the death of Lucifer, of his defeat. The official version of the Bible no longer contains those verses in which Evil is destroyed and humiliated. To begin with, they were there. And every pope has to confirm their cancellation in order to keep his power."

Joseph shot me a look of defiance. "There is a secret pact between the Catholic Church and the Voodoo religion. That is fact. But the evangelical churches will succeed in breaking it."

"Have you seen this video with Aristide?"

"No, but we can buy one if you like. However, I remember very clearly having seen a meeting between village heads on television, when Aristide brought them together in the presidential palace. The president had convinced the Americans that it was a meeting of politicians, but in fact he had invited all the leaders of the Voodoo secret societies. They were all wizards, all *hougans*. And Tontons Macoutes too, which is the same thing."

We listened in silence while Joseph continued to speak in the measured tones of a preacher delivering a sermon. The Protestant churches did indeed come to Haiti to rid the country of African superstition, described in their literature as the incarnation of evil. But it now seemed that the most convinced believer in Voodoo was none other than Joseph, the Baptist pastor. Maybe because of all the many attempts to eradicate Voodoo, none has ever succeeded, not even the bloodiest of all, which occurred after the fall of Baby Doc in 1986 when a thousand priests were killed by Protestant and Catholic extremists. It is said that many of them were killed with machetes or stones at the express command of Father Aristide, the Catholic priest who became president and whose behavior was at that time widely considered erratic. This seems like a contradiction, yet Joseph and magicians such as Max Beauvoir (who accuses Aristide of anti-Voodoo persecutions and even of teaching the peasants to kill babies in the wombs of the *mambos*) share a belief that is substantially the same in both cases, namely that appearances belie the truth, and that men, especially those with power, are guided by spirits.

Joseph's chicken was now cold. We decided to leave. Back at the Wahoo Bay Beach Resort, Joseph declared smugly: "Now I must go and read the Bible. I do so for at least three hours a day." Tomorrow we would meet again. The Poles were expecting us.

After their defeat at the hands of the slaves, the French and all the white people living in Haiti in 1803 were pitilessly massacred by Dessalines. The first of these massacres took place in the city of Jérémie in the evening of the very day of the French surrender. Thomas Madiou gives a chilling account of these events in his monumental work, *Histoire d'Haiti*. Having described how all the French inhabitants, even those who had fought alongside the blacks, were taken from the city and herded into the hospital on the orders of General Bazelais, who then sent in a battalion with drawn bayonets, he continues:

> The corridors of the hospital were ankle-deep in blood. At the same time, patrols were combing the city for any whites who were in hiding. The massacre continued the following day. Babies clinging to their mothers' breasts were torn from them and killed without mercy. There were corpses all over the city. Jérémie itself was surrounded by guards preventing the French from escaping and warning the Europeans in other cities of their danger.

Over the next few days, massacres of the French continued all over the colony despite the reluctance of some of Dessalines' troops to carry out such brutal orders. Pétion, for example, se-

cretly tried to save as many whites as possible and ordered his
three field adjutants to do the same. But the slaughter was horrendous. In Port-au-Prince the cold-blooded killing continued for
two days, on 16 and 17 March, involving a house-to-house man-
hunt. Dessalines' orders were to take every white and every mulatto to the square in front of Government House and kill them all
at once. Those who managed to evade the killers, by hiding during the day and swimming under cover of darkness to the safety
of friendly ships, fled abroad, forming white colonies on the other
Caribbean islands. In *A Way in the World*, V. S. Naipaul writes
about these gentlemen farmers who came to the English colony in
Trinidad, and how they cleared the virgin forest to make way for
sugar plantations with the help of slaves newly imported from
Africa. Their eyes still reflected the terror of the black revolution
in Haiti, identified with one name: that of Dessalines.

But the Poles stayed put. Madiou writes:

> Dessalines gave orders that none of the Poles who had
> served in the French ranks was to be killed. On the con-
> trary, he instructed his officials to grant them Haitian citi-
> zenship. Boisrond Tonnerre, Dessalines' ferocious secretary
> and ideologue, added that they (the Poles) were brave peo-
> ple whom despotism had armed against liberty, but that in
> their own country they had fought long and hard against
> tyranny.

Polish troops were even formed into special battalions to
guard the prisons overflowing with French people awaiting exe-
cution. A few officers managed to leave the island in ships under
French command, and were taken to Cuba or the United States
from where they wrote to the generals in Warsaw pleading to be
repatriated. Only 160 Polish soldiers asked Dessalines for permission to leave Haiti, and this was granted. They were put
aboard a British frigate, the *Tartare,* commanded by a Captain
Perkins, and taken to Jamaica. Unfortunately they were not welcomed by Governor Nugent, who offered them a stark choice:
enrollment in the English army or immediate return whence

they came. When they refused to a man to serve under the English flag, the governor sent them back to Haiti with a recommendation to Dessalines to expel them. But the leader of the revolt, the "black Jacobin," received them with most untypical warmth and sent a tart message to Jamaica: "The Poles are free citizens of a free nation, Haiti, so I cannot oblige them to leave."

No contemporary documents record the fate of these 160 soldiers. They probably merged with the several hundreds of their compatriots who had begun to spread out over Haiti and form rural communities such as that of Casales. It is said that the original name of this village was Canton des Plateaux, and that the name changed with the arrival of the first Pole, a soldier with the name—or nickname—of Zal. But from this point on, the former enemies who owed their lives to Dessalines began to slip gradually into the mists of history, hardly touched by what happened subsequently in a Haiti with which they were losing all meaningful contact.

For a century and a half very little was known about *les polonaises* except for the fact that with the inevitable intermarriages (most of the Poles were men, but a few had brought their wives with them) their skin became darker. They were "rediscovered" in the 1950s. When Papa Doc Duvalier, the sworn enemy of the mulatto elite and its French trappings, was seeking symbols for his pro-African, anti-European stance, he publicly eulogized the Poles' patriotism and dubbed them "European white negroes."

One day in March 1983, a car made its way up the steep mountain road to Casales. On board were two priests from the diocese of Port-au-Prince whose brusque, matter-of-fact manners belied the mysterious nature of their message. They instructed the half-naked peasant men and the women in their light cotton dresses to prepare themselves for an extraordinary event, a great celebration. They were to wear traditional Polish costume, nothing else would do. The Casales peasants looked at each other, completely mystified. They had no idea what the priests were talking about. The clothes they wore were the clothes they, and their parents before them, had always worn. But the two priests insisted. They must dress like Poles, or at least wear the best clothes they had. "We shall come for you in a few hours," they said.

The story becomes confused at this point and there are discrepancies of time in the various accounts. The inhabitants of Casales, accustomed to obeying orders without asking too many questions, remember that the two mulatto priests did not return that day; they reappeared a week later, with a van, and said they were taking a group of fifty people to Port-au-Prince immediately to take part in an important ceremony. They wanted the community leaders, those with the fairest skin, and, indeed, anybody else who cared to go along.

The date was 18 March. A few hours later, a group of fifty-odd tired, hungry Poles, wearing long trousers, straw hats and their Sunday best shirts, were decanted onto the scorching tarmac of François Duvalier International Airport. A special space had been reserved for them beside a crowd waving the flags of Haiti and the Vatican. Foreign priests thrust flags into their hands too: red and white, the colors of Poland.

When John Paul II emerged from the plane and kissed the ground, it all became clear to the Casales group. The Polish pope had remembered them at last and had come to rescue them. he was about to invite them aboard his white plane and take them back to the land of their forefathers.

"Yours is a beautiful country, rich in human resources, but Christians cannot be unaware of the divisions, the injustice, the deteriorating quality of life, the poverty, the hunger and the fear suffered by the majority. Things must change in this country." Such was the substance of the pope's admonitory speech subsequently printed—in French—and distributed to the faithful in hundreds of leaflets as his "Speech to the Haitian Nation."

Then it was time to meet the people gathered to welcome him and to shake hands. Belaizaire Eliazaire—seventy-eight, hollow-cheeked, deeply wrinkled, gray eyes irritated by the sun—told us what happened next. "We had time to ask him for help and explain that no one had ever given us anything since our ancestors arrived in Haiti, that we needed food, schools and medicines. A few managed to shake his hand. To others he promised that he would send assistance, because, he said, we were all Poles and should help one another. Then he went on to speak to another group. . . . Wait a moment, I've got something to show you."

The old man, whose face bore the sad expression so typical of Polish peasants, hurried off and returned with a framed photograph, the only one in the village, showing a still youthful Pope John Paul shaking his hand at the airport while other leaders of the Casales community wait their turn watched suspiciously by fat Haitian army officers in uniforms rather too heavily encrusted with gold braid. Ignoring them, the Poles stand to attention for all the world like brave infantrymen during an inspection by their general. "From that moment to this," said Emile Magloire with a sad shake of the head, "we have heard no more. No aid has come. Even His Holiness has forgotten about us, like all the rest."

"Were you disillusioned? Were you angry?" I asked.

The little group of men with lined faces and straw hats clutched on their knees exchanged glances. We were sitting in the shade of some trees, and had been joined by others who had shared that brief moment of illusory hope. There was a moment's silence before anyone spoke, then two or three spoke up at the same time, denying they had been disappointed because they were sure that sooner or later the pope would send someone. They knew he must be very busy, but nevertheless a promise was a promise and they were sure he would keep his word and do something for them. Perhaps, they suggested, we might jog his memory when we went home. . . .

It was not easy to explain that although we were white and although we lived in Europe, we were not exactly on terms of day-to-day intimacy with the pope. Moreover it seemed incredible, given the length of time that had elapsed, that no one had ever succeeded in getting through to the powers that be in Port-

au-Prince. Had they never, I asked, tried to contact the papal
delegate, for instance? No, they replied, because Baby Doc was
against any contact with the Vatican. And his Tontons Macoutes
prevented them leaving their village. It was now too late and
they no longer had *les moyens,* the means. I proposed an alternative solution. What about trying to interest the Polish
embassies in Italy and England? This idea was received enthusi-
astically by Chantal Cherestal, the schoolmistress, who longed
for the children of Casales to have a proper school. She
promised to have official documents ready for us by the next
day, "with signatures, seals and all."

Next morning the "documents" were ready. The first we
were shown was the only remaining copy of a letter sent six
months previously to a minister in Port-au-Prince—and still
unanswered. In the ornate French of a bygone age modernized
with the use of abbreviations, it ran:

> *Monsieur le Directeur,* we wish herewith to solicit the
> assistance of your department in the building of a new
> school to replace the ISMA [Institution St. Michel
> Archange] of which we have the honor to be the govern-
> ing body. The present school, which has been housed in a
> dilapidated building since it was set up in 1990, serves the
> deprived children of this area and the surrounding dis-
> tricts such as Lacosse, Belac, Lamy, etc.
>
> We already have the land; we pray you to provide the
> wherewithal to start building our school, the plans for
> which we enclose.
>
> Signed by the chairman Jimmy Albert, general secretary
> Marie Andlène Garcon, councillor Marie Chantal Cherestal
> and committee member Emile Yves Jeanbaptiste.

In the financial projection for the school, contained in a
binder with teddy bears on the cover, the plan's promoters describe infant mortality in Casales as being strongly on the increase
and the whole area as "impoverished to a degree that must arouse

concern in any observer possessed of humanitarian principles."
And it goes on to analyze the causes: *"Pas de production agricole,
pas de dispensaire, pas d'écoles, pas d'électricité."* [No agricultural
production, no dispensary, no school, no electricity.]

The matter-of-fact, official tone of the document nevertheless
has an underlying sense of disillusionment with a revolution that
started out with such fine ideals and then failed. It even awakens
memories of Toussaint Louverture calling on the slaves on the
French plantations to rebel, and is pervaded with the rhetoric of
desperation found in many official documents of independent Haiti
in passages such as the following: "We must create a new generation
of men and women capable of shaping their own destinies."

There is even a hint here of Duvalier-style rhetoric. The local
doctor, who called himself "the black, savage slave in search of
the pure beams of the radiant sun" and, in 1964, proclaimed
himself "Professor of Energy and Napoleonic Electrifier of
Souls," had invented the cult of *noirisme* and encouraged the
blacks to "once more take charge of their own destinies." In
other words, he was telling them to expel the mulatto elite and
return to the revolutionary ideals of Dessalines.

The people of Casales, those *nègres blancs* cited by Duvalier
as the most shining examples of Haitian patriotism, never really
backed Papa Doc or his son. As they explained, life was difficult
in those days, so although they naturally sided with the rebels,
they never had the power to act in any way.

Their situation was unique. And dangerous too. While they
were carrying out their great purges of the mulattos, the Tontons
Macoutes tended to forget that these strange peasants with fair
skin and blue eyes were not part of the hated francophile *bour-
geoisie.* For the mulatto elite, the privileged ones who played
tennis, danced the waltz and sent their children to study at the
Sorbonne, they were a different species; not only were they
poor, but they had lived with the blacks too long to be considered European and, most important, were descended from the
traitors who had sided with Dessalines.

"That's enough talking for now," decreed an old man with

European cheekbones and fair streaks in his hair. "We still haven't offered you anything to drink." Speaking in Creole, he sent two young lads off on an errand. When they returned a few minutes later they were carrying three coconuts just cut from the tree. The old man took a machete from his belt and gave it to the boys to split the nuts. All three were for us, *les visiteurs.* One of the boys, little Stanley, showed us how to drink the clear liquid. This was a true present in a mountain village where the only drinking water is the spring that feeds the stream, and coconut trees are few and far between.

We were somewhat embarrassed, because the little group of children who had decided to follow us everywhere—Stanley, John, Marie, Michelle and Joseph—were gazing at us in silence. "Drink it, drink it," advised our divine, who had suddenly emerged from his trancelike state. "They consider it a great honor that we are here, and would be deeply insulted if we refused this gift, which is a big one for them."

Just before we left, a second document arrived. We took delivery of it as of a relic. This was a handwritten letter with a large stamp on each side of the sheet of paper bearing the legend: "Community of Saint Michael Archangel." The center of each stamp showed an open book similar to a Bible, and a crucifix. The text of the letter—in French apart from the final sentence—was as follows:

> From the Poles of Casales to the Polish Embassy in Italy.
> *Monsieur l'Ambassadeur,* we are descendants of Poland. After independence a group of Poles came to live in Casales and remained here with their descendants. Our present situation is very difficult, as we all live in extreme poverty, there is no road, no hospital, no food. We beg you to help us resolve certain problems and implore you to deliver this message to the pope. Enclosed with this letter you will find plans for a school for disadvantaged children. *Help us to build a school for the poor.*

Signed on behalf of the community by:
Joseph Similein, Pierrilus Pierre Khesner,
Garzon Marie Andlène,
Darcelian Celimise,
Yvonne Beau Brun, Mme. Elius . . .

From a letter sent by Lieutenant Romanski to Citizen Jan Henryk Dabrowski, general in command of the Polish troops, dated 27 November 1803:

After the suicide of battalion commander Jasinski, Citizen Zymirski assumed command. But because of his disastrous orders, the battalion was destroyed. His ineptitude was the direct cause of 400 soldiers and eight officers being taken prisoner by the Brigands, while he and the General took to their heels without a word to any officer about the imminent embarkation. The unfortunate men have since remained in the Brigands' hands being unable to pay the ransom demanded, which particularly affects those who—like me—have received no pay since the day we disembarked. Abandoned by everyone, we have tried in various ways to escape from the Brigands. After many appeals, the Brigands' General, Fero, gave us boats and permission to embark just two officers and 20 men, while our unfortunate brothers are to this day still in the hands of the Brigands. I and the second officer who was freed, Grynski, reached the island of Cuba with our men and were here for some time until we found a French General, Sarrasin Trissinet, who, however, refused to help us in any way. So we returned to the island of Saint-Domingue, to the port of Mole which until very recently had been under the command of General Noel, the last to surrender with his Division, since Commander Rochambeau and the city of Cap have already capitulated before the English.

The battalion colors of the second Armata are here with us. Blumer, the captain in command of the *Département* of Jérémie, left as soon as he had sold off the possessions of the Second Battalion officers who died. Or rather, he fled together with General Trissinet, stayed for a while in Cap, where he met up with Kobylanski, captain of the 113th demi-brigade, a man of similar character to himself, who had amassed and then sold off the belongings of the dead officers of the 113th demi-brigade, and appropriated the officers' wages, backdated for 6 months and sent to Palo-Prima, and also eight months of wages due to the soldiers.

These two men then joined up with the pirates, or rather the *souprakarga*. . . .

The letter continues with a list of the officers killed and survivors:

Major Jasinski committed suicide, ADC Biernacki succumbed to a fever at Jérémie, Major Joscicki fell ill and died at Kay, Captain Madrzycki was blown up by a grenade.

Captain Szylewcz died of fever at Jérémie.

Captain Gawlesinski died of his wounds.

Captain Berenzdorf died at Dan-Marya.

Captain Ziemierski deserted with Captain Blumer.

Lieutenant Orzelski is being held by the Brigands.

Lieutenant Szumski was killed in the field at Kay.

Jozef and Michael Zader left for Europe without permission.

Lieutenant Wiszniewski died at Jérémie.

Lieutenant Plechtowicz died at Koray.

Lieutenant Rusiecki took ship with General Trissinet.

Bialoszewicz and Laskowski are held prisoner by the Brigands.

Golinski and Ilnicki are being held prisoner by the Brigands at Jérémie.

Sub-lieutenant Bialkowski was killed in battle at Kay.

Sub-lieutenant Grvedy died in battle at Petit-Trou.

Sub-lieutenant Tokarzewski died at Jérémie.

Glinski, a sergeant major, died at Jérémie.

Captain Mechance of the Grenadiers, Major Krulikiewick and Sub-lieutenant Wegiel, both of the 1st Battalion, were killed in battle at Kay.

Officers in General Noel's Division are as follows: Citizens Romanski, Zukowski, Wielohorski, Woroniecki, Billewicz, Orleski, Grynski, Zaleski, Myszakowski, Sergeant Winkler and a further four sergeants, one orderly, twelve corporals, sixty privates, two drummers, one drum-major and a shoemaker.

In Casales, Mass is celebrated at ten every Sunday morning. The celebrant used to be the sacristan, but he promoted himself because the ordained priest, who lives in Cabaret, has no time for the Polish savages up on the mountain. A builder throughout the week, on Sundays he puts on a silk shirt, preaches, distributes the Communion bread and wine, and hears confessions in a church where the floor is of beaten earth, the walls of plaited straw and the roof sheets of corrugated iron supported on wooden posts.

The Mass we attended lasted at least an hour and a half, but no one dared allow his or her attention to wander. The pews—those that had survived the collapse of the church—were packed, and many of the mothers had dressed their children in their one and only frock or suit and pair of shoes. The men sat in blue chairs nearest to the altar, which was a Formica-topped table covered with a grubby cloth.

At the end of the service, the sacristan-*cum*-priest invited Joseph to speak *à la communité* and explain why the two foreigners had come to Casales and what they were doing. Our divine, who had even put on a tie for the occasion, acquitted himself well in his improvised sermon. Afterward, one of the leaders, his straight hair slicked back smoothly in the manner once common to South American soccer players, rose clutching his straw hat and addressed his people like a good drill sergeant to the troops. "If anyone would like to stay behind after Mass, our guests would like to ask them some questions to which they are free to reply."

Everyone stayed, silent and well-disciplined.

It was already hot, the mountains shimmering in the sunshine. For many of those present this plateau was their whole world and very few knew what lay beyond the plantations clinging to the steep red slopes. I stood up to speak while Pia played with the children and kept them occupied. "What," I asked, "do you know of the other Poles living in Haiti? Have you ever established contact with the other communities? Have you ever tried to join up with them?"

It was a woman—one of many with the limpid blue eyes of the Slav and the curly black hair of the African—who replied to my question. "We know that there are relatives of ours living somewhere very far away, possibly in the Jacmel district. There are other Poles in several villages in the south, and my parents told me that once, in the past, a delegation from here managed to reach a place called Fond de Blanches, and that many Poles like us lived there. But we lost all contact with them a long time ago. You see, *monsieur,* Haiti is a poor country. We haven't got the means to travel, not even as far as Cabaret or Port-au-Prince, let alone to places so far away. I've been told that it costs over a thousand dollars to go to Poland. Imagine! But the people from Fond de Blanches could come to us. We've heard that they are well off and even have automobiles."

"But if you have had no contact with them, how do you know that they are well off?"

One of the men replied. "When I was a boy I took it into my head to go and see the world. I spent years wandering all through the regions of Haiti, and even went to Miami. And I saw the people at Fond de Blanches. Many others live in Vayes, which is a city. So it's up to them to come and visit us. We are poor country people. But if they did come here one day they would still be welcome."

From the back of the hut a little boy winked at us and put a hand over his mouth to smother a laugh. This was Smith Clermont, and he was a friend of ours. Eight years old, Smith lived in a wooden hut the other side of the river, and when we met him on the mule track on our first day in Casales, neither Pia nor I could quite believe our eyes. Nearly two centuries after the arrival of the Polish soldiers in Haiti, and after generation upon generation of mixed marriages, the imponderable laws of genetics had endowed Smith with a skin as fair as that of General Leclerc's soldiers, smooth Slavic hair and a pointed face that stood out in sharp contrast with the round, dark features of all his playmates.

On that occasion Smith refused to be photographed, and his intelligent eyes became surly and suspicious whenever we tried to make friends with him. Our curiosity had only annoyed him, yet now, when the questions and answers around the altar had been exhausted, Smith, for whatever reason, decided to trust us and offered to take us to meet his little sister.

When we arrived, Madame Clermont said we would have to wait, the child was not ready. She ran back into her hut (where all we could see were a few pots and pans and four or five hens scratching around the floor), picked up the little girl and carried her down to the river for a wash. Then, having dressed her in a freshly laundered red jumper and white skirt, she wiped her mouth and eyes and presented her to us with a shy, proud laugh. The girl's eyes were of a deep, strangely disturbing green, her hair smooth and pale blonde, her nose as aquiline as that of any other child from Eastern Europe. Gathered in the shade of a tree in the courtyard was a group of housewives exchanging little cries and winks. Becoming aware of the presence of strangers, a girl who had been with them came running toward us. Another of Smith's sisters, she was older and her hair, although curly, was so blonde that the color looked almost unnatural. One day, if they survive hunger and disease, these girls will become extremely fascinating young women.

The latest generation of the Casales community seems to be more "Polish" than its immediate predecessor. Many of those involved suffer from a sense of being different and are teased by the black children. "We have never," said Michelle Belno, "suffered from racial prejudice here in Casales." Michelle is a large and very self-confident lady who now lives in the capital but returns to Casales for holidays. Her house is a substantial, orange-washed building in the center of the village, close to the ford at the point where the earthen track begins its steep descent. Sitting in an armchair on her verandah, she explained that Belno was one of the commonest names among the community, deriving from Belnowski. "We modified it in order to integrate ourselves more easily with the black Haitians; others have changed their names completely. But there has never been a problem. My grandfather was a Pole with very fair skin, my grandmother was black and my mother half-caste. You see, we Poles have been fortunate never to have been in power like the ruling mulatto class, and never to have had their superiority complex. So no one has ever hated us. There was a time when we lived really well. This house, for example, was built by my grandparents. In those days, finding money and building materials was no problem. Latterly the community has become poor, as you have seen. A few have had an education and found work in the city. There's a magistrate and a couple of doctors with Polish names in Port-au-Prince. To tell the truth, they're all dark-skinned. You see, this is what happens, as time passes the race disappears and only the surnames remain."

Michelle Belno spoke with the confidence of a city-dweller, her voice in marked contrast to the submissive tones of the peasants. Inside the house, a man—a poor cousin or nephew—was playing a pianola, all that had survived of a more gracious past. In another house, scarcely more than a hut, Madame Chalmai was plaiting straw. Blue-eyed but with skin as black as night, she had braided her hair as Nordic peasants did many years ago, in a style that no Haitian woman of today would copy. "My mother's family was Polish," she told us. "The only name I remember is Gamisto Vassily." Then, without pausing in her work, she added, "And there was a time when the young people danced the polka." But she was too tired to search her memory any further. Once the basket was finished, she would take it to the market at Cabaret and sell it for ten *gourdes*. With this money she would buy rice.

Another woman, with a kerchief tightly knotted over snow-white hair, was sitting on the concrete floor of the verandah washing clothes in a tin bowl. Were it not for the poverty, she might have been a Nordic tourist with a good suntan. "You ask me if I'm Polish? Take a good look at my face and you will have your answer."

The history of Casales is all there, in the skin of its inhabitants. No one in the village has kept documents or photographs. As the heads of families explain, rather vaguely, "The political situation destroyed everything." The reference is to the final, bloody years of the Duvaliers' regime. In 1979, many houses were burned, records vanishing without trace in the scramble to escape or to destroy compromising material such as newspapers and pamphlets. But even in the previous decade, during the dictatorship of Papa Doc, the rhetoric of nationalism had failed to deter the Tontons Macoutes in their dark Ray-Bans from searching the houses of the Poles of Casales for mulattos who might have fled Port-au-Prince intending to merge into this peasant community, which, though poor, was still white.

The man who had shown us the photograph of himself with the pope told us, "I still remember the day, it was the twenty-seventh March, in '69, when the Tontons Macoutes arrested a large number of people, and killed many of us. There is a little memorial to eleven of them down by the river, with an inscription that says 'The community of Casales will not forget.'"

So the old documents have been destroyed. Or perhaps they are preserved in some place well hidden from the eyes of strangers. And in the absence of written records, the deeds and the rituals that provide Haitians with their real spiritual nourishment are mulled over in the long dark evenings, and become transformed into symbols of great potency.

The pope's kiss, for example, when he arrived in 1983, was dismissed by the rest of the world as a merely routine act of homage, even banal when one remembered in how many airports in how many countries the act had been performed by Karol Woytyla. But in the imagination of Haitians both black and white, descended from Polish soldiers or African slaves,

that singular gesture, unusual for any man of power and inconceivable for any Haitian politician, continues to generate the
most widely different interpretations even to this day. It could
not possibly have been a mere kiss. There must have been something behind it, something hidden, perhaps something with
magical connotations.

"The pope kissed the ground because he knew that this
country, Haiti, was the home of his Polish compatriots," was the
explanation given to us in the church by Luis Joseph Rosier, a
small man clutching a tattered Bible. And he added, "He sent
the money he promised, but it never reached us. Someone in
Port-au-Prince got hold of it." He was interrupted by Celestine.
"The pope embraced me and gave me a crucifix." The implica-
tion was that a Pole, who doubtless had relatives among them,
could not possibly betray them.

The inhabitants of Casales are convinced that only kind people who long to help them live in the Poland they have never
seen. Amon, the magic-man, is not generally liked. The attitude
toward him was summed up by a cousin of his as he took me to
see the land designated for the building of the new school. "We
belong to the same family, but he is what he is and we are what
we are. Why? Because he has always refused to tell us what
Poland is like even though he is the only one who has been able
to go there." "And to think," commented another, "that our
families are there waiting for us."

Isolated and forgotten, the peasants of Casales are immersed
in the melancholy of their Slav ancestors. But the hope lives on
that this is all a nightmare, and that one day they will awaken in
that magic land called *Lapologne*. Of this, however, they must
not speak too much or the spirits of the forest could come seeking revenge.

Haiti has been invaded by missionaries of every sect, from Mormons to Jehovah's Witnesses. The one most envied by our friend Joseph is Pastor Wallace Turnbull, a Baptist from Minnesota who arrived half a century ago and built a hospital and church at Fermathe, in the hills surrounding Port-au-Prince. He then added a supermarket, a restaurant (because "we must nourish the whole man"), a museum and a private villa with panoramic views.

"Wallace," said Joseph, "is very, very rich. And very powerful. Anyone who disagrees with him is thrown out immediately."

Wallace himself continues to preach that "the people of Haiti are held prisoner in Satan's claws. Voodoo sows hatred and incites to unnatural acts."

Apart from having hosted the baptism of several hundred Haitians, Wallace's *Eglise Battiste Conservatrice* runs the best souvenir shop selling the work of local craftsmen, and is also generally acknowledged to be the most up-to-date place to eat in the whole country. The Mountain Maid Tea Terrace serves hamburgers made with "delicious pure beef imported from the United States," portions of "pure tender chicken imported from the United States and delicately pan-fried" and his famous MM Big Boy, "a double hamburger of pure beef U.S.-imported and flamed." "Prices exclusively in dollars, with ice cream and milk shake available. Credit cards accepted."

A group of Canadians wearing the blue berets of the UN arrive at midday, park their white Jeep with its blue flag in front of the supermarket, buy peanut butter in the air-conditioned shop and devour stacks of filled rolls. Wallace was careful to print on his menus the somewhat overused Chinese saying, "If you see a hungry man, give him a fish. But if you stop and show him how to catch fish, he will have a meal every day of his life." But faced with all this "delicious" meat imported from Minnesota, one wonders what the local cattle breeders think of the slogan.

In his museum, Pastor Wallace has not forgotten the Poles "who fought for liberty together with the Haitians." And among old Christmas lanterns made in the first rural communities of *polonaises* and souvenirs of imperial Haiti, he has included a proverb still extant in the countryside, which in Creole runs: "M-ap fe Krako," which translates as "I do as in Krakow," implying good workmanship. The houses in Casales hardly bear this out.

Half a mile lower, in a cool, calm oasis in the center of Port-au-Prince, we came across another Haitian proverb connected with the Polish "tribe." This oasis is the library belonging to the Catholic missionaries of St. Louis de Gonzague, a group of elderly, rather discouraged-looking Frenchmen who have been responsible for educating the elite of the whole island in their private school.

Father Ernest, a tall, thin man who tries hard to present a gruff exterior, is one of the few to have visited Casales, many years ago. Nowadays he is content to protect his library. "The Poles' church has fallen down? Really? I must inform the Vatican Embassy immediately. Let's hope we can do something about it. No one here, not even the Catholic Church, has any money. We'll see. I'll try to pull a few strings. The country isn't what it used to be. . . ."

We came across the proverb at the end of a cyclostyled book written by Laurore St. Juste and Frère Enel Clérismé in 1983 under the title *Présence Polonaise en Haiti.* The cover showed photographs of John Paul II and Dessalines, each with his right hand raised in blessing. Clérismé was one of the two priests who went to collect the Poles and take them to the airport on the occasion of the pope's visit. The book refers to them as *un hommage de l'intellectualité haitienne à Sa Sainteté le Pape, d'origine polonaise* [homage from the Haitian intellectuals to His Holiness the pope, who is of Polish origin]. The phrase *"Chajé kou Lapologn,"* charge like Poland, means attack in large numbers. It is now used, we were told, by students about to sit an exam.

Describing himself as *mouin chajé kou Lapologn,* a student implies that he expects to pass with flying colors.

The most curious section of this rudimentary essay in anthropology is the final one, consisting of four pages of photographs taken in Haiti's Polish communities and one illustrating faces typical of different white ethnic groups. Beside the peasant women of Fond de Blancs, St.-Jean du Sud and Port Salut, all with long blonde plaits and resembling Nordic dolls wizened by the tropical sun, are their Finnish and Siberian sisters, dressed in national costume and patently lifted from some Soviet encyclopedia, with faces rounder but otherwise identical to those of their Haitian counterparts. The men logged by the researchers all wear either side-whiskers or the long drooping moustaches fashionable in Paris and Warsaw during the nineteenth century, apart from a few of the younger ones who sport the comical goatee (without moustache) still seen in provincial Germany and Holland to this day.

The bureaucratic pomposity, the arrogance of the document, beggars belief. In what they probably deemed a fine patriotic flourish, the representatives of the *intellectualité haitienne*—the Haitian intelligentsia—concluded their study by proposing some 'practical suggestions' for the consideration of the governing authority, which in this case happened to be Baby Doc. Described by his enemies as even more brutal than his father, Papa Doc (but also nicknamed "Empty Head"), Jean-Claude Duvalier had, three years earlier, married a mulatto woman, Michèle, in a ceremony costing seven million dollars—extorted by his Tontons Macoutes by means of roadblocks and raids—and the country was beginning to feel the grip of terror. Yet No. 5 of our two intellectuals' concluding suggestions proposed, with no sense of irony, "To encourage private initiative in those localities inhabited by the Poles for the construction of restaurants, tourist shops, hotels and motels, or privately owned *pensions* for foreign and native tourists."

༺❀༻

Haiti will go down in media history for having caused CNN to suffer one of its few public embarrassments. The morning in September 1994 that saw the arrival in Port-au-Prince of twenty to thirty thousand American troops spearheading a contingent similar to the occupying force of 1919, the world was expecting a massacre in old Haitian style and CNN was ready to record the bloodletting. "We were all barricaded in our homes. I can't deny it. We were all armed and prepared for the worst. We expected the blacks to really cut loose, to attack the Americans, the army—which is dominated by mulatto officers—and us foreigners as well," recalls Joanni de Matteis, great-great-great-nephew of a nineteenth-century ambassador of the Kingdom of the Two Sicilies who came to Port-au-Prince as the representative of the Bourbons.

On 19 September CNN cameras were covering the airport where dozens of American helicopters were landing. General Raul Cédras had just left to begin his exile in Panama. One month previously, in line with mulatto tradition, he had wanted to show the world that "Haiti is in Europe, not Africa" (the phrase was coined by the mulatto officers who dethroned the black emperor Faustin Soulouque on 16 April 1849). Cédras had supplied photographs to the foreign press showing his wife and daughters sitting on an elegant terrace sipping tea with well-manicured hands. Madame Cédras had declared: "I would rather die than leave. The Americans can shoot me if they want to." But eventually the American ex-president Jimmy Carter had persuaded them to go into exile.

When the marines sprang from their helicopters in full battle dress with their faces blacked, their radios crackling and their arms at the ready, Haiti met them with the most subtle weapon of all: total silence. The airport was deserted. The streets were empty. All weapons had suddenly disappeared. And, live on world television, the Americans were made to look like Boy Scouts on a camping trip. The only person there to welcome the most powerful army in the world was a minor customs official. He might have been a character from a Graham Greene novel. With total impassivity he introduced himself to the marines and asked to see their passports. With nothing better to do, they arrested him.

"For the next few days, the Americans guarded the most important buildings, standing motionless in the broiling sunshine," recalled De Matteis. "And the Haitians, a warm-hearted people, decided that the poor Yanks had to drink or they would die of thirst. So they distributed cold drinks. But the good people of Port-au-Prince only lined up in front of the marines who were white, while the black ones, many of whom were of Haitian origin, were ignored. And to think that the Americans had included them especially, hoping to create a friendly atmosphere with the local people! But the Haitians had decided that if they had to be invaded, at least it should be by real marines, the A Team."

Hotel Oloffson. The starting point, or at least transit camp, for everything written about the mysteries of Haiti, this colonial-style hotel with its tropical garden and empty swimming pool has always been a magnet for foreign intellectuals. It is still floored with creaky boards, the bar hung with photographs of the famous people who have sipped rum here while keeping an ear cocked for the noises of the night and talking about Voodoo. The present proprietor of the Oloffson is Richard Morse, an anthropology graduate of Princeton University, son of an American university professor and of a famous Haitian *danseuse,* Emérante de Pradines. Ian Thomson heard from Morse's own lips the story of his buying the hotel for twenty dollars in 1985 from a Voodoo priest with whom he was sharing a taxi. At the time, he was studying the *méringue,* a form of Haitian music. With his Haitian wife he now sings at the hotel every Tuesday for an audience of artists, wealthy owners of Pétionville villas and foreigners working with humanitarian organizations.

Morse's group, the Rams, recorded the soundtrack for the film *Sleepless in Seattle,* starring Tom Hanks. "I've got an American passport, but the others just have Haitian ones, so we can only go to the States when they give us visas, which isn't as often as we would like," complains this hotelier-*cum*-anthropologist-*cum*-musician. But he still rations the Haitians to one performance a week, when he gives them music high in decibels and with a powerful beat, redolent of sex and magic, of religious ritual and slaves at work in the plantations.

In his office Morse has hung his trophies, notably letters from all over the world thanking him for having saved the famous hotel from the threat of demolition. He also treasures cuttings from American newspapers that ran ironic profiles of him at the time of the acquisition.

One evening, after we had dined at the Oloffson and watched the floor show, we decided to return to our hotel, El Rancho. It was eleven o'clock, and not having a car we needed a taxi. Every number we rang from Morse's office elicited the same reply: *rien.* The drivers had gone home for the night. Then a power cut left the hotel not only without light but without the phone line. We went out into the garden, which was pitch-dark. The porter regarded us unsympathetically. "You want to get to the Rancho at this time of night? A bad idea, a really bad idea. Impossible on foot. Brigands, thieves. Dangerous road." He adopted an expression of concern, but the sheer absurdity of the idea evidently struck him as richly comic. "Ask for a lift, it's the only thing you can do. If I find someone who's going that way, I'll let you know." But no one was going that way.

We waited for half an hour. The music continued, Morse sang, the crowd applauded. At last a Jeep appeared out of the darkness. I flagged it down. "Could you do us a favor? We need your help. Would you take us to the hotel El Rancho? It's only a ten-minute drive. I know it's a lot to ask, but there are no taxis and the phone's not working." At the wheel was a black man wearing an Armani sweater. He looked straight past us and barked a few words at the porter. "He'll do it for fifty dollars. American dollars." "Fifty dollars for half a mile? It wouldn't cost that much even in Tokyo!" The Jeep jerked forward. I ran after it. We climbed in and the wheels skidded as it lurched at speed up the road into the hills.

Ten minutes later we were back at base, greeted by the perennial smile of Señor Albert Silvera. The driver of the Jeep had not even said "good night," but before leaving he had very carefully counted the five ten-dollar notes. As everyone knows, you can't be too careful when dealing with *blancs* who go on foot.

5
Namibia
How the Basters Lost the Promised Land

And Abimelech said unto Isaac, Go from us: for thou art much mightier than we. And Isaac departed thence and encamped in the valley of Gerar, and dwelt there. [. . .] And Isaac's servants digged in the valley, and found there a well of springing water. And the herdsmen of Gerar strove with Isaac's herdsmen, saying, The water is ours [. . .]. And they digged another well, and they strove for that also [. . .]. And he removed from thence and digged another well; and for that they strove not: and he called the name of it Rehoboth; and he said, For now the Lord hath made room for us, and we shall be fruitful in the land.

—Genesis 26: 16–22

Rehoboth, June 1995

"Have you ever had a good look at the flag flying outside this building?"

John Heinz was angry. The veins on his neck stood out, his face was red and there were dark patches of sweat on his checked cowboy shirt.

"It's the flag of our own state, the Free Republic of Rehoboth, recognized by the League of Nations no less. A rectangle with three concentric bands. The outer band is black, like the unknown future of our forefathers when they left the Cape in 1868 to look for an uncertain Promised Land. The middle band is red, for the blood shed defending us from all our enemies, of whatever nationality, German, South African, Ovambo, Herero, Nama. The inside one is white, signifying our desire for peace. But this could be wiped out any time. If the Ovambo government continues to confiscate our grazing land and farms, then we'll fight. Don't you believe me? We've all got guns at home, they only need oiling. Throughout our history we've had to fight; once more won't make any difference. We'll be into the saddle and off to the front."

The men seated in a semicircle exchanged glances then nodded at him to proceed. And John Heinz resumed in his metallic, guttural English: "You know, we're the only people in the whole of this cursed Namibia to have documents that prove we purchased our land legally? God's truth. We Rehobothers bought it, paid for it with our own sweat. When the others arrived, they took something that wasn't theirs. Not us. Like honest souls, we bought legitimately and paid up front because we respect the law and like to have official seals on our documents. Maybe we were stupid. But at least we can prove to the whole world our title to the land. Let them try to deny it, let them just try! We'll die rather than give in!" John laughed sardonically. "Now they're in power, the Ovambo are spreading the word that Namibia always belonged to them. But when they arrived in 1932 we'd already been here for decades."

An old, dark-skinned man as tall as a basketball player rose to interrupt him. "That's enough, John. We shouldn't provoke the thieves in the Windhoek parliament. We'll act when the time's right. The Ovambos want to take everything away from us, even our souls. But if we stick together, we're stronger than they are. As our motto says, *Groei in Geloof,* 'Grow in your faith.' Now I'm going to take our foreign guest to visit our ex-Parliament, my ex-residence, and then the school the Ovambo closed and the hospital that went the same way. I'll show him how ethnic cleansing can go on in democratic, independent Namibia without the world even noticing. You lock up here and put away the documents, because one day they'll be more use to us than guns."

"*Ja, Kaptein.*"

The members of the council of war followed their "captain" out of the building and into the open beneath the tall sky of the African desert. The building that accommodates the "provisional seat of the free government of Rehoboth" is furnished with plastic chairs and Formica-topped tables. It stands on the outskirts of a city with a name so biblical that only a nineteenth-century Calvinist missionary could possibly have ferreted it out from the pages of Genesis.

Around the city stretches the vast expanse of Namibia, with its white dusty plains, its ochre deserts, its flat savannah crisscrossed by roads as straight as airport runways, seemingly drawn with a ruler on a map that showed no natural obstacles. You can travel for hours through this limitless, unbounded space without seeing anything of the farms that lie across your path apart from a single fence and the start of a rough track.

The apparently empty vastness is in fact inhabited by herds of lumbering, wet-nosed kudu and zebra that gallop between the acacias. Termite hills, ten feet high, are in perpetual construction like Gothic cathedrals. In the entrails of the rocky hills that occasionally jut up from the horizon of scrub, veins of colored marble continue to form in secret as they have done for millennia.

Sixty miles to the north, at fifty-five hundred feet above sea level, are the Windhoek breweries known as *Bierhalle.* The oldest of them lie close to Independence Avenue, which everybody continues to call Kaiserstrasse.

Windhoek is one of the most orderly, calm capital cities in the world, and the least African in all Africa. John Gunther, visiting the city in 1955 while compiling his weighty report *Inside Africa,* noted—incredulously—the presence of "Hohner mouth-organs, cuckoo clocks, Adler typewriters, Zeiss binoculars and vinyl records labelled '*langspiel.*'" If you compiled a list today it would be almost identical. One might add that although the colony of South West Africa became independent Namibia in 1990, the new government has still not bothered to change the name of the street called after Hermann Goering's father, who was governor during the last phase of German rule. This oversight has perplexed many people, including the investors and German entrepreneurs now slowly returning to their former colony.

Goering, in point of fact, was under orders from Bismarck to exterminate the Herero, an ancient people originating in the Nile delta who had come south many hundreds of years previously, and the Nama, ferocious hunters of Hottentot descent, both of whom rebelled against the Reich and posed serious obstacles to the expansion of the German empire overseas.

In one of the darkest episodes of colonial history, the behavior of the Germans toward the Herero between 1904 and 1907 came close to foreshadowing the "Final Solution." Surrounded during a battle near Fort Namutomi at the foot of the Waterburg plateau in what is now the Etosha National Park, they were simply massacred. By the end of the campaign their numbers had been reduced from eighty thousand to fifteen thousand. Suffering from disease and starvation, the survivors were led into exile by their leader, Samuel Maherero. Many months later, having crossed the Kalahari Desert, they reached safety under English protection in what is now Botswana (then Bechuanaland).

Ninety years after the genocide, independent black Namibia has no interest in revenge. And Heinrich Goeringstrasse is still there, a remnant of colonialism that no longer arouses any emotion at all. On the contrary, the past is providing publicity for today's commerce. New hotels built in the last few years for tourists heading for safari parks have been given names redolent of provincial Germany, such as "Pension Kleines Heim" and "Thueringer Hof." Hotel Henitzburg, in the residential quarter Klein Windhoek, is a restored castle originally built in 1914 by the Graf von Schwerin for his fiancée, Margarethe von Henitz.

Not only is the fortress built at the beginning of the century on another of Windhoek's hills still known by the German name *Alte Feste* ("ancient manor"), but no one has thought of removing the ornament that stands at the entrance, an equestrian statue of the Unknown Soldier unveiled on 27 January 1912 for the birthday of Kaiser Wilhelm III and dedicated to the German soldiers who fell in the conflict with the Herero.

Monuments are not all that the Reich bequeathed. Windhoek's supermarkets sell *Wurst* and *Speck,* and Namibia is the only place in the world outside Germany where beer is brewed according to the *Reinheitsgebot,* a law passed in 1516 to ensure the "purity" of the product. The three national brands, Tafel, Holsten and Windhoek, proudly claim to use "only malt and hops directly imported from Germany."

It is as if the brief colonial episode left traces too deep to be expunged. Even the Herero, having returned to Namibia after the defeat of the Germans in the First World War, still copy the style of dress of their one-time enemies, having transformed it into national costume. The women wear the forty feet of material recommended in 1844 by Frau Emma Hahn, wife of the Lutheran missionary Hugo Hahn, with a view to concealing every hint of female shape, and when the men march in September through the streets of Okahandjia, the town in which Samuel Maherero is buried, they do so in the Prussian uniforms of a hundred years ago.

Herero women, stout and slow-moving, alight from the bus in Windhoek in their circular skirts, living monuments to the prudishness of colonial times. They walk through a city where nothing much ever happens and failure to put money in a parking meter will be met within ten minutes by a ticket made out by a policeman wearing a rigid visor and as incorruptible as his counterpart in Stuttgart.

My first sight of Basters was in a pedestrian precinct beside the Kaiserstrasse. They were standing in a silent queue outside the Telecom public phone booths, huddled together and ill at ease in the urban environment. These workers from a construction site—Basters are much sought after by construction companies because they are considered the best builders in Namibia—were calling home to their families in Rehoboth at the end of a day's work.

At first it was difficult to tell whether they were poor whites, like those found on run-down farms in the Kalahari, or "colored" immigrants from Capetown. Pale-skinned but thin to the point of emaciation, with fair, curly hair cut short, they had broad noses and cheekbones and eyes of a startling green yet almost Oriental in shape. I found the eyes disconcerting. They seemed to be reading my mind.

When we asked a passing student about these strange men with hands caked in plaster dust, he muttered, "They're the Basters from Rehoboth," with a disapproving grimace. It sounded like an insult. I had yet to learn that Baster, or Baaster, is an ancient name of which the tribe from Rehoboth is very proud.

Coming from the eighteenth-century Dutch spoken in Cape Colony in the days when it was an outpost of the Dutch East India Company, it means "of mixed race." But the reference nowadays is not to a casual cross between black and white. The Basters are descended from unions between Dutch pioneers and Hottentot or Nama women, resulting in a genetic and cultural mix that exists nowhere else in Africa. For three centuries they have been an ethnic entity in the truest sense, a tribe that came into being as a result of historical accident but has since developed a sturdy self-sufficiency and an identity distinct, both psychologically and genetically, from the peoples who unwittingly founded it.

The Baster story began in the middle of the nineteenth century, when nomadic Dutch farmers from the Cape Colony—the *trekboers*—were being pushed further and further north in search of fertile valleys by the arrival of English settlers in the south. They found few black people in those valleys and on the savannahs apart from San tribes of Bushmen hunting antelope with poisoned arrows as they had done since the Stone Age, and surviving on the juice of wild melons.

Khoi-Khoi, too, appeared in their frontier camps. These Hottentots, as the whites called them, were herdsmen from the north of Africa who had been almost wiped out in the eighteenth century by a smallpox epidemic. The survivors formed themselves into robber bands moving from place to place in the savannah with their herds and stealing cattle. But, too weak to survive in such depleted numbers, the Hottentots were ever more frequently pressed into service with the *trekboers*, finally becoming absorbed into their rudimentary farms as slaves, laborers, lovers and relatives. They even helped the farmers to hunt down Bushmen like wild animals. The bond between Boer and Hottentot was a union of losers, an alliance of the poor, in one sense a marriage of equals.

The Dutch colonists, themselves nomads because they were constantly seeking new land, were increasingly isolated and rebellious. In 1795, during the Napoleonic wars, Holland had lost her Cape province and London had immediately intervened to forestall any attempt by Bonaparte to seize Cape Colony and its valuable trade route. The new administration tried, unsuccessfully, to subdue the white adventurers who had begun to call themselves Afrikaners and who spoke a form of Dutch increasingly influenced by African languages.

To English eyes, the isolated and semi-wild Boers were guilty of two mutually contradictory but equally unforgivable sins: they used slaves as laborers on their farms, and they procreated children with these same slaves, Hottentot and Bushmen who expressed themselves in a language of clicks and snapping noises.

In a cyclostyled document distributed by the Museum of Rehoboth (housed in an old colonial-style building on the outskirts of the city), the extraordinary story surrounding the beginnings of the Basters tribe is recounted as follows:

It was a world dominated by men. . . . Similar to colonial situations elsewhere in the world, extramarital intercourse and intermarriage between the male colonizers and indigenous women was hardly frowned upon or disapproved. The children born from this association were often judged by their appearance. Until only very recently a person of mixed origin but with a marked Caucasian appearance would have been classified as white in the segregated South African society. Those children whose mixed origins were too obvious were called "coloreds" or "bastards." They were kept apart from the colonizers' social structure, resulting in an identity crisis; the desire to be identified as white remained. The colonizers' language, religion and surnames were adopted with pride. Those who were not employed by or otherwise associated with the colonizers, in some cases developed their own settlements—Often in very remote areas outside the control of the colonizers.

By the middle of the nineteenth century some five thousand people were calling themselves "Basters." They had settled on unsurveyed Crown Lands in places they called Komaggas, Leliefontein, Amandelboom, Rietfontein, Pella and De Tuin. They were farming with goats, sheep and cattle.

These names now represent quiet little South African towns each of which began as a frontier village with only a wooden church and a few farms. When the Basters arrived and founded them, the English seemed very far away. But as the decades passed they came closer, and with them came the threat of laws against slavery, an institution that the Boers held to be directly sanctioned by Holy Writ. So many of them started out again, heading north with their ox-drawn wagons and their Hottentot women clad in the lace-trimmed costumes of old Flemish paintings. Like Isaac, they found their Rehoboth in the middle of the Kalahari Desert.

Not all, however, abandoned the farms so laboriously carved out on the edge of the desert. A few small Baster communities survive to this day in South Africa, close to the early settlements. In Steinkopt they still call themselves Basters and subscribe to a constitution similar to that once in force in Rehoboth. The Vilanders of Ritfontein, near the Kalahari Gemsbok Park, are also a minitribe. The last Griquas, pale-skinned African cowboys, live in Griquatown. A Mr. Edwards of the London Missionary Society, writing in July 1802, described them as follows: "They are more peaceable than the Bushmen, the men have cattle and are very lazy and hunt with lances and short knob sticks; the women labor in the field and sow a sort of corn which they call Mabaela."

The more adventurous *trekkers,* however, went further north in successive waves. Having passed beyond Rehoboth, many crossed the great Okavango River, one of the natural borders that has helped shape the history of northern Africa. By 1902 groups of Basters had reached Angola, founding rural communities destined to survive for many decades isolated from the rest of the world in a cruel, desolate land. John Gunther wrote of them in 1955: "These are white men, Afrikaners of the poorest type, who derive from Boer trekkers who refused to stay in the Transvaal under British rule and pushed up north and west into the Kalahari Desert. They have been called 'the last dregs of the Great Trek.' Some rather unkindly remark that 'they are still surprisingly white, all things considered.'"

Between 1928 and 1930, the South Africans, who administered the colony as a mandated territory, forced almost all the Basters in Angola back to Cape Colony. They were incapable of understanding that these illiterate and deeply religious people with whom they shared a common ancestry actually wished to live among the *Kaffirs,* the savages. Some Basters, however, evaded deportation and now live in southern Angola, in the city of Lubango, which the Portuguese call Sa Da Bandeira. They have converted to Catholicism and joined forces with families of dispersed Portuguese settlers also impatient of colonial rule and in search of the wide open spaces. Living alongside the routes trodden by the ancient Boer *trekkers,* although known as the Ouivumo they are still part of the Baster nation.

According to the government in Windhoek, the Basters of Rehoboth—the spiritual capital of the diaspora—now number thirty thousand. According to the Basters themselves, the number is between forty thousand and forty-five thousand. They once owned all the savannah between their city and the ocean, close to a million square miles. They patrolled the land on horseback and drove their cattle from one well to the next keeping a wary eye out for hyena and cheetahs. Like the Masai in Kenya and the Tutsi in the region of the Great Lakes, the Basters love their cows as individuals. They know the name and character traits of every one, and regard them as prized possessions. Now the pastures have shrunk. The government of new, independent Namibia has issued a decree outlawing the body that administers the Basters' land and has begun to confiscate hundreds of thousands of acres of the Rehoboth "kibbutz."

The Basters believe that only God can help them now. The same God who guided them beyond the Orange River, far from the heretical English, must now show them the road to survival.

"There are more churches in Rehoboth than in any other city in Africa," said Karl Budack. "The Basters compare themselves with the ancient Hebrews, a chosen people, faithful to the Lord, but also unfortunate. Everyone has a Bible in the house, and on Sunday they sing hymns identical to those heard in Utrecht in the seventeenth century. One day, the head of one of the most important families came to me and said: 'Doctor Budack, if you only knew the squabbles, the disputes that divide us under our surface solidarity! But religion is one of the things that has held us together up to now.' If you ask me, another bond has been their strong sense of discipline, that strict internal hierarchy typical of those who have always been a minority, for whom survival has depended upon solidarity. Everything is regulated by laws, written and unwritten. Did you know they've even got their own unofficial aristocracy? It's a fact. The most highly regarded and wealthiest families are those which, by coincidence or not, happen to have the whitest skin and the surnames of the original trekkers who came from the Cape in their ox-drawn wagons."

Karl Budack is a German ethnologist who, with the pig-headed determination of one born and bred in the mountains, has founded an amazing museum in a small colonial bungalow behind the post office in Windhoek with exhibits including rare books, sepia photographs, maps, documents, and diaries recording events from the arrival of the first Portuguese explorers to the victory of SWAPO, the guerrilla army led by Sam Njuoma before he became president.

Dr. Budack arrived in Namibia in 1966 when it was still a South African protectorate known as Suid-West Afrika. It was virtually the fifth province of the Union and despised as nothing more than a bucketful of sand with the odd diamond lurking inside. Gradually realizing that Namibia was an anthropological encyclopedia that would take more than one lifetime to read, he never went away again. He also came to realize that in this large and underpopulated country where apartheid was not an indigenous disease and the desert bloomed with uranium and precious stones, there was room for everyone. The blacks have never thrown out the whites, let alone the "old Germans." So Dr. Budack stayed, and won the confidence of the Basters.

"An emotional people, *ach,* how emotional! With a nasty temper, too. And when you go to Rehoboth, take a good look at the hands and feet of the young girls. They may have the fairest of fair hair and European faces with a bone-structure identical to that of a German or Italian woman, but their hands and feet are very small. Tiny, *ja!* Do you know why? They're the hands and feet of the Khoi women, the Hottentots. And, if you see a white peasant with a strangely Oriental face, take a good look. You're looking at a descendant of the Bushmen, the San. But he'll be more of a Calvinist than Calvin himself!"

The following extract is taken from an article in the September 1906 edition of the review *Zeitschrift für Kolonialpolitik, Kolo-*

nialrecht und Kolonialwirtschaft, written by a German captain, Maximilian Gustav Stephan Bayer (1872–1917), under the title *Die Nation der Bastards* and translated by Professor Carstens:

> The Basters have excellent military qualities. Because they are accustomed to living in the open, because of their passion for hunting and their knowledge of the land, they have great advantages as soldiers in the field. They ride superbly and are well acquainted with all the tricks of the natives. They are masters also of the difficult and, in African warfare, all-important practice of stealing horses and cattle from the enemy. Their talent for tracking can be traced partly to the fact that they are frequently forced to catch and bring back lost or runaway animals in order to preserve their herds. Here, practice is the best teacher, and the results are incredible. A Baster once told me that a band of Hereros had crossed our path on a certain day at a certain hour. He described the band as if he had seen it with his own eyes: how many men, how many women and children, how many goats and how many head of cattle they had with them. I was later able to verify this description which, at the time, I had listened to with mounting scepticism. Every detail the Baster had told me was confirmed when the band was tracked down and captured.
>
> Nor do the Basters lack courage. "It was a joy," wrote Captain Boettlin in his letter to me after a battle, "to observe the Basters charge, as they rode toward the Herero, over boulders and crags with a speed and dexterity that could not be matched on this terrain by any white corps." On that occasion victory was complete. The Hereros, who had stolen horses and cattle, lost their booty and their own animals as well. In general, however, the Basters' way of fighting is more cautious than our own. Bold decisions and victories like the one described therefore do not often occur. The reason lies partly in the shortage of fighting men who can be marshaled by a nation that is still weak. This small corps cannot afford great losses. . . .
>
> To irritate the enemy and provoke him into an unplanned attack, they shout obscenities in the Hereros' language into the bush. This is a custom that the indigenous peoples have inherited from past generations, understandable considering that battles in the thick African forests frequently happen with the two sides within earshot of each other or even closer. . . . The Herero use the same trick to

deceive or annoy us, too. [. . .] On [one] occasion, we heard the heads of the opposing factions inciting their troops to action. This was very convenient because it revealed their plan of attack in advance. [. . .]

The Baster contingent returned to Rehoboth on 22 October 1904. It had camped in the open for 356 consecutive nights, taken part in 22 battles and mounted 42 patrols, nearly always with Captain Boettlin! This is certainly an impressive accomplishment. Six Basters died in the fighting, five died of sickness and seven were wounded. For them, this was a serious loss of men and indicated the profound commitment of the Baster nation to our war. One-third of all Baster soldiers were decorated for bravery in battle. The soldiers who returned to their homes and to civilian life scattered immediately over the whole country to look after their flocks and herds, though a few soon returned to work for us as wagon-drivers or messengers.

Afternoon in Rehoboth. The roads are wide and only the occasional pickup truck passes along them, raising a cloud of white dust. There are no traffic signals or roadside billboards. The impression is of a town in the Far West where cattle-breeders go once a week to buy cases of beer in the supermarket, deposit money at the bank and collect their letters from the post office. The square, unadorned buildings are spaced well apart, because in Namibia—which, having a total area of 318,261 square miles, is as big as France and Italy combined—the only thing that everyone has in abundance is space. Even in the town center, where two main streets intersect and the scent of *Krapfen* and cream cakes wafts from the *Bäckerei,* there are tracts of savannah apparently belonging to no one between one house and the next.

The big event today is a rugby match between two school teams. The sports ground is at the end of one of the longest roads. Catherine De Koe and her friend Ilse are due to meet their schoolfriends on the terraces of the little stadium, but they are in no hurry to get there. Both are fourteen years old, and had they been walking down a street in Amsterdam or Cologne, no one would guess that they were *nth*-generation Africans.

Catherine has blonde plaits and wears flip-flops, Ilse is wearing denim jeans and a blouse and has eyes as blue as the Atlantic. They chat quietly to each other as they walk, and greet the other children coming, like them, from their homes to attend the match.

As soon as one leaves the city en route for the sports ground, Namibia stretches away boundlessly on every side. The natural landscape appears disorganized and repetitive: clumps of bushes, white sand in the arid areas, red earth in the humid ones, for mile after mile. But the African bush has its own strict logic, and everything has its significance, its role, real or mythological. Take the moringa trees, for example, with their shiny trunks, spindly branches and sparse foliage giving the impression of the work of an abstract artist. According to a legend of the Bushmen, the thunder god refused to give these ugly trees a place in heaven and tossed them back to earth. The poor moringas landed in Namibia and planted themselves upside down.

Until a generation ago, when the citizens of Rehoboth wanted some amusement they would take down their guns and go hunting on horseback or on foot, following the spoor on the ground and noting broken branches on the trees. The Basters created their own reserve in a particularly dense part of the bush. The number of animals that could be killed was controlled by the Kaptein's council, and the cattle-breeders kept their herds away in order to avoid crowding the wildebeest, the kudu and the gemsbok who grazed between the acacias and the *kokerboom,* the *Aloe dichotoma* that provided the Bushmen with wood for their quivers. Then the reserve was requisitioned and came under the control of central government, not as a national park but as a game reserve for the government's guests of honor. The last giraffe were killed a few months ago. The antelope chose to scatter among the farms, forming new herds and learning to live alongside the cows with their curved horns. No one knows when or if wild animals will ever return to this little Eden a few miles away from the rugby ground.

"Where is Italy?" asked Catherine and Ilse, giggling at the sound of the strange name.

"In Europe."

"Ah, Europe." They exchanged glances.

"Have you ever been there?"

"No, but my grandfather worked in Europe—in Germany, I think," said Ilse.

"We too, one day we shall go," added Catherine, her stilted English sounding like that of the German tourists.

"At home we speak Afrikaans, like everyone here. But they teach us English at school because they say that we are all Namibians now and must all speak the same language."

"And when are you going to Europe?"

"When we leave school, if our parents give us the money to go to university. And then to work. But not forever. I want to come back to Rehoboth."

"And where do you want to go in Europe?" I asked. "London? Paris?"

Ilse shook her head.

Catherine exchanged a remark in Afrikaans and a laugh with a pair of girls going in the opposite direction and then turned back to me with an expression of mild sympathy. "We want to go to a place called Holland, the nicest of them all."

"Yes," said Ilse, "and perhaps marry a real Dutchman!"

Evening in Rehoboth. The roads of the Promised Land are deserted and the darkness creeping in off the savannah brings with it the barking of wild dogs or, perhaps, jackals.

Behind the "Ego" petrol station is a small supermarket selling sacks of rice, dried meat and dark honey from the Kalahari farms.

At Club 45 they are playing billiards beneath lamps dangling on very long wires from the ceiling. "Entertainment every Thursday, Friday and Saturday evening. Music, restaurant, board games. The liveliest place in Rehoboth," declares the optimistic poster outside. But on this Tuesday evening the lively clientele is represented only by George and his two friends sitting round a table covered by a green cloth with holes in it.

I order a Tafel beer and then a glass of bilious-yellow Fanta. The boys play, ribbing each other in Afrikaans. The empty beer bottles pile up on the plastic chairs. The boys are builders or truck-drivers with slender, muscular arms and pronounced, almost Oriental cheekbones. A woman with dyed blonde hair comes up to the table. The boys tease her and then, after exchanging glances with each other, overcome their shyness enough to speak to me.

"Have you come from Windhoek?" asks George, a tall young man with drooping moustaches.

"No, I'm a foreigner. Italian."

"Italian. Like our friend Bertoh-Leni."

"Who?"

"Haven't you met Rehoboth's Italian? The one who works at the bank?"

"An Italian? Here? Who is he?"

"Well, his grandfather was Italian. He spells his name B-E-R-T-O-L-I-N-I. Excellent billiard-player before he got married. But why are you here? Business?"

"I'm doing some research on the Basters."

"Do you play billiards?"

"Very badly."

"Then you're not a real Italian. Come on, grab a cue. We're all amateurs here. Diet, let's play doubles. I'll play with the foreigner, you play with Hans."

We play some feeble shots and I find great comfort in the tattered state of the cloth before we start. I would hate to pass into the history of Club 45 as the Italian who couldn't hit the ball.

The smell of charcoal-grilled meat wafts from an upstairs room.

"The Kaptein told me that you were prepared to fight to defend yourselves. Is that right?"

"*Ach,* so you've already met old Diergaardt. Yes, of course, *Der Kaptein* is right. Take the matter of language. The blacks want to make us forget Afrikaans. They would like to impose English on us. But we grew up speaking Afrikaans, and if they take that away we shall lose our identity. If you want to understand, go to the museum."

The museum of Rehoboth is a red-painted building that used to be the family home of one of the heads of the Van Dyk clan, descendants of the first Kaptein. It was donated to the community so that the last of the wooden wagons used in the trek from Cape Colony could be preserved there together with old photographs, mementoes of Rehoboth's brief independence, flags and samples of local crafts. Every exhibit is accompanied by a little typewritten label.

The curator, Niko Kisting, wears the round spectacles that are de rigueur for all black intellectuals fresh from university. Niko started by fighting for SWAPO, then the organization gave him a scholarship to study for a degree in America. He has persuaded children from the local schools to construct paint and collage panels describing the story of the Basters, which, according to Niko, has reached the point where it should be consigned to the historical archives. Namibia's new and splendid future must not, he explained, be compromised by a few old fanatics.

When schoolchildren come on outings to the museum for an hour of civic education, Niko makes them read the following exhortation: "The three languages spoken in Namibia are English, German and Afrikaans. Especially now with independence, it's even more essential that all inhabitants of our beautiful country should stand together, co-operate and establish a united nation of proud, respectable and enthusiastic Namibians, who are eager to worship our Creator, educate our Youth."

"They'll never succeed," says George dryly. And, after a

mouthful of beer, he looses a shot that pots three balls at once. Compared with Niko Kisting in his well-pressed jersey and spotless jeans that could have stepped straight out of a Benetton poster, George looks grubby and unkempt. "They'll never succeed in wiping out Afrikaans. And you know why?" He belches once. Twice. "Because we Basters got our brains and our knowledge from white men. But we've also got the strength and resistance of the Khoi-Khoi."

The Reho-Megastore and the First National Bank stand next to each other. As in all frontier towns, the supermarkets in Rehoboth are stocked in a way that city-dwellers would find grossly disproportionate to their needs. The long shelves in the Reho-Megastore are stacked with tins of fish, cans of beer and frozen vegetables in plain five-kilo packs. Farms and villages within a very wide radius depend on Rehoboth for their provisions and collect them in wholesale quantities every two or three weeks.

Inside the bank the air-conditioning is super-efficient. Everything is new: the green plastic counters, the automated cash dispensers, the thick windows, the ashtrays, the posters explaining to the farmers how to raise a mortgage to enable them to survive the drought that has been scorching their grasslands for the last three years. In his office on the first floor, ensconced behind a computer and dark glasses, Otto Bertolini pretended not to know why I was there.

"You've come from Italy?" Mr. Bertolini squirmed nervously in his designer chair imported from Germany. "Why?" The question sounding ineffectual to his ears, he enlarged upon it. "For what reason?"

"I'm collecting information about the Basters. And people told me about you, who have such an Italian-sounding name. What is the story of your family?"

"To tell the truth, I don't know. I would have to phone my sister, Palmira, who lives on a farm a long way from Rehoboth. Or my brother Cornelius."

I smiled at him encouragingly. Sighing, my fellow Italian consulted the phone book. From her kitchen far away in the bush, his sister Palmira nudged his memory of names, circumstances, family ties.

"*Ach so, ja. Herr Tamburini, Herr Calzenitto . . .*" He began to jot down a list and then replaced the receiver with hardly a salutation.

"You see, the problem is that we don't know exactly. My sister believes that our grandfather was an Italian prisoner of war, but that wouldn't tally with the dates. His name was Giovanni Giuseppe Bertolini, and he wound up in South Africa at the beginning of the century, or in what was then South West Africa. Walvis Bay, to be precise, which used to be a resort and has always had a high percentage of South Africans. In 1903 six more Italians arrived on board a ship. Perhaps my grandfather brought them here. Their names were Tamburini, Calzenitto, Scolara, Tubello, Catolini. They were in the construction industry, I believe, building dams. Or they might possibly have tried their luck on the Skeleton Coast, where small businesses were sprouting up to mine diamonds or sell guano. They could have got involved with any of the myriad small companies—all failed—set up to make a profit out of that godforsaken place."

"But how did they end up here, with the Basters?"

"There was a certain Mr. Humann in Rehoboth who used to meet the Italians arriving at Walvis Bay and take them to work on his farm. The others may have gone with him, I don't know. But my grandfather didn't. He had married a Baster girl and stayed put. And that's about it. Old stories that no longer make much sense. And now you must forgive me but I have to leave you. We've got an important meeting today. As you may know, the bank is expanding very rapidly."

Several days later I was back in Windhoek talking to Dr.

Budack in his museum, sitting at a table surrounded by tall bookcases crammed with books. "*Ach,* so Bertolini didn't know his family's history? That's bad, very bad. But did you know that on the Skeleton Coast there used to be a mining station, long since abandoned, called Toscanini? Lots of Italians were working there at the beginning of the century. Heaven knows how it got there, so far from the emigration routes to the Americas. Many more Italians arrived here after the Second World War, having been prisoners in South Africa. However, one should remember that marriage with a Baster girl was the ambition of many people in this part of the world. Bertolini was not alone."

Dr. Budack was right. Captain Maximilian Bayer, a German colonial officer who was the first to write a scientific paper about the Basters but then became the Wilbur Smith of imperial Germany, achieved immediate notoriety by writing: "The truth is that these mixed marriages between Germans and Basters are nearly always happy marriages and that is what matters most."

This created a sensation in 1906 among the bureaucrats of the colonial administration. Sitting in their ministerial offices in Berlin, they found it inconceivable that subjects of the Kaiser could contemplate union with "natives." And they decided to put an end to the scandalous situation.

"Bayer had really set the cat among the pigeons, but he had company. Rehoboth was the Mecca of many matrimonial pilgrimages. Coloreds used to come from Cape Colony as well as Germans from Germany itself in search of a bride who was devoted, religious, white. And beautiful. Because the Baster girls have more than their fair share of beauty."

Even though he lives shut up with his books, Dr. Budack is a gentleman of the old school and susceptible to feminine charm. Just like Captain Bayer. "According to old Baster laws enshrined in the Constitution of Rehoboth, when a white foreigner came to town he had to make a formal request to marry a girl belonging to the community. He had to apply to become a resident in the

community, and then began the long, slow process of naturaliza-
tion. After six months he could get a permit to stay. To begin
with he became a *Bekerm,* entitled to the simple right of protection. Finally, after a certain number of years, if the Kaptein gave
his consent, the foreigner became a Burgher, or resident. But not
a Baster, because citizenship was never conferred on a foreigner.
Citizenship was tribal, a matter of blood-ties. In fact, there were
a number of fathers with beautiful daughters who asked these
suitors to go and work on their farms in the middle of the bush
before asking for the hand of the daughter."

Dr. Budack smiled at the idea of this autocratic society func-
tioning like a kind of Calvinist Utopia. "The time came when the
colonial authorities—diplomatically, of course—encouraged
young soldiers, or unmarried public officials, to marry Basters.
I've studied all the documents of the time and found that there
was a precise point at which policy officially changed. German
girls began to arrive specifically to provide wives for the Germans in the colony. So Rehoboth lost its claim to the title of City
of Love."

Kaptein Hans Diergaardt was twice elected chief of the Basters,
but on the third occasion his election was vetoed by the government of Namibia, by whom he is considered a private citizen
(and not one of the most exemplary). When this man with the
face of a Nama warrior strolls through the streets of Rehoboth,
the blacks lower their eyes, still afraid of him and of his title
although it no longer has legal currency. When Namibia held its
first free election he stood as a candidate and won, but resigned
after only two sessions, realizing that the life of a parliamentar-
ian was not for him.

"It's all over, all destroyed," he said, looking around him and
shaking his head incredulously. "They've taken everything,
everything we were proud of. There's nothing left." To the

naked eye Rehoboth was sleeping in the sun as usual. But for him the tragedy was apparent in every stone.

"We tried to sue the government over the confiscation of our land," he continued. "No one would help us. Two lawyers of Baster origin, qualified men, have a law practice over in Windhoek and work for the government. They refused to represent us because, they said, the Ovambo government wouldn't allow it."

The Rheinisch Mission church, surrounded by a white fence, was still open, but the mission hall was shut. Even the mission hospital had been closed one day without warning. "We built it all ourselves, with materials specially shipped from Germany," said the Kaptein. It was, in fact, in 1904 that the Basters traveled their forefathers' route in reverse, to Capetown, to collect the special bricks, the church furniture and the roof-tiles designed to withstand snowstorms in the Black Forest. Everything was transported to Rehoboth and delivered to Hermanus van Wyk, the charismatic Kaptein who had led them through the Kalahari decades previously. But Wyk, an old man, died in 1905 and the Germans used his death as an excuse to abolish the office of Kaptein even though they had already recognized his son Cornelius as Voorman or community leader. Despite the community being under the protection of a foreign power, the Wyks had been fast turning it into a hereditary autocracy.

The church was completed in 1906 and stood four-square and solid, the focal point of the community. It is now closed.

Every now and then Diergaardt has managed to appear on new, independent Namibia's state television and call for the restitution of the church. Viewers regard him as a character out of an old, bad history book, whingeing about rights of which few have ever heard. "That madman Diergaardt," they mutter. But as he walks through the city where he was all-powerful until recently, he looks merely old and resigned. Only when reliving past battles does he come alive.

"On 8 May 1915"—he quotes the date as if it had been only

yesterday, and he could probably tell you the time of day as well—"the Germans, with whom we had co-operated for a long time and with whom we had even signed a bilateral treaty of friendship, declared war on us. Why was that?" The Kaptein stopped in the middle of the road and held up a sheaf of papers in his calloused hands. "Why? Because we had refused to enter the war and fight with them against the Allied Forces, meaning the South Africans and the English. When we told Colonel Grancke what we had decided do, he called a meeting of all the heads of families and told us to do our 'duty,' as he put it. But that was a white man's war, a European affair we did not want to get involved in."

The sun shone. Rehoboth seemed deserted. "The Germans sent in their troops against us. There was a battle at Sam Kubis, and, while we were fighting, our wives and children, who had fled to safety in the Kubis mountains, prayed for us and for victory. On the morning of 9 May, after attacking all night, the Schutztruppe retreated on their camels to a farm the other side of the border, sixty miles from Rehoboth. They realized they hadn't a hope of winning. So, according to international law, we were the victors."

Some historians of the period maintain that the Basters were saved by the arrival of General McKenzie and that on their return to Rehoboth they looted houses and shops belonging to the Germans. The Kaptein preferred to overlook such minor details. "The South Africans, who had fought with the English against the Germans, were given a mandate by the League of Nations to administer South-West Africa. For the next forty-five years they ignored all our requests for independence and quelled the revolt of 1925. Then, in '79, they offered us the right of self-determination in exchange for our help against the SWAPO guerrillas. The usual story. They only remember our existence when it suits them. And I told them, yet again, that we wanted nothing to do with the SWAPO communists. That was their problem."

Diergaardt pronounced the word "communists" with a bitterness that suggested the Cold War was still being fought in the middle of the Kalahari Desert. "When the SWAPOs won they didn't even want to speak to us. What ingratitude! And on 16 October '91 they requisitioned 250,000 acres of our land. A quarter of a million acres! They accused us of being racist, of having collaborated with the oppressor, while we'd been the first in the whole of South-West Africa to open our schools and hospitals to black people. Now the Namibian government refuses to recognize us as a nation. All the other tribes, yes, but not us. And they flood the city with useless civil servants in order to alter the ethnic composition. Twelve hundred of them! It beggars belief!"

Standing apart from other buildings on a hill outside the city is an empty, dilapidated, barracklike building that enshrines a chapter of history often omitted by Captain Diergaardt. This is the Parliament House for the Basters' homeland that the government in Pretoria built to comply with the Rehoboth Self-Government Act.

The Parliament itself was almost clandestine. South Africa was happy to publicize the existence of the "independent states" of Bophuthatswana or Ciskei, which were never recognized by the international community, but kept quiet about the existence of the Baster ministate, a *bantustan* for second-class whites. But inside the Volksraat—as if on a surreal film set—every procedure of parliamentary democracy was respected. Soberly dressed men in jackets and ties and bearing solemn, biblical names such as Izaks and Christ, sat around a table presided over by a Speaker in a curled wig. The deputies (whose numbers varied between five and nine) wore jackets of red, black and white silk, the colors of the Baster State or Gebiet as it was called in Afrikaans. Every now and then they drafted some innocuous law, which always met with approval in Pretoria.

The Parliament, with its own tiny bureaucracy and its own hierarchy, was the modern equivalent of the acacia under which the Kaptein and his council members had gathered from time immemorial. "A two-thousand-year-old acacia, dead like everything else," mourned Diergaardt inconsolably. But it is the Parliament that he really misses, with its air-conditioning and long tables sent from Pretoria. The memory moves him still. "Just think," he said, "we even forbade smoking in the Parliament building that was a symbol of our autonomy. Now it has been degraded, like the residence the South Africans built for the Kaptein. It was a beautiful house, it even had a swimming pool, no less, yes, a swimming pool, up there." He pointed to another part of the hillside. "Now it is empty, no one lives there. Even the furniture has been looted."

I could well imagine the furniture, of the kind found in South African public buildings in a style somewhere between Scandinavian and Prison, that some minister must have been well content to dispatch in a truck for delivery to the "semisavages" of Rehoboth when the time came to refurbish a second-class suite of offices.

Out of season, the spa at Rehoboth is deserted. Hot water gushes from the spring at a rate of thousands of gallons an hour and from the tiled swimming pools you can hear baboons calling as they chase each other through the gardens, and the hooked-nosed hornbills shrieking in the trees.

The spa with its water at a constant temperature used to attract South African tourists and provide a steady income for the coffers of the Gebiet. It is now run by game wardens employed by the government of Namibia, dressed in khaki uniforms with green facings. Having rented one of the prefabricated cottages built around the springs, I bathed every evening in that immense natural jacuzzi welling from the heart of the savannah.

"Mister Riccardo?"

The Kaptein appeared at the edge of the covered pool carrying a cream-colored folder labeled in two languages—"Onderwerp-Subject"—and secured with a rubber band.

"I thought this might interest you."

I climbed out of the water, slightly embarrassed by the amused glint in the eyes of the Kaptein, who was almost standing to attention beside the pool. The folder he handed me came from the Chancery of the pro–South African Parliament and had been intended to contain a ruling of the Peri-Urban Development Board of the Gebiet of Rehoboth, one of the countless directives spawned by the Pretoria bureaucracy concerning the Kaptein and his faithful cohorts. In fact it contained a report by John Viall, a former "magistrate" of Rehoboth, in 1959. "Magistrate" was the title given to the representative of South Africa standing in provisionally for the traditional Kaptein.

From the photocopied sheets I learned how the South Africans managed, for the first time since the great trek, to split the Baster community into two rival groups, creating a division that has not healed to this day. On page 23 John Viall set out his premise:

> In 1913 the population of the Rehoboth Baster Gebiet numbered about three thousand Basters and two thousand Natives. The Basters possessed 600 horses, 5,500 head of cattle and 42,000 small stock. Eugen Fischer, the German anthropologist, describes the Baster community at the time as follows. "The community is divided into a distinct 'upper' and 'lower' class. I was not able to determine whether, in the days of their white ancestors, the Van Wyks, Moutons, Beukes, Koopmans and Diergaardts were more prominent and respected than the Vries, Orlams, Engelbrechts and Vreys families. But today at any rate the first-mentioned call themselves the 'good' or the 'old' families and are almost all well-to-do, some of them even wealthy . . . and have their own 'Volk,' or servants whose job it is to look after the herds. The better-off live in houses built of stone, the others in round huts. The houses usually consist of two rooms, living room and bedroom. . . . The Baster nation is superior to any pure Native race as far as industry and administration are concerned, but they are totally incapable of competing with European men."

The division between the old families directly descended from the original pioneers and the "new" families of those that arrived later has had a dramatic consequence for the Basters.

"I'm going to tell you a secret. We have always maintained our contacts with the United Nations ever since we presented our petition in 1952. Until 1915 we were a sovereign state and according to international law we have never lost that status. Had it not been for the stupidity of some, we would still be a Republic. The captain? What Kaptein? Hans Diergaardt is a nobody. His office was illegal. A puppet of the South Africans. I am the Basters' spokesman. It was I who went to negotiate with the South African head of state, Botha."

Hermanus "Maans" Beukes paused to observe my reaction to the name. Seated on a patriarchal high-backed chair, he bore a definite resemblance to the photograph of his father Johannes "Oupa" (meaning "Grandfather") Beukes, also known as "Der Griet," The Great One, which hangs in the museum. In the photograph "Oupa" is wearing suspenders and a wide-brimmed hat. Hermanus was wearing identical suspenders. "Anna," he said to his wife, who was standing silently beside him waiting for orders, "show him the map of our territory as it used to be recognized by everyone."

The Beukes, like the Diergaardts, are one of the old Baster families. The house is dark, with old calendars on the walls, a large crucifix and embroidered lace runners on the battered table. Anna addresses her husband deferentially as "Headman." She has Nama blood in her veins and speaks the language of the Hottentots, but the scarf wound around her head and the shawl over her shoulders are those worn by the burghers' wives in Flemish paintings.

"Diergaardt and his followers accepted the South Africans' proposal to create a Bantustan, which meant renouncing complete autonomy in our territory." The aggrieved tone of Herr Beukes's voice testified to the fact that despite the advent of Nelson Mandela in South Africa and the demotion of Diergaardt in Rehoboth, this betrayal still stung. "We tried to rebel, but in vain. The South Africans decided to use force. And the world has continued to ignore my messages to Geneva and New York. Officially at least. Behind the scenes, however, there are many highly placed people who still advise me not to give in."

By now it was dark outside, the deep dark of the African night. For many Basters this is the hour in which the specter of their only defeat in battle returns to haunt them.

Hermanus Beukes became mired in the details of a legal controversy, his account now a confusion of names and dates and electoral results. Professor Peter Carstens of the University of Toronto has analyzed the Baster saga in a study with the stirring title *Opting out of Colonial Rule: The Brown Voortrekkers of South Africa.* He summarizes the affair as follows:

> In 1923 most Rehobothers voted against accepting an "Agreement" regarding their relationship with the new ruling powers. The outcome of a complex situation was that the administrator of the territory issued a proclamation which transferred all the powers and duties of the captain to a magistrate, and made it an offense to attempt to usurp these powers. The Basters rejected this action and elected a new captain and councillors. The South West African Administration and the South African Government took retaliatory action immediately. Police, troops, and three airplanes were sent to Rehoboth to capture the town, and over four hundred people were found guilty of acts of unlawful assembly.

Not until 1961 did South Africa try to persuade the Basters to accept parts of the 1923 Accord by offering a minimum degree of autonomy in return for their recognition of South Africa's sovereignty over the territory. But in a referendum the Basters refused the Accord yet again, unwilling to be politically integrated with South Africa. Peter Carstens again:

> A new Constitution was also drawn up, but this too was rejected in a referendum held in June 1963. . . . In February 1975, a draft Constitution was put before the Advisory Board. Five of the seven members resigned their seats rather than accept it. . . . In a by-election held in April, a more "moderate" group was elected, and the Constitution accepted. Subsequently the Rehoboth Self-Government

Act was passed by the South African Parliament. Doctor
Ben Africa won the election for captain, but his victory was
contested in the courts by the other candidate, Mr. Hans
Diergaardt. It was alleged that irregularities in the registra-
tion of voters had taken place. A new election was ordered,
which Diergaardt won. He was officially installed as Kaptein on 25 June 1979.

Intrigues, vendettas, jealousies. For the Basters, the accounts
are still not settled. Ben Africa, representing the "inferior" families, is now a doctor in Capetown. In contention with the people
of Rehoboth, he has returned to the land his forefathers left.

Hermanus Beukes has stayed, not having the means to go
anywhere else. "This," he said, "is what white people do." And
he stressed the "white." "First they sign a pact and then they
break it. The Germans could never give us one good reason for
imposing their rule on us. And the South Africans went so far as
to claim that they had no money for digging new wells. But
when it suited them, they transformed our land into Bantustan
in a couple of days." History, for Hermanus Beukes, can still be
rewritten. "I have the original map," he said, "that proves the
extent of our land before it was taken away."

The map was on a sheet of yellowed paper that Anna slid out
of a tube. They used to have it hanging on the wall like a picture,
but today it's too precious and they keep it in the bedroom, probably under their bed. "With this in my hand, if I were younger, I
would go to the United Nations and ask them to intervene. Do
you know I'm in touch with the American government too? We
also have the Vaderlike Wette, the Paternal Laws of our forefathers, on our side. And South African–style Apartheid is something that the majority of our people have never wanted."

Postcard No. 1. Rehoboth, *D.-S.-W.-Afrika.* Undated. Two women in front of a round hut, one
seated, one standing. The seated woman is wearing a

cone-shaped headdress and a long white pinafore. The one standing up has a kerchief over her head.

Behind them is a high-wheeled cart, designed to cross the desert. The women are peasants. They appear to be European. One wonders if they live in the hut beside the wagon, which is in perfect condition and covered with cloths of some kind to absorb the heat. It has a rectangular door. This hut is typical of the Nama, enemies of the Herero and the last tribe of the Hottentot people.

Postcard No. 2. From the cover of a monograph entitled *Die Nation der Bastards,* September 1906. In Gothic script. A German officer in the middle of a treeless plain. Standing to attention, holding a rifle with its butt resting on the ground. He looks straight ahead, away from the lens of the camera. Lying on its side, round-bellied, a zebra dies beneath his boot.

Postcard No. 3. "Wagons in Rehoboth," undated. Emerging from the door of the Basters' church, men in wide-brimmed hats walk with their eyes down. All wear buttoned-up jackets. The church is a farmhouse with a thatched straw roof. Two wagons with empty shafts.

Postcard No. 4. Husband and wife. Standing motionless. She offers him her arm, he stands stiffly, elbows turned out, hands resting on his chest. It is hot.

Postcard No. 5. The Baster regiment goes to war. The men's boots are dusty. Their trousers are tucked into them. The hats have curled-up brims and a cockade. Square-jawed, efficient-looking men with riding-whips. The troop-train is about to leave the station. Knapsacks on the ground. A dog watches. The women are at home.

Postcard No. 6. The German Imperial Schutztruppe, riding camels, walking two by two over the sand. They are on their way to fight the Herero. The camels were sent by the War Ministry from other German colonies in Africa. They arrived by ship. They feel at home in the Kalahari. The Basters follow on horseback.

Postcard No. 7. Prussian helmet, black skin. The pockets of an old bearded soldier are bulging with heaven knows what. Bullets, perhaps, or rolled-up maps. He holds a wooden stick for use with his herds and his enemy alike.

Postcard No. 8. Rehoboth, *D.-S.-W.-Afrika,* undated. A woman carrying a bucket of water and wearing a hood that falls to her shoulders. Church with a bell-tower. Two palm trees. Church room close by. The rest is flat sand with faint traces of vegetation.

Postcard No. 9. Samuel Maherero in a uniform with high collar and gold braid round the cuffs. Still not pre-pared to surrender, he is about to send in his troops against the combined German and Baster forces.

Postcard No. 10. Rathaus in Windhoek, 1915. In Europe, Germany has only recently commenced hos-tilities. In Suid-West Afrika she has already capitu-lated. About fifty gentlemen with pith helmets and walking-sticks wait in Windhoek's main street for the latest news. Finally the German officers emerge into the sunshine. People crowd up to the porticoed door. The announcement is made that from today South West Africa is to be administered temporarily by the South African army commanded by General Louis Botha and General Jan Smuts. Shivers run down linen-suited spines.

"Senile idiots," said Chris Benadi. "If you listen to people like the Kaptein and his friends you'll never understand anything about this place. Forget about the tribes, the war, the Germans. We're not a colony anymore. That's over. Finished. Why should we call for independence? As citizens of the new Namibia we're free to do whatever we like. Do you know what those people lack? The will to get up and do something. We've got to forge our own future. And all they can do is play at a Republic of Rehoboth. See this African-style hotel? They jabber on, blah,

blah, blah. I built this. The first in the whole region. With bungalows, swimming pool and open-air barbecue overlooking this wild natural landscape. And soon the tourists will be coming. With their dollars."

Dusk was falling over the hill behind Rehoboth. We were sitting under a roof of interlaced wands of cane known as *makuti*. About twenty bungalows, some only half-finished, were dotted along a stony path. Behind the bar overlooking the savannah, a black boy was cooking sausages. Chris apologized, explaining: "We've only just opened, and this is all I can offer you. But before long this place'll be terrific."

Chris Benadi turned off his mobile phone and frowned as he looked at the road leading up from the city. His colleagues were late. One a dentist, the other a businessman, both are white, born on farms in what used to be the Basters' Gebiet but of English or German parents.

While still in Milan, I had been advised to contact Chris by a Norwegian appointed as honorary consul for Namibia because he was born in Walvis Bay where, in the 1950s, his father was training South Africans in the art of whaling. "Chap with his wits about him, Chris," he had said. "President of the Rehoboth Chamber of Commerce, knows all the right people in Windhoek and has his finger in every pie. If you're interested in the Basters, he's your man. Benadi is a Baster himself."

"Benadi? Oh, you mean Chris, the businessman!" As soon as I got to Namibia I realized that the friend of my friend was everybody's friend. Or rather, that everybody knew him. The Kaptein had shaken his head and hissed: "Traitor!" Professor Budack had smiled in a strange, ironic way and said: "*Ach, Benadi. SWAPO.*"

Chris removed his dark glasses. "Do you want to see the plans for my lodge?" I declined. I hadn't come all this way up the hill to talk about business. "OK, you want to know if I really am a Baster? Yes, I am. My family is one of the old ones. But I prefer to think of myself as Namibian."

His colleagues arrived and called for cold beer. The sky was now completely dark. These were men used to the outdoor life. "I raise cattle, both as a hobby and to make money," said the dentist. Namibia for them means business opportunity. Chris's lodge could relaunch a city that, following the nationalization of the spa, had fallen out of the tourist circuit.

"But all the giraffe in the reserve have been killed," I said to provoke a response. "How can you attract tourists if there are no animals for them to see? You must admit that it was a mistake for SWAPO to seize that land from the Basters."

Chris shrugged his shoulders. "The land belongs to everyone. So it belongs to the government."

"So he says, but all the same that hotel is being built on land that used to belong to the community and was confiscated from us," replied the Kaptein when I saw him a few days later.

It was time to return to Rehoboth. I was not, of course, expecting street lighting, but for people used to living in Europe it is always a shock to find oneself alone in the night. The car bumped down the stony path. As it was after ten-thirty and no one is abroad late at night in Africa, the gates of the spa camping-site were shut. But I had an agreement with a portly game warden who had worked in all the game parks from Waterberg to the Skeleton Coast before coming to Rehoboth. I was to leave the car outside and use a special door. He would look the other way.

The prefabricated cottages designed for families on vacation were nearly all empty because at this time of year the children are at school and hardly anyone drives up the B1 from South Africa. Two cats with whom I had made friends were waiting for me, as they did every evening. It was too late for a swim in the warm, ceaselessly gurgling water, so I prepared for bed. Even on this desolate camping-site the African night is ushered in with a symphony of sound as the nocturnal birds and beasts awaken. I found myself thinking about the giraffe, killed by God knows who, and about the Kaptein. I decided to return to the museum the next day.

~᪥~

From time immemorial the Basters have been obsessed with the idea of buying uninhabited land and transforming it into their own homeland. As if the purchase, signed, sealed and duly registered with the authorities, could guarantee them protection from anything untoward.

Their first experiment on these lines was in 1865 when they were living in Pella and De Tuin, two South African outposts. The Parliament in the Cape had just passed a law obliging the occupants of any plot of land to register with the government office dealing with Crown property, so Willem van Wyk and Stoffel Lombaard, two authoritative heads of family, were charged with the responsibility of going to Calvinia (the nearest city) and offering two hundred pounds sterling for 750,000 acres of pastureland to be registered in the name of the Baster community as a whole.

The response of the authorities was cautious. First, the Basters were told, it would be necessary to canvass the opinions of all the heads of families and see if there were any objections. So Van Wyk and Lombaard had to make another journey to Calvinia, this time accompanied by a large group of Basters, for a kind of public hearing. There, before the Boer farmers, they realized that they would not be permitted to acquire the freehold. The loudest protests came from a Dutchman, Andries Struis, who argued that were the land to be sold to these halfbreeds, "It would bring about the ruin of the whole country."

The Basters left before the verdict was pronounced.

"That was when we decided to go further afield, seeking land that belonged to no one or that we could acquire without problems. To do that we had to become a real nation with our own laws and internal structure," explained Hans Diergaardt. By a simple show of hands in a shady clearing, Hermanus van Wyk became the Basters' first elected Kaptein. He and Giel Diergaardt, great-grandfather of Hans, were immediately sent to explore the north of the region, in what is now Namibia, where they obtained the permission of the Nama to stay in the Berseba zone for two years.

In February 1868, during an assembly organized in the village of De Tuin, ninety Baster families voted to signal the start of the trek. It was time to go, for they were being threatened by the neighboring Koranna tribe and the Boers were now openly hostile. Before they made their great leap into the unknown, the Basters decided to gather all the families in Pella. Four days later De Tuin was razed to the ground.

The column of wagons, some drawn by oxen and others by horses, set off in the morning beneath an overcast sky. Heidmann, a priest from the Rhine Mission, was with them, having decided to stay with his flock wherever it might go. On 16 November 1868 the Basters, led by Hermanus van Wyk, crossed the Orange River and the Great Trek had begun. Ahead lay a journey of many hundreds of perilous miles over mountains, through deserts, warding off the attentions of hyenas, jackals, leopards and fierce Nama tribesmen who viewed the incursion of these white strangers onto their territory, heading no one knew where, with the deepest suspicion.

Reaching the spring known today as Warmbad, Van Wyk and his Baster followers stayed put for a month before resuming their trek. In June 1869 they were journeying through places then unnamed but known today as Keetmanshoop, Berseba and Bethanien. Eventually they halted at Chamis, beside the Konkiep River, and there they stayed tranquilly until 1870, recovering from illness and fatigue and fattening their cattle. "It was only a temporary staging-post," Professor Budack explained to me when I visited him again in his museum. "The Basters knew that they must go as far north as possible, but in the north there were a whole lot of tribes warring among themselves, and before facing these new dangers they needed time to regain their strength both mentally and physically."

The principal combatants in these intertribal wars were the

Herero and a tribe of Hottentots of great ferocity for all their Christian-sounding names. These were led by Abraham Swartbooi, and the English and the Dutch knew them simply as the Swartbooi. Another band was actually led by a David Christiaan. The Swartbooi base was in what would eventually become Rehoboth. The outside world knew nothing of what was happening here. Europe had not yet occupied this vast, remote land and cared nothing about the conflicts that flared up one after the other, the U-turns, the shifting alliances that were in many ways the mirror-image of events affecting the colonial powers themselves.

On the morning of 22 July 1864, the Herero and the Swartbooi together attacked and defeated other Hottentot tribes in the mountains between Rehoboth and Windhoek. In retaliation the losers sought to destroy Rehoboth, but by the time they arrived (on horseback) the camp was deserted. The Swartbooi had fled to Otjimbingwe. But their enemies gave chase, overtook them on the banks of the Kuiseb River and massacred them. Among the few to survive was Abraham Swartbooi, who managed to reach the court of Kamaherero, the great Herero chief, who ceded to him the town of Bokberg, then known as Erongo. Rehoboth had therefore been abandoned since 1864. It awaited a new master.

The wars, meanwhile, continued, but now it was the Herero who had the upper hand. However, as neither contingent succeeded in prevailing definitively over the other, Jan Jonker appealed to what was virtually the United Nations of the time, the German and Finnish missionaries who had elected to carry their brand of Calvinism to the most sparsely populated parts of Africa. The mediation worked, and on 23 September 1870 the Herero and the Hottentots signed the Treaty of Okahandia, undertaking to live together without further fighting.

Hermanus van Wyk was present at the signing, with his wide-brimmed cowboy hat and his quasi-Oriental features as depicted in contemporary portraits. He had been invited by some of the Hottentot chiefs who respected his reputation as a just and authoritative man, chief of a small but important tribe.

In a letter to the German consul written many years later, Van Wyk recalled the following. "They had asked me to help them conclude the treaty. At the time I was still living in Chamis, in the Bethanien region. After the peace conference I went to visit missionary Hann and asked him to whom I should apply for possession of Rehoboth, a place I had already visited twice and that was, together with its vast surrounding territory, completely uninhabited at the time. I knew we would enjoy living there. Mr. Hann sent me to Abraham Swartbooi because he owned it. And when I went to see him, he ceded it to me."

The Basters, white with an admixture of Hottentot blood, not indigenous and therefore presumed neutral, were used like peacekeeping troops: by installing them in Rehoboth, the Swartbooi and the Herero created a buffer zone between their peoples. Accounts differ, however, as to how this diplomatic operation was managed. The Basters claim to have paid for the land with horses, one a year as stipulated in a written contract. Professor Budack maintains that the horses were only a form of "rent." J. D. Viall, the South African magistrate at the time, also writes that the payment in horses, made every year until 1881, was for the usufruct of the Rehoboth region.

In the end the Basters went back to Swartbooi and asked him to sell them the land. Without due title to the land—still the same obsession with ownership—they were wary of investing the money necessary for digging wells, and Rehoboth needed water desperately.

Swartbooi refused. After a great deal of persuasion he conceded that, should he ever decide to sell the land outright, the Basters should have first refusal. The Basters still disagree about what was said, maintaining that Swartbooi eventually agreed to sell, the price being one hundred horses and five wagons, the technological marvels of the epoch. More than a century later, the ghosts of these one hundred horses are still creating bad blood between the people of Rehoboth and the Nama.

Besides the need to invest in wells, there was another motive for Van Wyk's insistence on acquiring title to the land. He had heard that another convoy of Europeans and half-breeds had left the Cape heading for Angola. And yet more trekkers had started out from the Transvaal, also heading toward Angola, which was rumored to be an extremely fertile and healthy region. Both were destined to pass into history as the ill-fated Dorsland Treks, the "Treks of the Thirsty Lands." But the aging Baster peasant feared that, given the difficulty of reaching their goal, the Europeans would get as far as Rehoboth and decide to stay. He was determined to have the Basters' title to their Promised Land in black and white before anyone could snatch it from him. He could not know that the Dorsland Trekkers' faith in their dreams about the Humpata valleys was such that nothing would hold them back, not even the loss of more than three hundred men to illness and accident on the journey.

Poor soil, cattle, documents signed by African chiefs with Scandinavian names. . . . The history of the Basters and the other small turbulent nations in this corner of Africa between the Kalahari and the Namib Desert in the second half of the nineteenth century played itself out in a paradoxical equilibrium between brutal, fast-paced wars and legal lethargy, between the desire to get as far away from central authority as possible—to "vote with their feet"—and the determination to set up their own autonomous but strict authority, and between the insatiable thirst for adventure in the arid heart of the continent and an unshakeable faith in the timeless truths of the Bible.

In the background was always the burning question of cattle, the living gold of the epoch. For the sake of cows and horses, war was declared and lives laid unhesitatingly on the line. The story of the Basters' agreeing to pay their rent in horses and wagons but defaulting on the wagons part of the deal is a case in point. In 1926 the Baster vice-captain, Carolus Zwart, confessed to a South African commission that this omission was the direct cause of the Swartbooi attacking Rehoboth in 1882.

War, war, always war. But in the nascent Rehoboth, a village

where a few brick houses and many native-style huts were springing up, the Basters were tasting a measure of stability at last. The
first school was opened by Matheus Gertze, a schoolteacher by
profession. In 1872 some Germans set up the first store. Baster
farmers returned to Capetown to buy Merino sheep to introduce
into their new homeland and genetically improve their aging
herds. Rehoboth now had a judiciary whose officials were appointed to collect taxes and organize public works, see to the
provision of water, the maintenance of the church, and later the
construction of a small railway. Every now and then a little dusty
wagon-train would arrive carrying brothers, cousins and friends
who had heard about the birth of Rehoboth and now came north,
leaving the towns of Pella and Gibeon. For its time and place,
Rehoboth had become a minor power in the land. By 1876 its
population count was eight hundred Basters, twenty thousand
sheep and twenty-five hundred cows.

The peace, however, was not destined to last long. In 1880 the
Herero and the Hottentots were again at each others' throats.
Both appealed to the Basters, who were considered the natural ar-
bitrators. Hermanus van Wyk decided to remain neutral—it was
the first of many "other men's wars" that his people would decline
to fight—but after six Basters and one European (a certain Mc-
Nab, on an isolated farm) had been killed, the Kaptein gave in and
sent a contingent of fifty men to assist in setting up a coalition between Witboois, Afrikaners and the Hottentots of Berseba and
Bethanie. Shortly afterward, the Herero attacked the Hottentot
and Baster forces and defeated them decisively.

The Basters now being weakened, Jan Jonker and Abraham
Swartbooi also attacked. It was 21 July 1882, a date still recalled
with terror and memorized by every child in the schools of the
former Gebiet. The Hottentots stormed the center of Rehoboth
after raiding the nearby farms and carrying off hundreds of animals. Seeing defeat imminent, Kaptein van Wyk climbed onto a
rooftop and called on his men to make a superhuman effort and
mount a surprise attack by night.

By the following morning the Hottentots were in retreat. On 14 February 1882, the Basters and the Herero signed separate peace treaties.

The history of Rehoboth continued to be one of battles, coups d'état, quarrels and alliances almost up to the present day. Rough cattlemen with an almost mystical respect for official documents, the men of Rehoboth continued to turn out one constitution after another, perfecting, modifying and modernizing their patriarchal laws—until they were overtaken and defeated by a greater, a more important historical event, the overthrow of Apartheid in South Africa. In the new Namibia there is no longer space for them.

Every time I have been to Namibia, a gemsbok has trailed me from the moment of arrival to that of departure. His extraordinarily long horns appear when least expected, spiraling up into the sky from behind some screen of vegetation. He has galloped beside me over the sand dunes in the Namib, and leaped the barbed-wire fencing around a farm before crossing the road in front of my car.

The Basters know him well. From the time of the Great Trek until the creation of the white Bantustan he was always galloping behind their herds. Tall, massive, with two white bands girdling his athletic body, he is solitary like them, a hybrid like them, part gnu, part hartebeest, with a dash of sable antelope.

On my last morning at the Etosha we began the day together, shortly after dawn, beside a spring of water. He had slipped in among a herd of zebra; I slipped into a red Jeep. Then, as I drove along a deserted road between farm buildings and the windmills that draw water from beneath the bush, he came to say goodbye. Sensing that I was about to exchange the dirt tracks of the savannah for the tarmac roads that would take me to Windhoek, he overtook me at a gallop fifteen hundred feet before the last turning and waited for me by the side of the road.

It was a dignified farewell signaled by poking his moist nose out of an acacia. I returned his salutation with a toot of my horn.

6
Guadeloupe
Blancs Matignon, the Sugarcane Dukes

Behind the enigma lay a truth so stark, so tawdry, so unre-
deeming. It was like pushing aside a richly veined rock to
reveal, on its lichenous underside, a suppurating colony of
maggots. A secret which had been hidden for so long had
been dragged out into the open.
—Shiva Naipaul, *A Hot Country*

Pointe des Châteaux, January 1995

"Blancs Matignon? You're coming to Guadeloupe just for the
sake of a handful of incestuous peasants? No, I don't know
where they live exactly. Wait, it could be in the Grands Fonds,
up in the mountains. *Alors,* you're asking me, at this time of
night, if they really exist?"

Poor Carole. In her wooden bungalow at Pointe des Châteaux,
a strip of white sand jutting out from Guadeloupe into the
Caribbean Sea, the day was only just dawning. The phone line conveyed Madame Dejean's sleepy bemusement all the way to Milan.

Carole Dejean competes with the hotels along the coast by
letting a few chalets close to Guadeloupe's prettiest beach, far
from anywhere, at the end of a narrow sandy road leading to
Salines. For the new arrivals who stagger jet-lagged off the
planes, she is an adoptive mother, even though she hardly looks

the part. An elegant thirty-something, Carole teaches English in Point-à-Pitre, the largest town in the region, and has all the restless energy of a Parisian career-woman.

Perhaps we move her to tenderness, we pallid Europeans who drop from the skies into her warm, limpid world, and perhaps that is why, when she has time, Carole will pop a banana cake into the fridge as a welcoming gesture and leave four or five bottles of home-distilled rum, with hand-written labels, in the tiny kitchen. The rum comes in three different colors: white, red and yellow, flavored respectively with coconut, cinnamon and mango. And in the evening she invites favored guests to her verandah, littered with fashion magazines and plastic tractors, to play with *Petit-chou,* the chocolate-colored child who is now the only man in her life.

It goes without saying that Carole has met her share of foreigners making outrageous demands at impossible hours. Italians are, apparently, the easiest to please. Several are outstandingly loyal and make the journey to Salines year after year unhesitatingly, unquestioningly. All they want is *il mare,* the sea. No one had ever mentioned the Blancs Matignon. In fact, it only occurred to her during our conversation that she had never given them a thought herself.

It was a cold day in Milan, and the computers in the newsroom were pouring out the usual New Year stories. I had been delving into books and maps for some weeks without much enlightenment. Now, only a few days before departure, my concern was that the experts who maintained that the Blancs Matignon of Guadeloupe were only a myth, a legend created by the ethnic mosaic of the Lesser Antilles, might be right. Or that they had existed once but had become extinct decades ago. The *Lonely Planet Guide* talks vaguely about "descendants of white colonists" seen on the tracks across the high plateaux. Could this really have been them? Or had the writers merely encountered a few emaciated backpackers trekking through the interior of the island?

I had to persist with my questions. "Can the Blancs Matignon be approached? If we come, could you take us to them?"

Carole gave in eventually. "*Très bien,* I'll find out," she said. "But I warn you it won't be easy. The Matignon are odd and very racist."

"Ah, so you do know some of them!" I crowed.

The line all but conveyed her shiver of distaste. "No, no, I don't know any of them personally. But I've heard about them and I know that there's no love lost between us and them. Just imagine, they marry their own relatives! That's incest, do you realize?" Carole, wide awake by now, was obviously finding the subject repellent. But business is business. "Come on over and I'll help you. Leave it to me. Of course you'll need someone to translate from Creole, too! I doubt if the Matignon speak French. . . ."

Two weeks later we were with Carole in the dry, blazing heat of Guadeloupe. We had become friends immediately. Every morning she drove off in her Renault with the baby seat in the back just like any European working mother, parked the child with his grandmother and went to work. We, meanwhile, explored the creeks and sandy beaches on both sides of the peninsula. For lunch we retreated to the bars with their white or blue terraces and dishes of lobster and fried fish. The rhythm of life at Salines was blissfully natural and relaxed. It was reassuring, too, to know that in the evening we would be going home to Carole and Jean-Pierre. The child made us laugh by picking up his kitten by the tail, shouting, *"Miao miao,"* and slinging it across his shoulders like a knapsack. The kitten seldom objected.

The day finally came when, satiated with beaches, rainbow-colored fish and sunshine, we began to explore the winding roads leading up into the mountains. I told Pia that I was not intending to go as far as the village of the Matignon, just somewhere near. "You've just got itchy feet," she scolded. So, clutching a map sponsored by Coca-Cola, off we went. Whenever we lost our way and stopped to ask directions, the post office clerk or the mechanic in his workshop would look at us askance and mutter: "If you want to find the Matignon, first get on the *Numéro Cinq*. Ask there."

The Route Nationale No. 5 is a licorice-stick of tarmac slipping through Guadeloupe's sugarcane and banana plantations. In the still, hot air, with not so much as a billboard to spoil the effect, colors are stratified into the emerald of the hills at the lowest level, the vivid blue of the sky at the top and the white clouds sandwiched between them. And this is how it is, for weeks at a time; maybe forever.

We drove through the noonday silence, two Europeans on the trail of a little Caribbean mystery, until we came to a spot where the vistas of farmland were interrupted by a barren patch littered with debris. There seemed to be no one about.

We had come here after being let in to a secret, one of those secrets that tend to be kept for a long time because nobody is interested enough to delve into them. The rubble-filled patch was once a big sugar refinery called the Usine Blanchet, one of the first refineries founded by Europeans in the Caribbean. It had belonged to the Blancs Matignon and had been their sole link with modern civilization and technology. Now almost nothing remained. After generations of distilling minute globules of sweetness, the factory now distilled great mounds of rust—coincidentally the same color as cane juice.

The refinery was being dismantled by a group of silent, dignified workmen in overalls and suspenders. They had been working with excavators and dynamite for the past ten months under the impression that their contract to clear an old sugar refinery in as short a time as possible was nothing out of the ordinary. But this was the mausoleum of the Blancs Matignon, a lost white tribe that, on the eve of the third millennium, was dying in this corner of the Caribbean in exactly the same way that it had lived, in silence, almost in secret, peering at the rest of the world through a keyhole.

Very little has ever been known about the Blancs Matignon. Even now, when the network of metaled roads has reached every corner of the island, they still live in isolation in the mountains, ignored and despised by the rest of the population of Guadeloupe. No one, not even the Blancs Matignon themselves, can explain why, two centuries ago when Napoleon was ruling Europe, a small group of French colonists decided to abandon the ports and the farms of this wealthy colony and hide away in the furthest corner of the island, a prey to hunger and disease. One theory is that they were idealists driven into these remote valleys by a determination to build a perfect, changeless society uncontaminated by the revolutionary democratic and egalitarian ideas that were spreading even into the tropical areas of the empire. Another theory is that they were driven out for having committed some crime. But perhaps the truth is that they simply decided to try their luck in the virgin forest only to find themselves trapped in one of history's darker culs-de-sac. *Insabbiati* is the word the Italians used for colonials who could not bring themselves to go home. It means "stuck in the sand," and was only logically applicable to such colonies as Abyssinia and Eritrea. Here, in the mountains of Guadeloupe, there is no sand, only leaves, butterflies and tracks hewn out of the forest. Perhaps the Matignon have merely become "stuck in the jungle."

The reason *why* it happened is not, however, that important. It is much more interesting to find out—or imagine—*how* it happened. And one can almost see them, those first rebel families, doggedly setting out with a few wagons along these paths bordered with lush vegetation, their black slaves following on foot with machetes tucked into their belts, straw hats on their heads and trousers rolled halfway up their legs. Before them rose a wall of wet, densely wooded hillsides to be cleared.

The flight of the Matignon recalls the Boer trekkers' long march through the African bush. But of the *blanc va nu pieds,* the "whites who walk barefoot" as the other inhabitants of Guadeloupe derisively call them, all we know is that from that moment they have never wanted to emerge from their own impenetrable jungle.

The Matignon used to go down to the Usine Blanchet in their ox-drawn carts four times a year to deliver the harvest of sugar-cane cultivated on the land cleared by their slaves. It had seemed indestructible, the old factory with its iron machines and steam engines. Yet when the demolition squads arrived, they found it already in a dangerous condition and choked with rubbish. For years the truck drivers who criss-cross the island (it takes half a day to negotiate the tight bends of the road from Point-à-Pitre through Morne-à-l'Eau and on to the pastel-tinted port of Anse-Bertrand) had been dumping bald tires in it and empty bottles of ginger-beer, the Caribbean beer that tastes of disinfectant.

Even in the immediate neighborhood there were many who had forgotten all about this flotsam of colonialism. Only the minister for education, in his distant office in France, had remembered about the old Usine Blanchet, and there was a rumor that he had once toyed momentarily with the thought of using it to house the new elementary school. But this was eventually built a couple of miles away.

Anyone who travels to the factory cannot help noticing the school, a four-square cement edifice built precisely to the specifications set out in ministerial circulars. Low-ceilinged class-rooms with pale yellow walls, playground-*cum*-sportsfield surrounded by high wire netting. Some trees had been recently cut down at the edge of the car park, but their indomitable roots, like varicose veins, were still pushing up the tarmac.

The school is perfect for those who will shortly be living in the defunct factory, because a certain Michael Clavery, a wealthy man with an office in Point-à-Pitre and—reportedly—little use for nostalgia, has bought the land where the old refinery once stood and is in a hurry to clear away the debris and start building apartment blocks and shops in the style of almost-poor Nice, or, if you prefer, almost-rich Dakkar. There will be balconies with striped awnings, a few spindly palms and a great many video-entryphones.

We parked beside a narrow road where wagons loaded with freshly cut sugarcane used to pass. Until twenty years ago the white peasants brought their cane to the Usine to be stripped, milled and then fermented. Such images are not entirely lost even today. The wagons still jostle each other along the roads of Guadeloupe. You only have to leave the main highways for the rough tracks to see them lumbering along, pushing and shoving one against the other in a confusion of axles and wheels, drawn by oxen, powerful beasts with the skin hanging from their necks in great loose folds.

The wagons no longer go to the Usine Blanchet, but during the harvest they still queue patiently in front of the Damoiseau distillery of *rhum agricole* at the head of the series of valleys known as the Grands Fonds. At least thirty wooden wagons, some drawn by tractors, others by oxen, wait their turn to unload.

We once saw them scatter in panic. There had been a blow-back and the alarm sirens went off. Alcoholic fumes from the rum had ignited, causing a great sheet of flame to spurt from the furnace. The manager of the distillery, a white man in shorts and little else, had appeared and shouted some orders. Suddenly everything was back to normal. A couple of silos had been blackened and a couple of old driving-belts in the main shed put out of action, but the Damoiseau was once again swallowing one load after another of freshly cut sugarcane.

❦

During the lifetime of the old Usine the files of wagons were longer and moved more slowly, because the Matignon came from all the surrounding valleys. And in those days they were in less of a hurry to go home.

The road into the site is still rutted from their wagon-wheels. Having negotiated it, we walked into what had been the factory, looking about us and crunching the crumbling remains of old pipework noisily underfoot. A small group of men in neat blue overalls emerged from a house on the left and came toward us. These were the workmen employed to finish the demolition. It was immediately obvious from their bronzed faces, blue-black hair and little moustaches that they were not from Guadeloupe or any of the other French islands. They spoke English.

"Where are you from?" we asked.

"Trinidad and Tobago," they replied in a well-disciplined chorus.

Trinidad lies at the bottom end of the Milky Way that is the Caribbean archipelago. It is a splinter of India at a stone's throw from Latin America, but when the steel drums sound it becomes part of Africa.

They belonged to such a distant world, those Indian demolition workers, that we were almost tempted to find excuses for them. How could they know, Dulam, Kenny and all the others, that on that site littered with rusty boilers and dismembered machinery, they were about to bury the memory and the secrets of a little, doomed, people? Why should they care about a tribe of white peasants, obstinate and illiterate, whose ancestors came from an unknown place called Normandy? "Is that so?" they marveled when we told them the history of the Usine.

Perhaps they were right, Dulam and Kenny. How does one distinguish between a slight story that never made any headlines and a great adventure that deserves the status of history? Or a simple factory and a repository of dreams? There are no tombs, no crosses, no headstones, no plaques on the site of the Usine

Blanchet. Only four thousand tons of rusty ironmongery neatly divided into piles ready to be carted away. So the tribe is about to be buried forever in this silent yard halfway between the two small towns of Le Moule and Morne-à-l'Eau in the heart of an island shaped like a butterfly.

It all began two, possibly three, centuries ago when the Matignon began to trickle in to Guadeloupe as colonial immigrants and sailors with the French imperial navy, not knowing that they were destined to become a race apart. Like their companions, they fought, cut down trees and built in the name of the kings of Versailles and later in that of the République. Whites among whites, victors among victors.

Then came the mysterious flight, the decision to hide themselves away in the interior with their black slaves—French and African, both oppressed by the rigors of the pioneering life—and finally total isolation from the rest of Guadeloupe.

The last remaining descendants of these rebels—"Blancs" from the color of their skin, "Matignon" because this is at one and the same time the name of their village, the surname of the majority and the name of the aristocratic family from whom they claim their ancestry—still live near the defunct refinery, in the same valleys where their great-grandparents once lived. There is a degree of resemblance between all of them. The men are short and thin, with bony hands and blue-gray eyes. All wear long side-whiskers. The narrow-hipped women, all with bags under their eyes, wear their reddish-blonde hair in a bun.

The Grands Fonds where they live is a territory of extremes and of breathtaking beauty, and has been, until lately, impenetrable. School minibuses, shops, electricity and phonecards with microchips only reached them a few years ago. The world they rejected has now taken its revenge upon the Matignon. As soon as it discovered their hiding place, it stigmatized them for permitting sexual love between members of the same family. And finally it deprived them of the Usine Blanchet with the excuse that it was no longer profitable.

Modern Guadeloupe knows nothing about the fate of the Blancs Matignon. It is even unaware that emigration to Canada, Australia and France has brought the tribe close to extinction. There is a sense in which Guadeloupe has defeated the Blancs Matignon not with violence but by absorbing them via the process of "creolization." In the Grands Fonds, the children of some of the younger families are born not white but coffee-colored. Their color makes them automatically part of the great democratic family of Creoles, otherwise known as mulattos. When they go to school, they at least will never have to fend off taunts such as *fous montagnards,* stupid mountain-dwellers. They will be on a par with nearly all their companions.

"The Matignon don't deserve any pity. They're debased by intermarriage and isolation, abject folk who give themselves airs, and, as if that wasn't enough, lament the passing of slavery." This was the sort of remark we heard many times in Port-à-Pitre, spoken in the hushed tones of horror by the *Béké* on the coast when they heard that two apparently quite normal Europeans, one English, one Italian, intended to venture into the heart of the Grands Fonds to seek out these people.

The *Béké* are the wealthy, respectable whites, the tiny elite of Guadeloupe that studies, accumulates and governs, maintaining strong ties with France. To them the Matignon are a blot on the landscape, an embarrassing anachronism reminding them of the time when all the white colonies—theirs included—exploited black African slaves on the plantations, killing them when they attempted to escape, whipping them if they interrupted their work to sing. The *Béké* would like to pretend that the Matignon do not exist.

Ironically, this attitude is shared by the blacks, themselves children of slaves. Hatred of the Blancs Matignon of the Grands Fonds is one of the few sentiments uniting them with the *Béké* in postcolonial Guadeloupe.

The island, or rather archipelago, of Guadeloupe is an integral part of the French Republic; it flies the blue, white and red tricolor and inscribes the words "Liberté Egalité Fraternité" over the doors of its municipal buildings. Its roads are populated with authentic Peugeot 304 vans on whose seats authentic crumbs of baguette grow stale. Everything is of genuine French origin. The *département* of Guadeloupe does not consider itself a colony, and does not refer to the mother country as "France." With a touch of hauteur, it calls it *la Métropole,* as if to imply that the real France is here, in this frontier garrison of *Francophonie,* the last empire on which the sun never sets.

"L'Usine Blanchet? Do you mean the sugar refinery? Yes, of course this is it. It was still standing when we got here ten months ago, though they told us it had been shut since 1979 and the walls looked most unsafe. It was a wonderful sight, tall and dark like a volcano. With the furnace, the rollers for crushing the cane, the office, the stores. Look over there, you can still see the cog-wheels. You wouldn't believe the amount of iron. Michael Clavery, the chap who's bought the old refinery, wants to ship all the scrap iron to Panama in a cargo vessel and sell it to a foundry. And he's going to build houses here. Look, that was a smokestack. The juice from the cane was fed through there, all thick and yellow, then it was collected in a vat and refined in the boiling pans. We come from Trinidad so we know all about these things. Ever been to Trinidad and Tobago? Beautiful islands, and when there's a carnival, boy, do we have fun! Once we had a whole lot of refineries like this one. Hey, don't go yet! We only speak English, and it's so difficult to find anyone else in Guadeloupe who speaks it. We only know two or three words of French, and we are a bit tired of only having each other to talk to. . . . So this is how our business works. We travel all over the Caribbean demolishing buildings. We're a specialized team. We dismantle something, like this refinery, then we go home, rest a bit and then we're off again to demolish another factory. Just out of interest, this Usine Blanchet, was there anything special about it? No, never heard anyone speak about the Blancs Matignon. White peasants, you say? And poor? If you say so."

The demolition men exchanged puzzled glances. Who, they were wondering, had ever heard of a poor white peasant? What were these foreigners talking about? In Trinidad it's the blacks and the Indians who are poor. The few remaining whites belong to the old families and are all government officials. Or landowners.

"Anyway, no, we've never met any of these people. And we can't wait to finish the job and get away from Guadeloupe. We're not fussed about sightseeing. Right, Kenny? Let me introduce my mate Kenny. He's calculated that the cost of living here is five times that at home. Believe me, we're better off in Trinidad. Come and see me next time you're there. I'll jot down my address on your notepad. No problem. Just ask for Dulam Katwaru in Felicity, district of Chaguanas."

Dulam and Kenny, Indians from Trinidad, products of the mysterious transoceanic hybridizations of the British Empire, breakers by profession, diggers of graves for an old colonial world powered by sugarcane, heroism and crime, enjoy their work. It is forbidden to regret the passing of this world, forbidden to remember it, forbidden even to curse it. In today's F.W.I.—this is how the French West Indies appear on business cards, in English to show off one's cosmopolitanism—everyone pretends that before the age of the time-share, and before the state subsidies that none dare refuse, there was nothing at all. Very simple, very reassuring.

For many, L'Usine Blanchet never even existed. Take the French sailor I met one day at the helm of a gleaming catamaran. Curly-headed, tanned and jocular—in the Trintignant mold—he had come to the Caribbean as a child. Every day he takes twenty tourists from Saint François out to the coral atolls lying offshore from Carole's house, then, on a beach of white sand, under picture-postcard palms, he produces the most delicious barbecued fish. Afterward he takes a coconut, opens it with a single blow— under the admiring gaze of the women—and presents the white flesh to the children first. In the evening he drinks rum with his friends in the elegant quayside bars between the yachts and the estate-agents' windows and the *zouk* music from open-air dance floors. It is like a scene from a soap opera set in Florida. He knows every breath of wind off the sea as well as he knows the breath of his own body, and picks up every last bit of gossip in Grande-Terre. "Heaven knows why it's called that," he commented, "when it's smaller than Basse-Terre, the other wing of the butterfly-island. Just one of those geopolitical injustices."

Yet when questioned about those four hundred desperate souls on the plateau, barely ten miles from his mooring as the crow flies, he looked blank. "No, I've never seen a Blanc Matignon in my life," he said. "Yes, occasionally I've heard talk about a few strange white people living in isolation up in the mountains beyond Château Gaillard and still cutting cane. Mysterious folk, apparently. Not much liked, so they say. And that's all I know. Incidentally, where do these crazy Blancs Matignon come from? And why are you interested in them?"

For Tatie, the sight of the Usine Blanchet in its death throes would have been unbearable. And we never told her about the curly-headed boatman, the carefree neocolonist of the Commonwealth of Tourism. Ill-health has made her a virtual prisoner in her tin shack on the Route Départementale No. 102 in one of the narrow gorges of the Grands Fonds. Madame Constance Bourgeois—and anyone who forgets to address her as "Madame" would do better to stay away—suspects, though without being able to prove anything, that her world is dead, swallowed up by shadowy modern devils calling themselves racial integration, democracy and welfare.

Constance is old and crotchety. And *simpatica*. She is bad-tempered because she knows that she only has a short time left. You cannot blame her for her ill humor. When we visited her she was wearing a shapeless skirt and an unfashionable strapless top. She had put all her pots and pans outside to dry in the sun on the verandah, and barred us from entering the hut as if there were untold treasure hidden inside—instead of nothing but a cream plastic telephone, which, she assured us, rang every now and then because the doctor at the hospital in La Mole liked to check if she was still alive and remembering to take her pills and eat her greens. She doesn't take kindly to such interferences.

"No one tells me what to eat and drink," she once snapped in answer to my well-meant question. "Of course, it's a while since I gave up champagne, but apart from that I deny myself nothing."

The narrow road where Constance lives is on a slope. Nothing exceptional in that: the same could be said for so many. But the vistas it affords her of the vividly green and dramatically steep hills of the Grands Fonds are truly magnificent. The hills are crowned with neat farmhouses, the valley floors carpeted with fields. Seen from a height, the steep hillsides and deep valleys seem to go on forever, a rollercoaster of jacarandas and palm trees. Wagons drawn by pairs of white oxen rumble past, and ancient sand-colored Peugeot vans jolt along the unsurfaced roads carrying straw-hatted peasants to the plantations.

These peasants, fair-haired youngsters in T-shirts, with pale faces and eyes of an unnatural green, titter with a mixture of embarrassment and insolence when they see a stranger on the road, then honk the horn loudly and raise the palms of their hands because this is how white men greet each other on the narrow tracks through the sugar plantations, united as they are by who knows what degree of blood relationship, by an instinctive bond of caste, or perhaps motivated by the desire for recognition. But then, they deride the stranger under their breath because he knows nothing about sugarcane and nothing about the Grands Fonds except that it is covered with lush vegetation, and is completely unaware of the problems involved in cultivating the hills, keeping the small holdings together despite the never-ending family feuds and delivering the best cane to the distilleries at every harvest. Because, without a shadow of a doubt, he comes from a city. And he has never held a machete. Because he will soon go away again, while they must stay, chained to their precipices and their solid, white, prefabricated farmhouses, too poor to "return" to Europe even if any of them still had a place to "return" to, too proud to admit defeat, relinquish the dream of a secret kingdom on the high plateau and retreat to the coast.

Constance's house is small, simple, hardly more than a hovel, and this embarrasses her. Three times in the past hurricanes have destroyed everything. Three times she has replanted the garden and rebuilt the walls. Her pale-blue eyes she inherited from her ancestors, who came from Normandy as did many of the first Blancs Matignon. They came to the Caribbean before the abolition of slavery, before the French Revolution, before the world changed.

With the passing years Constance's face has become encrusted with a dark, scabby puffiness which gives her the appearance of a Creole, as if old age were mocking or even punishing her. God, maybe, has turned his face away from the Matignon, tired of their obstinacy. Generations of Bourgeois have defended the color of their skin as if it were a priceless inheritance. They have protected it from the sun and from mixed marriages with slaves of African origin and later with the freed blacks, even at the cost of becoming a minority doomed to extinction, a lost tribe in the midst of a multiracial Caribbean community. Their skin was their only treasure, their banner. They might be poor, ignorant, possibly forgotten, but they were white.

"I have nothing against the blacks," Constance will protest with an ever-so-slightly supercilious expression on her face. "They're decent people, as a rule. We grew up together, so what can you expect. But we're white, we're different from them. I, for example, am in the process of selling the land on which my house stands. But I won't sell it to a black. I couldn't live cheek by jowl with black people. They might be heathen. We think differently. I know that the old times are dead and gone, but—forgive me—that's what I'm used to. No blacks ever entered my house, even if they were richer than us, while I've always had to earn my living dressmaking or cooking or working in a factory."

It had not been easy to approach Constance Bourgeois. She knows how to protect herself from unwanted callers.

"You must make an appointment. I can't receive you without due notice. What manners are these? And I speak only when I'm well enough. Today, for example, I don't feel like it. Come back another day. Yes, tomorrow. But at half past four, no earlier. I'm very busy."

We had asked her nephew, Emile Matignon, who lives only a stone's throw from her, to intercede for us. He had been encouraging.

"Emile told you to come?" she asked, puzzled. "Then go and tell him that I make appointments for Emile Matignon and not vice versa."

But eventually we had been admitted, and had discovered that old Constance knows many secrets, even if to reveal them all at once is not her way.

"Now I'm like this, old and ill. But we Matignon have a great past. I've met Prince Rainier of Monaco, who may be called a Grimaldi but is descended from the Dukes of Matignon, those that have a palace in rue des Varennes in Paris. Rainier came to Guadeloupe because he needed to re-establish links with his ancestors who fled to the Caribbean. It happened nineteen years ago. He came alone, without his wife Grace. We talked for a long time and went together to consult the parish registers of Fatima, our parish. He later gave the priest money to distribute to the community. He was such a kind man! A real prince."

Could it be true? And if so, why has nothing ever been said about Prince Rainier's mission in the tropics?

"It's true, I assure you," Constance insisted, "and he treated me like an equal; I could see how moved he was. If you ask me, he knew much more than he admitted. He knew, for instance, what my family has always said, that our great-grandparents were Bourbons, and that they fled Paris to escape the guillotine. And then, having changed their name to Bourgeois, with a touch of irony of course, merged with the French colonials who had emigrated to Guadeloupe to escape their creditors or avoid going to prison. My ancestors were penniless and obliged to work as farm laborers, but they were aristocrats by blood and by style, and the ways of Europe ran in their veins. I am a Bourbon, you understand. How could I consider myself no different from the children of African slaves?"

There is a document among the official archives of Guadeloupe that records the legend of the Dukes of Matignon. The Archives Départementales de Guadeloupe are housed in a modern building at the end of a dirt road in Basse-Terre, a sleepy little town lost among the banana plantations. The document is a detailed anthropological study of the Blancs Matignon. Any link with the Grimaldis or with the real family of the Dukes of Matignon is utterly refuted. Instead, the study refers to "romanticized origins" and "pure imagination," which it derides as typical of the megalomaniacs of the Grands Fonds, who, it asserts, give themselves the airs of impoverished princes. "Even they themselves know nothing of their origins," according to this study. But Constance has no fear of anthropologists.

"They can say what they like," she said. "I know that one day, when I was living in France, I went to Monaco and visited Prince Rainier without even having an appointment. And he invited me into the palace, just like that."

Further questioning got us nowhere. Constance refused to say any more: the rest was secret. But how could this old, ailing peasant know anything about the dynastic links between the Grimaldis and the Matignon? She could certainly not have read my friend Enrica Roddolo's book, one of the few works in which this long-forgotten dynastic affair is examined in detail. The gist of the story is as follows: Antoine I of Monaco, having no male heirs to succeed him to the monarchy, married his daughter "Coco" to Jacques François-Léonor de Goyon Matignon, nicknamed "le Grison." This was in 1715. The marriage was arranged by the two families in order to preempt the tiny principality's absorption into France. Thus "le Grison" renounced his family name and assumed that of his wife to prevent the extinction of the house of Grimaldi.

Matignon was heir to one of the wealthiest families in Normandy, the district from which the four hundred down-and-outs of Les Grands Fonds claim to have come. A strange coincidence. At least the first part of Constance's story seemed to tally with the truth: since the seventeenth century the princes of Monaco really are Matignon by another name. Maybe Prince Rainier really did make that pilgrimage. And maybe the other stories handed down through the tribe are also true.

But the anthropological study is implacable. It states:

> According to popular legend, a representative of the Goyon Matignon family came to Guadeloupe. Informed of the existence of individuals with the name of Matignon, the French nobleman decided to go and visit them. He went on horseback. On meeting them, he exclaimed: "Good day, Cousins."
>
> This possibly casual sally was reinforced by the arrival in February 1974 of a journalist from Monaco who took samples of blood from the most elderly members of the tribe, promising them payment should the eventual tests prove

their kinship with Prince Rainier's family. As if this were not enough, the members of this community are now all convinced that "they have a cousin who lives in the Palais Matignon." The plain truth is that these people are ignorant peasants who have concocted a story about the whites of the Grands Fonds based not on fact but purely on hearsay. And they have repeated this story to other white people who have believed them. Put simply, a few unsophisticated people have managed to deceive scholars and researchers.

Quite a put-down. But there is more. The study attacks the Matignon on the genetic front too, emphasizing the absence of aristocratic traits:

> The physical aspect of the women is distressing. Thin, pale, prematurely aged and toothless, surrounded by children, they move one to pity [. . .]. They live on the margins of a white society that knows little and cares nothing about them. They have not even integrated with the black peasants of the Grands Fonds, and have no intention of so doing. Cases of concubinage with black people are extremely rare, they marry exclusively among their own kind, and even when attending church at Morne-à-l'Eau of a Sunday, they stay together in one corner keeping their distance from the blacks.

"Enough, enough! I'm tired of listening to these wicked lies!" Constance protested angrily. "We deserve respect. I know the man who wrote this stuff. He's a Negro blinded by prejudice who came here to observe us and describes us as dirty, miserable savages. But if you till the soil you get your hands dirty! You can't help it. And we're proud that we still have our own land, even though some of us have had to sell."

With great deference, the Matignon call Madame Constance Tatie or even Mamie, because she is a kind of aunt to all, and so mad that her madness borders on wisdom. The last remaining white people on the high plateaux in Guadeloupe visit her in the same way that the black people visit their Voodoo priestesses, for advice, for mediation, to discuss marriage problems, for help if they are ill and counsel when they must decide whether to stay or emigrate to Canada or France before biological extinction or the inevitable curse of intermarriage brings about their total disappearance from the island.

They sit on the grass, listening to how things used to be when the Matignon tribe was still isolated from the rest of the world, before the coming of the tarred road, when nearly every family was still "pure" and still owned the land their ancestors had wrested from the forest. In those days nearly all of them, husbands, brothers and cousins, would eventually find themselves going to the Usine Blanchet either as workers or to deliver the harvested sugarcane.

"My father grew sugarcane as did the other heads of families. My mother was a half-caste, very pale-skinned and with a very strong character. My paternal grandfather was a rich gentleman who rode into town on horseback. When I was thirteen they sent me to school at a convent down on the coast. The school was right beside the sea and I spent a lot of time gazing at the ships. On Sunday we were taken to the beach in a wagon drawn by horses. There was a superstition that by bathing you could cleanse your soul as well as your body, and free it from the evil eye. The only journeys I had made before this were to the Usine Blanchet when I was six or seven. I would put on a big straw hat with ribbons tied in a bow under my chin, and then I'd sit in the wagon on top of the load of sugarcane. The canes pricked my backside, but that didn't stop me begging my father to take me with him. So we'd set off on the tracks through the plantations belonging to the other Blancs Matignon. When we got there we queued up behind the wagons that had got there before us and waited to deliver our load. And I used to chat to the people who worked in the Usine because they were nearly all young men from the Grands Fonds, by which I mean white lads belonging to our Matignon families who lived in the surrounding villages. We were all poor then, even poorer than we are now, but there were more of us and we felt safer, stronger."

And what about the refinery? What had happened to it?

"Go and see it, the Usine Blanchet. It's still there, I think. Wouldn't take you long to get there. It seemed a long way when I was a child, a real expedition. They were good times. Nowadays the blacks like to think they can boss the whites around, even though they're heathen and we're Christian and, what's more, of aristocratic stock. But maybe things aren't so bad. At least we're making mixed marriages now and lovely children are being born instead of the defective mites that still occur in more traditional families. Lovely children like my nephews and nieces who live in America, in Chicago, and write to me every now and then begging me to go and live with them, to leave this island as I did so often when I was young. But I'm going to stay here. I can't leave the Grands Fonds where my ancestors were born. I need this countryside around me, and when all's said and done I've got all I want. I'm ill, but they look after me very well. Yes sir, they look after me. Doctors even come from Le Moule to see me. And can you see that big iron pot?"

One could hardly miss it, this pot half as big as the house itself. It looks like the cauldron of Asterix and Obelix; heaven knows what would happen if anyone fell into it. Perhaps it contains a bard who could explain the mystery of four hundred pig-headed peasants who, on the eve of the second millennium, thought they could stop time itself.

"That pot is a family secret," said Constance. "It was left to me by my father who in turn inherited it from my grandfather. It has been in my family for generations. There's a legend associated with that *vielle chaudière,* but I have sworn never to reveal it to a stranger."

Princess "Tatie" was getting tired now, and irritable. She was also wondering what these two foreigners really wanted of her, and regretting that she had allowed them to see her swollen face. But she continued. "I was pretty as a young girl," she said. "My parents' friends kept asking why, since I was so pretty, they hadn't found a husband for me. So when I was sixteen they told me I was going to be married. To a man I'd never met, a chap who worked at the Usine in Saint François, a sugar refinery on the coast. In those days the Blancs Matignon lived in many villages, and not everybody knew everybody else. My husband, for example, originally came from the valleys, but had gone to the city to seek his fortune. Or so they told me. Then I found out that he was a cousin. And I hated him from the start. I told him that I would never give him children. Every night I prayed to God asking him not to let me become pregnant. It worked. God heard my prayer. The first day he left the house I waited until he had disappeared down the road and then set out myself, back to my parents. I said: "Take me back." But my mother sent me back to him. Six months after my mother died I asked for a separation. There was a big scandal, people talked about it for a long time. Such an act of rebellion was unheard-of at that time, even in my family, which was more sophisticated than many others and counted some doctors among its members. I suffered a good deal, but in the end I won."

Darkness falls swiftly over the Grands Fonds, and now, as Constance spoke, a strange melancholy descended on the world outside, covering the farms and plantations like a veil.

Families, which may include a large number of children, gather for a meal of rice and salt pork—the same food as that eaten by the black people. Conversation in the Matignon homes is sparse, turning on the work in the fields and disputes between the six clans that bear the only names to have survived in the community: Matignon, Bourgeois, Boucher, Ramade, Roux and Berlet.

I had found the following words in an old document: "Here, magic is important. The white people learned about it from the blacks and made it their own." But no one wanted to talk about it. Perhaps Constance is a kind of witch.

The houses in the village are scattered, following the line of the road but set well back from it, often on top of little hills known locally as *mornes*. There is no village square, no center of gravity; even the church is tucked away at the end of one of the many switchback roads. Genetic ties are so close that the four hundred Matignon seem to feel no need for physical closeness, and even when passing each other on the road seldom exchange more than a greeting, as if unaware of the fact that everyone else is a cousin if not a brother.

When a boy or girl reaches marriageable age, the search for a partner becomes of overriding importance. In traditional families, the unacceptable risk of producing mentally defective offspring and so weakening the whole tribe dictates that the choice falls on the candidate with the fewest shared genes. Anyone who disregards this rule risks ostracism and may even have to leave the tribe and become part of the black community.

"For us white people the father's authority was absolute," Constance explained. "The only way in which I could rebel was by refusing to have children." She knew that the clan needed her children. Without new members, the Blancs of the high plateau would die out. Her memories were bitter, but as a Bourgeois-Bourbon she had to keep a stiff upper lip. You did not cry in public like other people.

"I had been separated for a few years when my brother died in a road accident leaving a daughter of three and a half. I reared her as if she were my own child. When she was grown up she married a Latin-American half-caste. And she repaid me with five beautiful grandchildren. They're all in Chicago. Mixed race, naturally, but you should see how beautiful they are. And I, meanwhile, traveled the world, to work and earn a living, of course, but also because I was curious. I liked adventure, and I didn't want to live and die in one place. I took some liberties, I was a natural rebel, and what a life I had! First Paris, then Santo Domingo for fifteen years, then the island of Saint-Barthélemy for ten, then the United States."

It was easy to imagine the conversations that must have taken place in the Parisian *atélier* where Constance sewed buttons onto the silk blouses of elegant women. "Where do you come from, with your strange, old-fashioned French?"—"From Guadeloupe, in the Antilles. A district known as the Grands Fonds, Madame." —"Guadeloupe, did you say? But you're not black!"—"I am French, Madame."—"But as a child of one of our colonies, why did you come here to ruin the sight of your blue eyes by sewing on mother-of-pearl buttons? What was your parents' name?"—"Bourbon, Madame. Their name was Bourbon. Do you know the family?"

To explain that her parents were indeed white and French but had sacrificed everything to live alone in the mountains with their slaves, which they both loved and hated, would have been too difficult.

"I discovered what it was like to live in France," she said, as if needing to justify her actions. "I tried it. But the cold!" She broke off and opened her blue eyes wide before repeating, as if one had to be convinced, "The cold!"

Thus it came about that she went as a cook to St. Barts, the other French island of the Lesser Antilles where the natives are white and therefore similar to the Blancs Matignon. There Constance opened a little restaurant, in a place where she no longer had to explain about being both poor and white. Because the Grands Fonds and St. Barts share much of their history, two ships navigating the same route through time.

The determining factor, as always, was sugarcane. In Guadeloupe it was synonymous with life itself, making and devouring vast fortunes, while on Saint-Barthélemy, now within the same administrative and electoral *département,* there has never been any cane at all. The eighteenth-century French conquerors who transformed the Caribbean settlements into true colonies once they had won the argument with the British Navy decided that, in the case of the islands best suited for growing sugarcane, manpower in the shape of strong African slaves would be needed to tame the tropical vegetation, clear the forests, plant, cut, dig over the ground and replant. On the other islands a small white nucleus would be sufficient to man the garrison and the port. Where necessary they could always import *engagés,* indentured workers from northern France. These were workers determined to seek their fortunes in the New World, who, in return for their travel, would engage themselves as slaves to a colonial estate owner for three years. The debt discharged, they were free to penetrate ever deeper into the virgin forests of the interior, find unoccupied land, chop down the trees and become landowners themselves.

The Dutch had a name for these people in search of adventure and land. They called them Burghers. When the oceans of the world were little more than private highways for the vessels of the Vereenigde Oost-Indische Compagnie—United East India Company—trading in competition with the English East India Company and the Portuguese throughout the frenetic years of the seventeenth century, the Company was more than a commercial enterprise. It was an army, a family, a clan, a church. Betrayal was unthinkable. The company men voyaged, traded and died only in the name of the supreme good. Each one of them was the exclusive property of the council of administration known as the Seventeen Gentlemen of Amsterdam, which imposed minutely detailed rules of behavior on every employee no matter how humble or how far away. If an employee wished to cut the company's apron strings and take on the challenge of the unknown forest, savannah or archipelago on his own, he had to seek special permission—like a priest seeking papal dispensation before renouncing his priesthood.

The Burghers, whether in Kaapstadt (Capetown) at the southern tip of Africa, or in Borneo or Ceylon, were first and foremost rebels and misfits and possibly, at heart, entrepreneurs. The Norman and Breton peasants and fishermen who sailed in the colonial trading ships as *engagés* were in fact Burghers too, in the sense that they aspired to be free citizens or even free pioneers, even though the word "Burgher" (from the Dutch *Burg*) would have been unknown to them.

Sugarcane was never planted in Saint-Barthélemy. Someone in Paris must have decided, for some obscure reason, that the climate and soil were unsuited for its cultivation. So there were no black slaves, only civil servants and colonists, white, of course. And so they have remained. The occasional mixed marriage has, in a very few cases, darkened the skin. But the four hundred Blancs Matignon look upon them as far-flung members of the same family and acceptable marriage partners. So every now and then someone makes the journey from the Grands Fonds to Saint-Barthélemy, a sliver of Paradise only six miles long and, at most, two and a half miles wide, and settles there, or perhaps finds the perfect partner and eventually returns to Guadeloupe with a new family.

In the 1950s, when few people had ever heard of Saint-Barthélemy, it was a favorite holiday destination of the Rothschilds and Rockefellers, who, attracted by the unusual combination of Caribbean sun and the reassuringly cosy atmosphere of provincial France, built villas overlooking its loveliest beaches.

The attraction has endured to this day. Even the capital city bears the name of a European village: Gustavia. The first white man settled here in 1648. He came from nearby St. Kitts. In 1656 the Caribs razed the small French settlement. This was one of their last victories before being exterminated by the European newcomers. From that moment Saint-Barthélemy became a haven for buccaneers, and the great fortunes began to be amassed.

While Saint-Barthélemy prospered, Guadeloupe remained poor. This has been their respective fate ever since. So even today the Blancs Matignon set off for the smaller island seeking treasure, the most precious treasure of all, a life partner with whom to carry on the race, to survive.

"They sign a two- or three-year contract as a waiter or farm laborer, and look around. To marry someone from Saint-Barthélemy is like winning the lottery. It puts new life not only into the family, but the community too. And when they come home they bring in new blood and their children are a precious gift to the village," explained one old Matignon woman.

The emigrants go singly, but on behalf of the tribe. All who are able to do so make the journey with the aim of increasing the strength of the tribe, as if following an ancestral instinct. Besides, the islands of the Lesser Antilles have always been staging posts in that long and intricate Odyssey undertaken by the merchants of every European sea power.

The first cosmopolitan European community in the Caribbean was created here. Among the five thousand Saint Barts (the local name for the inhabitants of Saint-Barthélemy) not all are of French origin. Many come from Scandinavia. "The Saint-Barthélemy blood is good because of the high percentage of Swedish people," say the Blancs Matignon, experts in the genealogical analysis of every red blood cell in the archipelago. "The genes are more mixed than ours, they're fresher." And the more extrovert talkers wave their hands about animatedly as if seeking a graphic description of the meeting between these lively, bubbly cells inherited from dynamic Viking warriors and the tired, broken-winded ones originating from northern France.

In 1784 King Louis XVI ceded Saint-Barthélemy to his friend and ally King Gustav III of Sweden in return for the right to trade with the port of Gothenburg, rather more strategically placed than the faraway, underpopulated outpost in the Tropics. Until then the port of Saint-Barthélemy was called Caranage. The Swedes changed it immediately to Gustavia and declared it a free port. (The authorities in the smaller Caribbean islands do the same today to attract offshore capital and facilitate the laundering of dirty money.) The population of the Burghers of Saint-Barthélemy immediately increased from eighteen hundred to six thousand.

Swedish rule lasted until 1878, when the Stockholm monarchy sold the island back to France for 320,000 francs. Then the Blancs Matignon could once more think of it as home away from home. This was crucial in and after the 1950s, when the alliances between various Matignon clans were breaking down and consanguineous marriage was not only reducing the size of the community but filling the classrooms of the little school with a quite unacceptable proportion of mentally and physically handicapped children. For fear of discovery by the outside world, these cripples and mental defectives were being hidden away in houses that became secret, illegal asylums. Constance recalled how the heads of families prevented their handicapped offspring from leaving the house, afraid lest a stranger might see them and inform the authorities about the barbarous practice of incestuous marriage. "They were also afraid," she continued, "that the curious or the mischievous might invade our mountains and poke their noses into our affairs, our traditions." The fear still lingers.

We returned to Matignon on another still, hot day. This time Carole came with us, embarrassed but unwilling to admit it. For someone who had traveled the world from Paris to New York, a visit to these mountains, a racist stronghold, was proving strangely problematic. Our intention was to knock on a door at random and ask whoever lived there to tell us the history of his family and of the tribe. But the sight of foreigners in their midst, let alone foreigners accompanied by an elegant black woman with positively nothing of the rustic about her, was the signal for a general stampede.

The village is divided into three parts, called *sections*. The only bar in the area is a small eatery run by two black women, where other blacks congregate to play checkers, the great passion of the islanders. The Matignon have no public meeting places, and it would be impossible to go into a private house without the whole village hearing about it. Suddenly, everyone seemed to have remembered an important appointment elsewhere.

Undoubtedly news of our visit had gone before us as the whole tribe was in a state of alarm. Their pallor and excessive thinness make them fearful of prying eyes. This fear is exacerbated by the behavior of some tourists for whom hunting Matignon has become a cruel sport in which the chase is only relinquished once the terrified face of some wretched "degenerate" has been sighted.

We had learned that once, many years ago, a Frenchwoman decided to go and see for herself these strange people she had heard about. Reaching the village of Rousseau, she stopped at a house belonging to a Blanc Matignon woman. When the woman appeared, with sunken cheeks and a kerchief on her head, the Frenchwoman asked, "Is this where the whites of the Grands Fonds live? You see, I'm from Brittany and some friends told me that that was where these white people originated." Without a hint of embarrassment she continued, "They said they were all albinos, and I just wanted to see if they were right. . . ."

The Frenchwoman was, of course, talking about albino blacks, the true *nègres blancs*. Looking for an example of genetic deformity, a sport of nature, what she had found was a woman like herself, though wearier and weaker from carrying on her peasant shoulders centuries of isolation in the Caribbean jungle. "Take a good look at my face, *madame*," said the Matignon woman, "and then tell your friends what the Blancs Matignon are really like."

We were anxious not to wound their pride. The tribe's situation has been made even more difficult over the last few years by the flight of so many of its young people. The number of handicapped children has risen enormously. The clan feels itself to be on the brink of disaster.

"Let's see if we can take a few photos," I suggested as some skinny, fair-haired children ran out of a farmyard. Our camera was an automatic, a veteran of African safaris, and absolutely silent. It was time to make use of it.

"I'll try," Pia replied. "Park at the side of the road and look innocent. We must give the impression we're admiring the scenery."

"Go on, take it."

Too late. Our attempt had failed before it started. A mother ran out onto the verandah and called her children indoors. The indignant glance she threw in our direction made us feel like peeping toms.

I began to wonder how Prince Rainier could ever have traveled along these roads without inspiring terror. But perhaps it is different where "cousins" are concerned. The Matignon had welcomed him like a long-awaited prophet, one who would at last make sense of their lives in the isolated mountains.

Carole directed her questions at the few people prepared to answer them. One boy pointed to a house, saying, "Try that one, because only a little while ago the lady who lives there talked to a television team. Perhaps she could help you. Me? No, I don't know anything."

"You see," said Carole, "they haven't forgotten that somebody blew the whistle. In my opinion we're trying to get blood out of a stone. I think we should leave."

I refused. Our work had barely begun. Outside the house indicated by the boy stood a young woman with dark blue eyes in a pale face, wearing a dress with "Yves Saint Laurent" printed on it. The farmhouse, a white prefabricated block standing ten feet below the level of the road, looked dark inside, but with so much light outside this was probably a blessing. We approached the woman, who spoke hesitantly yet was obviously more used to dealing with strangers than the other Matignon women. The reason for this became clear when she explained that before marrying and returning to the village she had worked in the city as a nurse. She told us how she had discovered that by revealing her Matignon origins at Point-à-Pître she had laid herself open to floods of abuse, to hearing her people dubbed spastics, racists and degenerates. That was how the outside world regarded them.

Carole said nothing—despite having come along as our interpreter! When we told the young woman that we were gathering information about the Matignon, and would like to talk to her in a general sort of way, she nodded and invited us in. However, after a few banal exchanges, the conversation flagged. I decided to be bold, and said (with a fair stab at wide-eyed innocence): "We've heard that there are those, mischievous or badly informed undoubtedly, who accuse you of incest. Do you know anything about this? How would you respond?"

"By saying that it is true, absolutely true."

Pia, Carole and I tried our best not to look flabbergasted.

"Yes, there was a time when our community was becoming genetically impaired, was even in danger of extinction. I think the phenomenon is known as endogamic degeneration. We had to find some fresh blood to inject into the veins of our children. Our chromosomes were going round in circles, they were out of control. You must realize that, while marriage between close relatives is regrettable, there was no alternative for us if we wanted to survive. We're European, we're different from the rest. Do you know that my grandfather's grandfather was the best friend of the mayor of Marseilles? I once received two visitors who came from Marseilles in search of their own roots. They told me that my grandfather was their grandfather's cousin. Or something like that."

Until that moment I had believed that all the Matignon came from Normandy. I told her this, and—thinking to give my statement the seal of authority—that the information had come from Constance. "Ah, Constance. Yes, I know her." The pale woman said no more, but it was enough. Could there really be rivalries, jealousies, among these four hundred forgotten people? She preferred to take up the thread of her argument. "There aren't any Normans. There used to be a small group from Marseilles. The Matignon come from all over France, not from any one region."

From behind a colored plastic curtain came the sound of heavy footsteps and Monsieur Boucher, the head of the household, appeared. He was wearing an undershirt and denim shorts and went barefoot as many peasants used to do during the summer in Normandy. The nurse, who had lost her clan identity by marrying a mulatto, Laposte, was his daughter. She stiffened on hearing him, but as he disappeared she resumed, telling us that she had nine brothers and sisters scattered throughout the Caribbean. "Racism is now a thing of the past," she said. "The barriers have fallen." It was not clear whether the barriers she was talking about were their own prejudices toward the blacks or those of the blacks toward them. Perhaps both. "Many of our people have left their own land. I have stayed because I love the Grands Fonds and the tranquility of the place. Yes, our reputation has been bad for a long time, but it is nevertheless true that our origins are aristocratic."

Carole smiled with polite, if frosty, skepticism. Lucienne Laposte pretended not to notice. Ignoring Carole completely, she spoke only to Pia and me.

Outside, the afternoon blazed in all its glory; inside, we sat around the kitchen table. Lucienne (who had only grudgingly told us her name and that she was married to a mulatto) offered us a glass of water; it was quite clear that she was enjoying the chance of talking to someone different. But then grunts started to come from behind the door and Père Boucher lifted the curtain, allowing us a brief glimpse of a poorly furnished bedroom. The heavily built peasant began to shout in the bastard French of Guadeloupe. "Lucienne, I told you not to answer any questions! I don't want anyone in my house! I'm sick and tired of people nosing around! What's so special about us? We are what we are and no one has the right to judge us."

Lucienne tried to calm him down, glancing at us as if to say, "He always goes on like this, but his bark's worse than his bite, so don't worry." But the peasant prince was not going to give up. "We're just ordinary people, not animals in a zoo. Why does everyone want to stare at us? Leave us alone!" Then another idea struck him, and without even looking at us, he yelled: "You want to know something? I come from a family of Negroes, I'm a Negro too. OK? Happy now? A Negro, that's what I am."

Carole signaled that she thought perhaps we should go. Lucienne rose, whispering, "My father is a simple farm laborer. He never went to school. What else could he do in life?"

A few days later we were sitting round the table in another farmhouse, listening to Lucien Ramade, a smallholder in the Matignon *section* (at the top end of the road leading up from the telephone kiosk), explaining the tribe's survival strategy. "I've got four daughters and I've married all four to men from Saint-Barthélemy, nice boys just like our own Matignon. You see, in this way whites stay with whites, and that's how it should be."

Recalling her fifteen years in Saint-Barthélemy, "Tatie" Constance shakes her head. "There's a popular saying that goes: Poor as a Blanc Matignon. Hardly surprising, when all that outsiders choose to see is a poverty-stricken people, worn out, thin, pale. They 'know' that we of the Grands Fonds are destitute, that we have to go abroad to find marriage partners and that we have all these mongoloid children." Constance screws up her old face into a mask of disgust, a cruel mimicry of the deformed children of her people.

And yet for the Blancs Matignon of the high plateau the solution is, theoretically, very easy and close to hand. That solution is Les Saintes, an archipelago of eight small volcanic islands in which God has amused himself by setting, as in a precious miniature, some of the loveliest jewels of the Caribbean. The largest island, Terre-de-Haut, is a three-mile-long succession of breathtaking bays and coves and beaches opening gracefully one into the other like a suite of rooms in Versailles. There is even an odd, vivid green Sugarloaf Mountain that looks like the younger brother of Rio de Janeiro's. The mountains of the island are covered with compact, dense greenery interrupted only by a few houses along the coastline.

The archipelago has been a French possession since 1648. The first colonists were thirty men employed by the Compagnie des Iles d'Amérique (the great commercial enterprise founded by Cardinal Richelieu), who came over from Saint Christophe (now known as St. Kitts) to prevent the English getting there first and occupying it.

In fact, the interminable see-saw struggle with England for possession of Les Saintes lasted until 1816. In the meantime prisoners had arrived, and soldiers to man the garrison of Fort Napoleon, which, being high enough to dominate the surrounding sea, was once considered strategically important.

Last to arrive were the Norman and Breton fishermen who now number fifteen hundred and call themselves Santois. They are, therefore, a tribe within a tribe. Separated from the *continent,* which is for them neither France nor America but Guadeloupe, their nearest city is Basseterre, nearly ten miles away over frequently rough seas. At the start of the academic year a special ferry carries a few dozen unwilling, pasty-faced children to the school, children with a reputation for never answering questions in class but staring blankly into midair with expressions of mingled scorn and indifference.

The "Saints" are considered the best fishermen in the Antilles; with neither fear nor scruple they follow the schools of tuna into foreign waters if need be, but they are thick-skinned and their eyes are unfriendly. Perfect marriage partners for the whites of the Grands Fonds? Too obvious, too banal.

The mere idea makes Constance shudder. "The Santois? But they're vulgar, common people, not aristocrats like us. Plain, ill-mannered fishermen. How could we associate with such coarse, primitive people? And even if we wanted to, they would refuse. Don't you know that if a Matignon goes to Bourg des Saintes, the town on Terre-de-Haut, they slam the door in his face? They even refuse to speak to us! They regard everyone who lives in Guadeloupe as an enemy, whatever their color, whatever they do. They live in those godforsaken islands because they can't live anywhere else, and all they can do is catch fish. We're different. We came to the Grands Fonds of our own free will, no one made us come."

Such are the whims and follies of the Tropics, where there is squabbling between clan and clan and hatred between island and island regardless of the fact that their predicament has already been sealed by history. The perpetual silent feuds are still fueled by a particular fragment of land having dared to surrender to England or Spain two centuries ago, or having dared to become independent. Or a plantation having changed hands two weeks ago without regard to the unwritten rules of precedence and the right of preemption favoring relatives. Because, in the Caribbean, everything changes, but everything leaves its mark.

Today Les Saintes is a little paradise of elite tourism. There are chic restaurants run by French people from Paris itself, like the fat gay couple, owners of a Creole villa called "Les Petits Saints." The restaurant is on the verandah. Inside, the rooms are stuffed with more or less exotic objects from an antique piano to a large wooden parrot, all for sale. In an infinity of affectation, everything is pierced, inlaid, engraved or miniaturized and the air is heavy with the smell of incense.

In the bay below, yachts are moored in ever-increasing numbers, local artists sell hand-painted T-shirts at exorbitant prices, policemen imported from France stroll around in tropical kit. The "Saints" speak only to each other and look askance at visitors. The shops are like those of St. Tropez twenty years ago, with today's prices. The bronzed faces of the shopkeepers are inscrutable, less emaciated, less uniform than the Matignon, but cold and aggressive. The "Saints" regard themselves as a living museum. The taking of photographs is forbidden, so is the asking of questions; look but don't touch. They also regard themselves as living in paradise, and are afraid someone might spoil it. Visitors who come to spend a few hours on the island are definitely second-class.

All the children on the island are under orders never to speak to strangers. If one yields to temptation an adult will invariably appear to whisk it away. "He has done nothing wrong, leave him alone," I remonstrated with a large man removing a child from my vicinity. He responded with a stream of menacing Creole.

Visitors coming off the ferry see women and girls wearing mushroom-shaped straw hats selling *"tourments d'amour,"* coconut sweetmeats that sound a lot nicer than they taste. The hats are very odd, like mushrooms with chinstraps. Brought to the West by French mercantile traders in the days of the empire, the hat originated in the Far East, probably China, and is called a *Salako.* It became popular because it was easy to make out of dried banana leaves and also because it happened to be fashionable among the ladies in Tonkin and Cochinchina during the earliest colonial days. The name is Vietnamese. How did it get here?

The question is completely unimportant, but I thought it might provide a useful opening gambit in conversations with the people of Terre-de-Bas. "How should I know?" replied a boy in a baseball cap, hastily starting up his scooter, the most common means of transport in the island. A group of children did not even waste their breath, but ignored me as completely as if I had been invisible. An old man walking about the town barefoot muttered some imprecation in Creole. All I could do was consult the *Guide pour Voyageurs Curieux,* a publicity brochure that conceals the natural beauty of the island under a welter of smarmy smiles and posed photographs. According to the guidebook the mushroom hats arrived soon after 1848, when the abolition of slavery led to laborers being imported from China. It also alludes to a legend according to which a cargo boat carrying a quantity of these hats for a destination unknown was driven by a storm to seek shelter in the bay. The "Saints" saw them, fell in love with them and offered to accept them as payment for repairs to the ship, and immediately decided to adopt them as their symbol.

Even though tourism has made them rich, the Santois are still seafaring folk today. Every afternoon the fishing boats are launched from the dazzling white sand of a little beach, perfect for snorkeling, behind the village. The islanders' hair, plaited Rasta-fashion, is fair, their skin reddened by the sun, their noses straight and narrow like the Matignons'. But every face seems deformed by something that has got under the skin and is spoiling the basic bone structure. This almost gives them the appearance of cartoon characters. But they never laugh.

"You'll never find out anything about us," a fisherman shouted at us one day. His weathered face was European, but with hints of Chinese and Negro. Returning from a fishing trip with a tuna fish slung over his shoulder like a knapsack, he was on his way to one of the houses with windows identical—so they say—to those common in northern France three centuries ago. The outside walls are painted in bright pastel colors, but the rooms inside are small, dark and shuttered as securely as bank vaults. The furniture is similar to that found in the homes of Corsican fishermen, there is sometimes a black and white television switched on for the news and a calendar hung on the wall, but the atmosphere is that of a hut in the African bush.

You are right, fisherman. We common sinners will truly never know anything about you saints.

"Are you in the habit of reading the Bible? Would you like to read it with me, now if you like? I know a very interesting passage, let's see if I can find it straight away."

Emile Matignon, high-school teacher in the daytime and Jehovah's Witness in the evening, has, by joining the sect, widened his horizons from being one of the chosen 400 to one of the chosen 144,000. An enormous step forward.

When, as a boy, he had to suffer the taunts of his schoolfellows calling him a pervert, a filthy Matignon racist who probably slept with his sister, pure self-defense drove him to believe that only the four hundred pure, steadfast Blancs of the Grands Fonds had a hope of reaching heaven. They were the ones whose horny hands worked the plantations, who dressed modestly and seemed the only God-fearing souls left in a confused, chaotic world.

Then he found Jesus, in the shape of a courageous preacher who came from the city to his own rural *commune* of Rousseau, a few hundred yards from the Matignons' *commune,* and was converted. The former Catholic became a Jehovah's Witness. And it is, he would argue, all there in the Bible, in Revelations chapter 7, verse 4, where it says quite unequivocally that the number of those who will reach the kingdom of heaven is 144,000.

A man of character, Emile. A visitor comes all the way from Europe to talk about the Matignon, and he proposes a Bible-reading! "It is relevant, you'll see," he insisted. The passage in Revelations served to explain his views about the destiny of the Matignon tribe. It does mention that 144,000 souls will be saved and his own personal interpretation is that this means room for everyone, or nearly everyone. "A hundred and forty-four thousand is nearly half the population of Guadeloupe!" he exclaimed ecstatically. "The old people always said that mixed marriages were against the will of God, that to betray the clan was sin. But the people of Jehovah's elect will end up multicolored. White, black, Creole." What price racism, then! Paradise will be nothing like the Grands Fonds. If anything, it might be like Point-à-Pitre.

The arms protruding from Emile's undershirt are bony, his reddish whiskers rather longer than necessary, and he has the long thin face that his family has been reproducing unchanged under the tropical sun since 1665. Since, that is, the first Matignon stepped ashore in Guadeloupe, then still covered by virgin forest and inhabited by Carib Indians with soot-streaked faces.

The first colonists were afraid to venture far from the coast and their villages, which were originally groups of wooden huts built close to the beach. But they were all eyeing the volcano and the mountains that dominated their settlements, conscious that the real promised land, the frontier country that had to be claimed and tamed, lay beyond them. Emile's ancestor was one of those who, having survived debts and strange tropical fevers, had taken the plunge into the immense forests to seek out a parcel of land to call home.

Three centuries and three decades later, Emile still feels the same urge, although he has transformed it into a hobby. Every Sunday he goes into the garage beside his neat little house and takes down a machete from its hook. The house, immersed in a tangle of tropical forest, has a reassuring look about it. The verandah is littered with tricycles and toy cars, the living room has a lounge suite in brown velvet (doubtless straight from the catalogue of a *Metropole* wholesaler), a tape-recorder and several pictures of Jesus gazing ecstatically heavenward. But on Sunday Emile tucks the machete into his belt like any peasant, rolls up his trousers and goes off to cut cane in his field on the outskirts of the village.

The field is now only five acres. *"Tout partagé,"* he sighs. All divided up. "All the rest was split up between brothers and various members of the family. First the big families, then poverty destroyed our holdings, which are now only pocket handkerchiefs of land."

But if you expect a paean to the good old days and the glorious destiny of the tribe, Emile is the wrong address. He is a Matignon that many in the Grands Fonds describe (in whispers) as a traitor, having lowered himself to compromise not once but twice with the modern world. He insisted on a university education and now teaches at a school in the city, and as if that were not enough, he married a black woman, carefree and laughter-loving, by whom he has had two chocolate-colored children, Odile and Jérome, carefree and laughter-loving like their mother. They both adore him. He is aware of the criticism leveled against him and regrets it, but he believes there is someone up there who has so willed it.

We went to see him again one afternoon when we knew he would be at home. He was in very good spirits and reveling in the role of *paterfamilias*. First he offered us a "fruity milk-shake" of pineapple and banana on ice, one of the best we had ever tasted. Odile and Jérome, thirteen and nine respectively, were intensely curious about us and, once over their initial shyness, bombarded us with questions. They had heard about something called "snow" at school, but what was it really like? Had we ever touched it? Did it melt if you picked it up? We told them that sometimes our house in Europe was completely covered by snow. This met with skepticism, so we promised to send them postcards of winter scenes to prove we were telling the truth. Meanwhile, Emile was more concerned about his Bible, which was full of underlinings and bristled with bookmarks.

Emile and his Bible reminded me of a man who had sat next to me on a flight between Belize and Miami, a surly-looking South American; not, however, a Catholic. He had all the fervor, the conviction, that marked him out as a member of some evangelical church. While those around us read pulp fiction or sailing magazines, he pulled out a massive Bible in thick covers. That too had been heavily underlined with marker pens. The point had indeed been reached where there was more text underlined than not. I didn't know about the others, but I felt a little embarrassed about my own lightweight reading matter. I had my revenge eventually, however. When lunch was served, I refused it: it would have been the sixth in-flight meal in twenty-four hours and I was beginning to feel slightly nauseated. But my dour neighbor took his tray without a word of thanks and wolfed the food almost without chewing it. I was sorely tempted to ask him if gluttony were no longer classified as a sin.

Emile is different, though, his fervor overlaid with layers of serenity. Talking about it later, Pia remarked, "His family seems so happy. I'm sure that the other Matignon, despite their disapproval, must have noticed how cheerful they are." And she was right. Perhaps Emile's real sin in the eyes of the villagers is to have cast off the gloomy resignation that is the pride of the rest of his tribe.

Emile knew who we were before we met. We had slipped a note under his door the previous day, telling him that we would be back and that we wanted to ask him about the Matignon. We chose the back door rather than the door off the verandah, having noticed the entire family's sandals lined up outside it. Much later, he would tell us with great pride that he had built the house himself, and in such a way that not even a hurricane could completely demolish it.

Having received us, a day later, he had his lesson prepared. "Yes, of course I know the history of my people. I've found references to one Matignon, a certain Léonard, who emigrated to Guadeloupe in 1665 and died in Petit Bourg in 1707. At first my family lived in Basse-Terre, like all the other French colonists, because Grande-Terre, where we are now, was still uncultivated. Indeed, it was almost uninhabited and completely wild. Then, at a certain point, Léonard's sons went to Saint Anne, a small town on the coast not far from here, close to the Grands Fonds."

A little room, cool and shady, had been squeezed in beside the garage, and here Emile sat behind a desk facing a dozen or so plastic chairs ranged in rows as in a classroom. A hand-drawn genealogical tree, copied from some encyclopedia, hung on the wall. Emile Matignon was treating this little history lesson with the seriousness of a public lecture.

This is the room in which he usually preaches about Jehovah to his neighbors—who are well content to have an excuse for getting out of the house twice a week. One of his students is his cousin Philippe, a fair-haired boy who works on the plantations. On this particular day, however, there was to be no talk about

Jehovah. Instead, Emile spoke about the Matignon and the documents he had collected over the years. *Professeur* Matignon was every inch the schoolmaster. "I shall open the proceedings myself," he said, "with an introduction. My wife and children, if you don't object, will remain with us because it will do them good too to learn something about the family. Later you can ask questions. Or better still, would you like to write them down on this sheet of paper?" Emile cleared his throat and the lesson began in earnest.

"In 1816 my ancestors had seventy-seven acres near Saint Anne, along the coast. But then they fled inland. Why, I do not know. A certain Bienvenu Matignon arrived here in the Grands Fonds in 1835 and bought an enormous stretch of virgin soil. Then came the Ramades, the Bouchers, the Roux and all the others. We whites kept very much to ourselves."

But why did they choose to live so far away from all civilization? Could they not have stayed together with the other colonists?

"Maybe my great-grandparents were fleeing from persecution."

The persecution theory is one of the most commonly encountered among the tribe, but it is difficult to know if it is myth or reality. What, after all, could be the motive for persecution? A mystery.

"Some say that they were fleeing from the English, our traditional enemies, who occupied Guadeloupe from 1759 until 1763. Unwilling to submit to the new rulers, they hid themselves away, thinking—quite correctly as it happened—that the English would never dare explore the interior. But they stayed in the forests even after the Treaty of Paris, when Great Britain gave Guadeloupe back to France in exchange for her renouncing all claims on Canada." So it would appear that it was not foreigners whom the Matignon had feared, but their own compatriots!

Emile talked on and on. His wife and children had now lost

interest, but for him the subject was still one of burning immedi-
acy. He had obviously been turning the matter over and over in
his mind without finding an answer. Finally he shook his head.
"When you come down to it, the Matignon were not that stupid." He comforted himself, ruminating, "They did the right
thing, leaving behind all that chaos. Besides, during the French
Revolution the English went back on their word and invaded
Guadeloupe yet again. That was in 1794. The only one who
could drive them out was Victor Hugues, a black *condottiere*
who made himself leader of the bands of freed slaves and used
guerrilla tactics against the invaders."

Victor Hugues came to be known as *le Robespierre des îles*
and showed pity to no one. "The same day he drove the English
back into the sea," Emile said, "Hugues killed three hundred
royalists, by which I mean whites loyal to the monarchy, who
owned plantations here in the colony." The Matignon now had a
choice. They could accept defeat and return to France on the
same banana boats that had brought them to Guadeloupe, or
they could retreat to the forests inland. In his book *Quand les
Français Cherchaient Fortune aux Caraibes,* Louis Doucet wrote:
"It is said that among those who fled into the forests there was a
Bourbon, a Bouchard de Montmorency and even a Matignon
related to the Grimaldi of Monaco. No one could deny them the
right to take their own lives, so they decided to throw themselves among the wild boars and tarantulas and leave it up to the
Supreme Being to decide whether they should live or die!"

In 1826 Victor Hugues died, ill and completely forgotten, in
Cayenne. But the Blancs Matignon survived, and by transforming themselves into farm laborers and woodcutters almost
overnight, succeeded in transforming that "mountainous,
insignificant stretch of land" (as it was described by one registrar
of French colonial land in the seventeenth century) into fields of
sweet potatoes and sugarcane. And with the French *Restaura-
tion* they could even buy more black slaves to swell the numbers
of those who (free only in name) had remained with their old

masters. The bond between *planteur* and slave was reinstated, at least until slavery was definitively abolished in 1848.

"They were troubled times. My ancestors had made the right decision when they abandoned the chaotic conditions elsewhere and took themselves off to a place where no one would disturb them. One current theory is that they refused to give up slavery. But I don't believe that. The Blancs Matignon have always worked their own land. Certainly they had black slaves, but so did everybody else at that time. They were no different from the rest of the population."

Emile never exaggerated, never accused, never became incensed. In his account, even the epic history of the white tribe was reduced to a catalogue of perfectly normal events. But he too has his scars.

"As a boy I had problems because I was a Matignon. I can't tell you how many times I was called a racist, a backwoodsman. No one wanted to be seen with me, I was a social outcast. All because part of the tradition of my people was this presumption of nobility, as if being a Matignon were enough to make one an aristocrat. But it's ridiculous, and the young people no longer believe it. Just imagine, we're so poor that we have to leave the Grands Fonds to find work. We still have a great love for the land, but the land has gone. So many of our youngsters end up as cashiers or storemen and they no longer cultivate the cane."

Emile omitted to say that marriage outside the community often means social sidelining and sometimes being forced to leave the community altogether, and losing all rights of inheritance.

So were they aristocrats fleeing the guillotine, or small-time slave-owning farmers clinging to a traditional way of life? There are many for whom this question is no light matter. Serge Matignon, a *paysan planteur*, speaking to us on his farm buried in the middle of the Grands Fonds, regarded us with blue eyes that hid three centuries of mystery, slowly sipped a Ti-punch and said gravely: "I'm almost certain that the Palais Matignon in Paris is connected with my family." His wife nodded.

Lucienne and her father, the aged Tatie, Emile and his family, the children returning from school in the humid evening—all know each other, all are related, all live in the same labyrinth of vegetation. But the real bonds that unite them—the quarrels, the loves, the alliances, the marriages—are secret, their mysteries impenetrable.

Who knows, for instance, if a researcher from the University of the Antilles, writing many years ago, was right or wrong in stating that the Blancs Matignon had a tribal chief whose identity was never revealed to outsiders? When I asked Emile, he replied with a vague negative. Others smiled and shook their heads. One or two told us that the title had once existed, but no more; that it was among the many things taken from the Matignon by the French administration.

Years ago one or two French magazines tried to penetrate the world of the Matignon. The same television team that interviewed Lucienne went to record Emile's life and that of his family on film, getting him to talk about his rebellion from the clan. "The blacks I was at school with insulted me but were unaware that, even though I was white, I had different ideas," said Emile in conclusion. "Today my ideas are out in the open. If I had behaved like my grandparents, I could never have been saved by Jehovah."

The "ideas" of the good Emile, the T-shirted, red-whiskered Emile, are three in number, and always shown off at the earliest opportunity: his wife Jocelyne, as silent in company as any African wife, and his children, Jérome and Odile, who laugh like a couple of imps and have a beautiful tan. Geographically, Emile lives within the clan borders, but he has chosen not to be part of it any more. "I teach in the city, so I have to commute. There's no work here now. We have to look elsewhere."

Emile's name had first been mentioned to us by his sister, a deformed cripple with a strange face marked by inbreeding. When we first met her she was walking slowly along the road that runs through the *commune* of Matignon, wearing a light cotton dress that showed her petticoat and her orthopedic sandals. A few years earlier she would have been kept hidden indoors, but now she is free to let everyone see her misfortune. "If you want to know about the history of the Blancs Matignon," she said, "you must speak to my brother. He's always got his nose in books and concerns himself with such things. What would I know about them? I know that I am a Matignon, but that's all."

That day, dusk was now falling, transforming the plantations into rose-red lakes. A small group of fair-haired children on their way home from elementary school walked in single file along the tarmac road toward the farms scattered around the hilltop pastures and set among fields of sweet potatoes and rice. Like their African counterparts, they wore school uniform but went barefoot, their shoes slung around their necks. And their gait was that of people who do not expect to arrive, ever.

In front of the beige-colored parish church with its great iron crucifix over the door, Henry was getting ready to drive to the beach in his Peugeot 505 turbo. Although he has always lived in the *commune* he is not a Matignon; he is black, like the vast majority of the 340,000 inhabitants of the island. And he is a soccer enthusiast. In Guadeloupe the game known as *fut* sends the entire population wild with enthusiasm every Sunday, and Henry coaches the village team on the field opposite the church.

"A few years ago the Matignon wouldn't play *fut* with us, but now there are a couple of white kids in the team. And *fut* is important. The two groups used to discriminate against each other. Relations are still ambiguous, blacks and whites are still divided even if only by cast of mind. They used to make babies with close relatives and that horrified the rest of us. But since the

1970s things have changed. They can make fine kids too, kids who play well."

All very well, but why did these white people settle right here, in the mountains?

"I know they were escaping from something or someone, but no more than that."

This is the ongoing contradiction of the Grands Fonds du Morne. Everyone clings to history, but no one admits to knowing exactly what that history is.

Until recently the church was the center of the community, the place where the whites affirmed their superiority every Sunday. In 1952, when the priest at Morne-à-l'Eau gathered together 150 men on horseback to provide a fitting welcome for the bishop when he came to consecrate the new church dedicated to Our Lady of Fatima, the small machete-carrying army included a representative from every family in the colony. This was perhaps the Blancs Matignon's last public festival. Tarmac roads and electricity were still in the future; in the coastal regions the old colonial way of life was falling apart, but here in the mountains it still seemed indestructible.

"The Matignons used to regard the church as their private property," said Henry. "They would all keep to one side, on the left, and look us up and down. And heaven help any of us who dared sit near them. Nowadays there are no fixed places in church on a Sunday."

Caste solidarity, however, remains strong. Those who betray their own race risk expulsion even if they leave the community to make their fortunes; even, paradoxically, when they marry other whites.

A story is told in the Grands Fonds about a Matignon boy, the youngest of seven brothers, who married a *Béké* widow much older than himself in 1946. This marriage between a *"petit Blanc"* and a *"grande Blanche"* put the young Matignon at the head of a commercial empire comprising banana plantations, trade deals, ships. He needed a workforce, and where should he look for it if not in the Grands Fonds? So he summoned his cousins and brothers to come and work for him and his wife.

The *Béké* woman having died much sooner than expected, the man waited six months and then married again, this time choosing a young woman of twenty-six, white and a *Béké* like the first. But the girl attached conditions to her acceptance: he had to cut all links with the community into which he had been born, he had to repudiate his tribe and send back to their mountains the relatives he had summoned to work for him, who now constituted a source of shame for the sophisticated young bride. And what did he do? He gave in. He bid farewell to the Grands Fonds.

From that moment he became a member of the white elite of the island. He had accepted the state of *créolisation,* a word pronounced by his erstwhile tribe only with fear and loathing. He had become a common white man with no tribal identity.

In the farmhouses up in the mountains of the Grands Fonds, this story is told and retold on dark evenings as the parable of the man who sold his birthright for a mess of pottage and was swallowed up in a morass of white anonymity as a punishment.

At the eastern tip of the eastern wing of Guadeloupe's green butterfly is a spit of wooded land with beaches of white sand on either side. It's called Pointe des Châteaux. Right at the very end it becomes a rocky promontory facing the sparkling sea and the island of La Désirade in the distance. In this earthly paradise of forests and plantations of sugarcane lives an even smaller version of the Blanc Matignon tribe, descendants of the pioneering farmers who crossed the seas in the sixteenth century to colonize La Désirade. It is another almost invisible point in the Caribbean galaxy; another forgotten enclave.

By the side of the straight road that divides Pointe des Châteaux (where the only castles are those built and destroyed incessantly by the waves), a little chocolate-colored old woman sells melons and a one-time ballerina from Paris runs a very stylish but sometimes chilly fish restaurant. Behind the hand-painted board carrying the legend "Chez Honoré—Langoustes et Ti-Punch" is a single-story building open to the elements facing the Grande Anse, a long road running parallel with the sea. The "sand" with which it appears to be made is, in fact, fragments of shell ground small by waves and millennia.

Until ten years ago, Pointe des Châteaux was a completely neglected part of the island. Projecting far out from the mainland, it was too exposed to wind and sea. A few tourists and a few French émigrés have now found their way there, as have a builder, a decorator and an artist, all escaping from something. This is where Carole Dejean lives, too. Her blood a heady mixture of Vietnamese, French and African, her hair in girlish plaits, her eyes black, her culinary speciality fried-banana pie, Carole refuses to make a drama of the fact that her husband left her. She still has the sun, the sea and her three-year-old son chasing his kitten among the flowering shrubs. "Every morning when I wake up I find something different to be happy about," she says. She too, like the Blancs in the mountains, was in search of a corner of the world that would be hers and hers alone.

Aimé Césaire, the poet from Martinique, another speck of rock on the map of the Antilles, wrote: "Hurrah for all those who have made nothing!" He was referring to the Carib and Arawak Indians, the first inhabitants of these islands, a primitive people who came to a swift end crushed by colonists who appropriated their land at the behest of the European powers. "The English, the French, the Dutch, they had an idea of history based on absurdity: massacre, death. An idea of history as progress, as a march. The pioneer says: 'I own this land, I fenced it off.' But here there is only the primal, blessed experience of waking up in the reality of the earth." So said Derek Walcott, the Nobel laureate of St. Lucia.

Lost in their green mountains, the Blancs Matignon have

270 Lost White Tribes

ceased to be colonists. No longer Europeans in exile, they have become latter-day Arawak Indians. They create nothing, they possess nothing, not even the color of their skin. They are happy waking up every morning to the knowledge that they are still children of the high plateau.